Extending Puppet

Design, manage, and deploy your Puppet architecture
with the help of real-world scenarios

Alessandro Franceschi

BIRMINGHAM - MUMBAI

Extending Puppet

First published: June 2014

Production reference: 1170614

Published by Packt Publishing Ltd.
Livery Place
35 Livery Street
Birmingham B3 2PB, UK.

ISBN 978-1-78398-144-1

www.packtpub.com

Cover image by Alessandro Franceschi (alvagante@yahoo.it)

Credits

Author

Alessandro Franceschi

Reviewers

Dhruv Ahuja

C. N. A. Corrêa

Brice Figureau

Commissioning Editor

Edward Gordon

Acquisition Editor

Llewellyn Rozario

Content Development Editor

Azharuddin Sheikh

Technical Editors

Rohit Kumar Singh

Pratish Soman

Copy Editors

Sayanee Mukherjee

Karuna Narayanan

Alfida Paiva

Adithi Shetty

Laxmi Subramanian

Project Coordinator

Kartik Vedam

Proofreaders

Simran Bhogal

Maria Gould

Ameesha Green

Paul Hindle

Indexer

Hemangini Bari

Production Coordinator

Adonia Jones

Cover Work

Adonia Jones

Foreword

I first met Alessandro in person at the inaugural Puppet Camp in San Francisco, 2009, but by this time, we'd already chatted on IRC and the Puppet Users mailing list. This was a small event by the standards of Puppet community events today, with about 60 people in attendance, and it's been great to see how many of that original crowd have continued to be active participants in the community, especially Alessandro.

While I was running Puppet at Google, I kept getting a lot of questions from attendees about how we were managing to scale our Puppet infrastructure technically. Alessandro, however, was already prodding me about how I was managing workflow and code layout for reusability and shareability, a topic that he's been very much focused on over the last five years.

When I initially left Google and moved to Puppet Labs in late 2010 to handle products, it became even more apparent how much Alessandro cared about guiding the community towards standards for Puppet content that allowed for reusability and shareability, yet allowed sysadmins to work quickly. We saw this with his promotion of the "params pattern" to consolidate input variables in a single location, and to allow for a first step towards separating data from code, well before the existence of Hiera as a formal project.

Alessandro saw this need well before most of us, and regularly raised it with the community as well as just about every time we ran into each other at conferences and events. As new projects appeared that added to the capabilities of the Puppet ecosystem, he modified his thinking and raised new proposals.

I'm thrilled to see this new book by Alessandro on Puppet architectures and design patterns, and I can't think of a better person to write it. He's cared about these principles for a long time, and he's promoted them as a responsible community member.

Nigel Kersten

CIO, Puppet Labs

About the Author

Alessandro Franceschi is a freelance Puppet and DevOps consultant. Surviving IT battlegrounds since 1995, he has worked as an entrepreneur, web developer, trainer, and system and network administrator.

He has been using Puppet since 2007, automating a remarkable amount of customers' infrastructures of different sizes, natures, and complexities.

He has attended several PuppetConf and Puppet Camps as a speaker and participant, always enjoying the vibrant and friendly community, learning something new each time.

During the following years, he started to publish his Puppet code, trying to make it reusable in different scenarios.

The result of this work is the Example42 Puppet modules set, a widely used collection of modules based on reusability principles and with some optional, opinionated twists to automate firewalling, monitoring, systems' inventory, and application deployments.

For more information on Example42 modules, visit `www.example42.com`. His Twitter handle is `@alvagante`.

Acknowledgments

This is my first book. When Packt Publishing asked me to write a book about Puppet, I was surprised, flattered, and intrigued. The idea of sharing my experience about this wonderful tool was really attractive.

I have been using Puppet for seven years. I have loved it since the beginning.

I have seen a great community of people doing wonderful things with it, and I tried to credit as many people as possible, knowing that many worthy contributors have been forgotten.

I have assisted in its evolution and the tumultuous growth of the company behind it, Puppet Labs.

I have definitely not seen any attack ships on fire off the shoulder of Orion, but I think I have gathered enough experience about Puppet to have valuable things to write about and share.

Please forgive my approximate grasp of the language; if you are a native English speaker, you will surely find some sentences weird or just wrong.

I tried to avoid the temptation to build phrases based on my mother language constructs; I believe I have failed in more than one place.

Various people have helped me with suggestions and corrections; they couldn't solve all my language idiosyncrasies and content limitations, but their input has been very important to make this book better.

I'd like to thank in particular Brice Figureau, Joshua Hoblitt, and Azharuddin Sheikh for the invaluable help and corrections, and Nigel Kersten, Jon Forrest, Calogero Bonasia, Monica Colangelo, and Kartik Vedam for the precious suggestions.

A big hug to Chiara, who is always patient and supportive, and to all my family, even the younger one who is extremely skilled in kicking me out of the bed, encouraging early morning writing sessions.

It's time to enjoy some more weekends together, finally.

About the Reviewers

Dhruv Ahuja is a senior DevOps engineer at a leading financial data vendor. He specializes in orchestration and configuration management in an enterprise, heterogeneous setting. His first brush with Puppet was in 2011 when he developed a solution for dynamically scaling compute nodes for a multipurpose grid platform. He also holds a Master's degree in Advanced Software Engineering from King's College London, and won the Red Hat UK Channel Consultant of the Year award in 2012 for delivering progressive solutions. A long history in conventional software development and traditional systems administration equip him with aptness in both areas. In this era of infrastructure as code, he believes that declarative abstraction is essential for a maintainable systems life-cycle process.

C. N. A. Corrêa (@cnacorrea) is an IT operations manager and consultant, and is also a Puppet enthusiast and an old-school Linux hacker. He has a Master's degree in Systems Virtualization and holds CISSP and RHCE certifications. Backed by a 15-year career in systems administration, Carlos leads the IT operations teams for companies in Brazil, Africa, and the USA. He is also a part-time professor for graduate and undergraduate courses in Brazil. Carlos has co-authored several research papers on network virtualization and OpenFlow, and has presented at peer-reviewed IEEE and ACM conferences worldwide.

> I thank God for all the opportunities of hard work and all the lovely people I always find on my way. To the sweetest of them all, my wife Nanda, I thank for all the loving care and support that pushes me forward. Also, to my parents, Nilton and Zélia, for being such a big inspiration for all the things I do.

Brice Figureau works at Days of Wonder, a board game publisher best known for its award-winning train game *Ticket to Ride*, where he designs, manages, and programs distributed online game servers and the infrastructure they run on. In several previous job roles, he programmed 3D-rendering engines, Photoshop plugins, early mobile Internet services, and voice-recognition-based phone services and learned system administration. He likes to spend time contributing to various open source projects and has started some of his own. He's been using Puppet since Version 0.23.7 and contributed several major features to the Puppet core code that helped make Puppet what it is now. He also maintains `www.planetpuppet.org` and helps to organize the Paris DevOps Meetups and the DevopsDays Paris conference when time permits. You might find him hanging around in IRC under the masterzen nickname on Twitter with the `@_masterzen_` handle, or at different open source, DevOps, or Configuration Management conferences around the world.

www.PacktPub.com

Support files, eBooks, discount offers, and more

You might want to visit www.PacktPub.com for support files and downloads related to your book.

Did you know that Packt offers eBook versions of every book published, with PDF and ePub files available? You can upgrade to the eBook version at www.PacktPub.com and as a print book customer, you are entitled to a discount on the eBook copy. Get in touch with us at service@packtpub.com for more details.

At www.PacktPub.com, you can also read a collection of free technical articles, sign up for a range of free newsletters and receive exclusive discounts and offers on Packt books and eBooks.

http://PacktLib.PacktPub.com

Do you need instant solutions to your IT questions? PacktLib is Packt's online digital book library. Here, you can access, read and search across Packt's entire library of books.

Why subscribe?

- Fully searchable across every book published by Packt
- Copy and paste, print and bookmark content
- On demand and accessible via web browser

Free access for Packt account holders

If you have an account with Packt at www.PacktPub.com, you can use this to access PacktLib today and view nine entirely free books. Simply use your login credentials for immediate access.

Table of Contents

Preface

Puppet has changed the way we manage our systems. When it was released, other configuration management tools were around, but it was clear that it had something special. It came at the right time with the right approach. The challenges of IT infrastructures were beginning to step up to a new level, and the need to automate common activities such as a quick setup and configuration of systems was becoming a requirement. Puppet presented a sane model, based on abstraction of resources and the definition of the expected state of a system, using a clear and sysadmin-friendly language.

There are various books about Puppet around, and most of them are very good. This one tries to contribute with solid and no frills content (few pictures and few large blocks of copied and pasted text) and some new perspectives and topics. It begins with an intense technical overview of Puppet, Hiera, and PuppetDB so that you can use them to design appropriate Puppet architectures that fit your IT infrastructure.

We will explore where our data can be placed, how to design reusable modules, and how they can be used as building blocks for higher abstraction classes. We will try to give a clearer and wider view of what it means to work with Puppet, and what are the challenges we might face when we introduce it on our systems, from code management to deployment rollouts. We will dive into Puppet's internal details and its extension points, showing the multiple ways we can tweak, extend, and hack with it. We will also give a look to less traditional fields, such as Puppet as a configuration-management tool for network devices or cloud services.

The last chapter is about the future: how Puppet is evolving and what we can expect to do with it in the next years.

I'd dare to say that this is the book I'd have liked to read when I was trying to connect the dots and figure out how to do things in the "right way", struggling to grasp Puppet's inner concepts and reusability patterns.

Years of pain, experience, evolution, and research are poured in these pages and I really hope they can be useful for your personal adventure exploring Puppet.

What this book covers

Chapter 1, Puppet Essentials, is an intense and condensed summary of the most important Puppet concepts: the baseline needed to understand the chapters that follow and a good occasion to refresh and maybe enrich knowledge about the Puppet language and model.

Chapter 2, Hiera, is dedicated to how to manage our data with Hiera: how to define the lookup hierarchy, organize data, and use different backends.

Chapter 3, PuppetDB, covers the installation, configuration, and usage of PuppetDB, and explores the great possibilities that it may enable in the next generations of modules.

Chapter 4, Designing Puppet Architectures, outlines the components to manage when defining a Puppet architecture: the available tools, how to integrate them, how to cope with data and code, and organize resources to be applied to nodes.

Chapter 5, Using and Writing Reusable Modules, covers the most important Puppet element from the user's perspective, modules, and how to write them in order to be able to reuse them in different infrastructures.

Chapter 6, Higher Abstraction Modules, takes a step further and focuses on modules that use different application modules to compose more complex and wider scenarios.

Chapter 7, Deploying and Migrating Puppet, analyzes the approaches that can be taken when introducing Puppet in a new or existing infrastructure: methodologies, patterns, techniques, and tips for a successful deployment.

Chapter 8, Code Workflow Management, focuses on how to manage Puppet code, from when it is written in an editor to its management with an SCM, its testing and deployment to production.

Chapter 9, Scaling Puppet Infrastructures, covers the challenges you might face in growing infrastructures and how it is possible to make Puppet scale with them.

Chapter 10, Writing Puppet Plugins, covers the many available possibilities to extend the core code with custom plugins and gives a deeper view on how Puppet internals are organized.

Chapter 11, *Beyond the System*, takes a journey outside the traditional territories, exploring how we can manage with Puppet network and storage equipment and cloud instances.

Chapter 12, *Future Puppet*, is a step towards Puppet 4 and how its new features may influence the way we work with Puppet.

What you need for this book

You can test the Puppet code present in this book on any Linux system connected to the Internet. You can use the Vagrant environment provided in the example code and have your test machines running a VirtualBox instance on your computer. For this, you need both Vagrant and VirtualBox installed on your system.

Who this book is for

This book is accessible to any Puppet user.

If you are totally new to Puppet, be sure to have given a thorough read of *Chapter 1*, *Puppet Essentials*, and to have well understood its principles before continuing your reading.

If you are an intermediate user, enjoy reading the following chapters in order.

If you are an advanced user, you may pick in different pages' useful information and new insights on topic you should already know.

Conventions

In this book you will find a number of styles of text that distinguish between different kinds of information. Here are some examples of these styles, and an explanation of their meaning.

Code words in text, database table names, folder names, filenames, file extensions, pathnames, dummy URLs, user input, and Twitter handles are shown as follows: "For inline documentation about a resource, use the describe subcommand."

A block of code is set as follows:

```
:backends:
  - http
:http:
  :host: 127.0.0.1
  :port: 5984
  :output: json
  :failure: graceful
  :paths:
    - /configuration/%{fqdn}
    - /configuration/%{env}
    - /configuration/common
```

Any command-line input or output is written as follows:

```
puppet agent -t
puppet resource package
puppet resource service
```

New terms and **important words** are shown in bold. Words that you see on the screen, in menus or dialog boxes for example, appear in the text like this: "At the end of a Puppet run, we can have metrics that let us understand how much time the Master spent in compiling and delivering the catalog (**Config retrieval time**)."

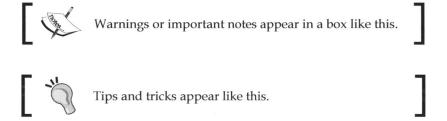

Warnings or important notes appear in a box like this.

Tips and tricks appear like this.

Reader feedback

Feedback from our readers is always welcome. Let us know what you think about this book—what you liked or may have disliked. Reader feedback is important for us to develop titles that you really get the most out of.

To send us general feedback, simply send an e-mail to feedback@packtpub.com, and mention the book title through the subject of your message.

If there is a topic that you have expertise in and you are interested in either writing or contributing to a book, see our author guide on www.packtpub.com/authors.

Customer support

Now that you are the proud owner of a Packt book, we have a number of things to help you to get the most from your purchase.

Downloading the example code

You can download the example code files for all Packt books you have purchased from your account at http://www.packtpub.com. If you purchased this book elsewhere, you can visit http://www.packtpub.com/support and register to have the files e-mailed directly to you.

Errata

Although we have taken every care to ensure the accuracy of our content, mistakes do happen. If you find a mistake in one of our books—maybe a mistake in the text or the code—we would be grateful if you would report this to us. By doing so, you can save other readers from frustration and help us improve subsequent versions of this book. If you find any errata, please report them by visiting http://www.packtpub.com/submit-errata, selecting your book, clicking on the **errata submission form** link, and entering the details of your errata. Once your errata are verified, your submission will be accepted and the errata will be uploaded to our website, or added to any list of existing errata, under the Errata section of that title.

Piracy

Piracy of copyright material on the Internet is an ongoing problem across all media. At Packt, we take the protection of our copyright and licenses very seriously. If you come across any illegal copies of our works, in any form, on the Internet, please provide us with the location address or website name immediately so that we can pursue a remedy.

Please contact us at copyright@packtpub.com with a link to the suspected pirated material.

We appreciate your help in protecting our authors, and our ability to bring you valuable content.

Questions

You can contact us at questions@packtpub.com if you are having a problem with any aspect of the book, and we will do our best to address it.

1
Puppet Essentials

There are moments in our professional life when we encounter technologies that trigger an inner wow effect. We realize there's something special in them, and we start to wonder how they can be useful for our current needs and, eventually, wider projects.

Puppet, for me, has been one of these turning point technologies. I have reasons to think that we might share a similar feeling.

If you are new to Puppet, you are probably starting from the wrong place, since there are better fitting titles around to grasp its basic concepts.

This book won't indulge too much in the fundamentals, but don't despair as this chapter might help for a quick start.

It provides the basic Puppet background needed to understand the rest of the contents and may also offer valuable information to more experienced users.

In this chapter, we are going to review the following topics:

- **The Puppet ecosystem**: The components, its history, and the basic concepts behind configuration management
- **How to install and configure Puppet**: Commands and paths to understand where things are placed
- **The core components and concepts**: Terms such as manifests, resources, nodes, and classes will become familiar
- **The main language elements**: Variables, references, resource defaults, ordering, conditionals, comparison operators, and virtual and exported resources
- How Puppet stores the changes it makes and how to revert them

The contents of this chapter are quite dense; take your time to review and assimilate them; if they sound new or look too complex, it is because the path towards Puppet awareness is never too easy.

The Puppet ecosystem

Puppet is a configuration management and automation tool. We use it to install, configure, and manage the components of our servers.

Written in Ruby and released with an open source license (Apache 2), it can run on any Linux distribution, many other UNIX variants (Solaris, *BSD, AIX, and Mac OS X), and Windows.

Its development started in 2005 by Luke Kanies as an alternate approach to the existing configuration management tools (most notably, CFEngine and BladeLogic).

The project has grown year after year. Kanies' own company, Reductive Labs, which was renamed in 2010 to Puppet Labs, has received a total funding of $45.5 million in various funding rounds (among the investors, there are names such as VMware, Google, and Cisco).

Now, it is one of the top 100 fastest growing companies in the US. It employs more than 250 people, and has a solid business based on open source software, consulting services, training, and certifications. It also has Puppet Enterprise, which is the commercial version that is based on the same open source Puppet code base, but it provides a web GUI that improves and helps in easier Puppet usage and administration.

The Puppet ecosystem features a vibrant, large, and active community that discusses it at the Puppet Users and Puppet Developers Google group, on the crowded Freenode's #puppet IRC channel, at the various Puppet Camps that are held multiple times a year all over the world, and at the annual PuppetConf, which is improving and getting bigger year after year.

Various software products are complementary to Puppet; some of them are developed by Puppet Labs, which are as follows:

- **Hiera** is a key-value lookup tool that is the current choice of reference for storing data related to your Puppet infrastructure
- **MCollective** is an orchestration framework that allows parallel execution of tasks on multiple servers. It is a separate project by Puppet Labs, which works well with Puppet

- **Facter** is a required complementary tool as it is executed on each managed node and gathers local information in key/value pairs (facts) that are used by Puppet

- **Geppetto** is an IDE that is based on Eclipse that allows easier and assisted development of Puppet code

- **Puppet Dashboard** is an open source web console for Puppet

- **PuppetDB** is a powerful backend that can store all the data gathered and generated by Puppet

- **Puppet Enterprise** is the commercial solution to manage Puppet, Mcollective, and PuppetDB via a web frontend

The community has produced other tools and resources; the most noticeable ones are the following:

- **The Foreman** is a systems lifecycle management tool that integrates perfectly with Puppet

- **Puppetboard** is a web frontend for PuppetDB

- **Kermit** is a web frontend for Puppet and Mcollective

- A lot of community code is released as modules, which are reusable components that allow the management of any kind of application and software via Puppet

Why configuration management matters

IT operations have changed drastically in the last few years; virtualization, cloud, business needs, and emerging technologies have accelerated the pace of how systems are provisioned, configured, and managed.

The manual setup of a growing number of operating systems is no longer a sustainable option. At the same time, in-house custom solutions to automate the installation and the management of systems cannot scale in terms of required maintenance and development efforts.

For these reasons, configuration management tools such as Puppet, Chef, CFEngine, Rudder, Salt, and Ansible (to mention only the most known open source ones) are becoming increasingly popular in many infrastructures.

They allow a centralized and controlled approach to systems' management, based on code and data structures, which can be managed via a **Software Change Management (SCM)** tool (`git` is the choice of reference in Puppet world).

Once we can express the status of our infrastructure with versioned code, we gain powerful benefits:

- We can reproduce our setups in a consistent way; what is executed once can be executed any time; the procedure to configure a server from scratch can be repeated without the risk of missing parts.

- The log of our code commits reflects the history of changes on our infrastructure: who did what, when, and if commits comments are pertinent, then why.

- We can scale quickly; the configurations we did for a server can be applied to all the servers of the same kind.

- We have aligned and coherent environments. Our development, test, QA, staging, and production servers can share the same setup procedures and configurations.

With these kinds of tools, we can have a system provisioned from zero to production in a few minutes, or we can quickly propagate a configuration change over our whole infrastructure automatically.

Their power is huge and has to be handled with care as we can automate massive and parallelized setups and configurations of systems; we might automate distributed destructions. With great power comes great responsibility.

Puppet components

Before diving into the installation and configuration details, we need to clarify and explain some Puppet terminology to get the whole picture.

Puppet features a declarative **Domain Specific Language** (DSL), which expresses the desired state and properties of the managed resources.

Resources can be any component of a system, for example, packages to install, services to start, files to manage, users to create, and also custom and specific resources such as MySQL grants, Apache virtual hosts, and so on.

Puppet code is written in `manifests`, which are simple text files with a `.pp` extension. Resources can be grouped in classes (do not consider them as classes as in OOP; they aren't). Classes and all the files needed to define the required configurations are generally placed in modules, which are directories structured in a standard way that are supposed to manage specific applications or a system's features (there are modules to manage Apache, MySQL, sudo, sysctl, networking, and so on).

When Puppet is executed, it first runs facter, a companion application, which gathers a series of variables about the system (the IP address, the hostname, the operating system, the MAC address, and so on), which are called facts, and are sent to the Master.

Facts and user-defined variables can be used in manifests to manage how and what resources to provide to the clients.

When the Master receives a connection, then it looks in its manifests (starting from `/etc/puppet/manifests/site.pp`) what resources have to be applied for that client host, also called a node.

The Master parses all the DSL code and produces a catalog that is sent back to the client (in the PSON format, which is a JSON variant used in Puppet). The production of the catalog is often referred to as catalog compilation, even if the term is not perfectly appropriate (there is no other program that is compiled from the source code to binary), and is going to be discontinued. In this book, we will still use it as it is quite common and widely used.

Once the client receives the catalog, it starts to apply all the resources declared there, irrespective of whether packages are installed (or removed), services have started, configuration files are created or changed, and so on. The same catalog can be applied multiple times; if there are changes on a managed resource (for example, a manual modification of a configuration file), they are reverted to the state defined by Puppet; if the system's resources are already at the desired state, nothing happens.

This property is called idempotence and is at the root of the Puppet declarative model. Since it defines the desired state of a system, it must operate in a way that ensures that this state is obtained wherever the starting conditions and the number of times Puppet is applied.

Puppet can report the changes it makes on the system and audit the drift between the system's state and the desired state as defined in its catalog.

Installation and configuration

Puppet uses a client-server paradigm. Clients (also called agents) are installed on all the systems to be managed; the server(s) (also called the Master) is installed on a central machine(s) from where we control the whole infrastructure.

We can find Puppet's packages on the most recent OS, either in the default repositories on in the additional ones (for example, EPEL for Red Hat derivatives).

The client package is generally called puppet, so the installation is a matter of typing something like the following:

```
apt-get install puppet # On Debian derivatives
yum install puppet # On Red Hat derivatives
```

To install the server components, we can run the following command:

```
apt-get install puppetmaster # On Debian derivatives
yum install puppet-server # On RedHat derivatives
```

> To have updated packages for the latest versions, we should use Puppet Labs' repositories: http://docs.puppetlabs.com/ guides/puppetlabs_package_repositories.html.
>
> To install Puppet on other operating systems, check http://docs. puppetlabs.com/guides/installation.html.

Both agents (clients) and the Master (server) use the configuration file /etc/puppet/ puppet.conf, which is divided in [sections] and has an INI-like format. All the parameters present in the configuration file may be overridden while invoking puppet from the command line. All of them have default values; here is a sample with some of the most important ones:

```
[main]
    logdir = /var/log/puppet
    vardir = /var/lib/puppet
    rundir = /var/run/puppet
    ssldir = $vardir/ssl
[agent]
    server = puppet
    certname = $fqdn # Here, by default, is the node's fqdn
    runinterval = 30
[master]
    autosign = false
    manifest = /etc/puppet/manifests/site.pp
    modulepath = /etc/puppet/modules:/usr/share/puppet/modules
```

A very useful command to see all the current configuration settings is as follows:

```
puppet config print all
```

With the previous information, we have all that we need to understand the main files and directories that we deal with when we work with Puppet:

1. Logs are in /var/log/puppet (but also on normal syslog files, with the facility daemon), both for agents and Master.

2. The Puppet operational data is in /var/lib/puppet.

3. SSL certificates are stored in /var/lib/puppet/ssl. By default, the agent tries to contact a Master hostname called puppet, so either name our server puppet.$domain or provide the correct name in the server parameter.

4. When the agent communicates with the Master, it presents itself with its certname (this is also the hostname placed in its SSL certificates). By default, the certname is the fully qualified domain name (FQDN) of the agent's system.

5. By default, the agent runs as a daemon that connects to the Master every 30 minutes and fetches its configuration (the catalog, to be precise).

6. On the Master, we have to sign each client's certificates request (manually). If we can cope with the relevant security concerns, we may automatically sign them (autosign = true).

7. The first manifest file (that contains Puppet DSL code) that the Master parses when a client connects, in order to produce the configuration to apply to it, is /etc/puppet/manifests/site.pp. This is important as all our code starts from here.

8. Puppet modules are searched for and automatically loaded from the directories /etc/puppet/modules and /usr/share/puppet/modules on the Master.

> Puppet Enterprise is provided with custom packages that reproduce the full stack, Ruby included, and uses different directories.
>
> /etc/puppetlabs/puppet/ is the main configuration directory; here, we find puppet.conf and other configuration files. The other directories are configured by default with these paths:
>
> ```
> vardir = /var/opt/lib/pe-puppet
> logdir = /var/log/pe-puppet
> rundir = /var/run/pe-puppet
> modulepath = /etc/puppetlabs/puppet/modules:
>              /opt/puppet/share/puppet/modules
> ```
>
> In this book, we will mostly refer to the open source version; besides, the previous paths, all the principles, and usage patterns are the same.

Puppet in action

Client-server communication is done using REST-like API calls on an SSL socket; basically, it's all HTTPS traffic from clients to the server's port 8140/TCP.

The first time we execute Puppet on a node, its x509 certificates are created and placed in `ssldir`, and then the Puppet Master is contacted in order to retrieve the node's catalog.

On the Puppet Master, unless we have `autosign` enabled, we must manually sign the client's certificates using the `cert` subcommand:

```
puppet cert list # List the unsigned clients certificates
puppet cert list --all # List all certificates
puppet cert sign <certname> # Sign the given certificate
```

Once the node's certificate has been recognized as valid and been signed, a trust relationship is created, and a secure client-server communication can be established.

If we happen to recreate a new machine with an existing `certname`, we have to remove the certificate of the old client from the server with the following command:

```
puppet cert clean  <certname> # Remove a signed certificate
```

At times, we may also need to remove the certificates on the client; we can do this with the following command:

```
mv /var/lib/puppet/ssl /var/lib/puppet/ssl.bak
```

This is safe enough as the whole directory is recreated with new certificates when Puppet is run again (never do this on the Master as it'll remove all the clients' certificates previously signed, along with the Master's certificate, whose public key has been copied to all clients).

A typical Puppet run is composed of different phases. It's important to know them in order to troubleshoot problems:

1. Execute Puppet on the client. On a root shell, run `puppet agent -t`.
2. If `pluginsync = true` (default from Puppet 3.0), the client retrieves any extra plugin (facts, types, and providers) present in the modules on the Master's `$modulepath` client output with the following command:

   ```
   Info: Retrieving plugin
   ```

3. The client runs facter and sends its facts to the server client output:

```
Info: Loading facts in /var/lib/puppet/lib/facter/... [...]
```

4. The Master looks for the client's `certname` in its nodes' list.

5. The Master compiles the catalog for the client using also its facts. Master's logs:

```
Compiled catalog for <client> in environment production in 8.22
seconds
```

6. If there are syntax errors in the processed Puppet code, they are exposed here, and the process terminates; otherwise, the server sends the catalog to the client in the PSON format.

   Client output:

```
Info: Caching catalog for <client>
```

7. The client receives the catalog and starts to apply it locally. If there are dependency loops, the catalog can't be applied and the whole run fails.

   Client output:

```
Info: Applying configuration version '1355353107'
```

8. All changes to the system are shown on `stdout` or in logs. If there are errors (in red or pink, according to Puppet versions), they are relevant to specific resources but do not block the application of other resources (unless they depend on the failed ones).

9. At the end of the Puppet run, the client sends to the server a report of what has been changed.

   Client output:

```
Finished catalog run in 13.78 seconds
```

10. The server sends the report to a report collector if enabled.

Resources

When dealing with Puppet's DSL, most of the time we use resources as they are single units of configuration that express the properties of objects on the system. A resource declaration is always composed by the following parts:

- `type`: a package, service, file, user, mount, exec, and so on
- `title`: how it is called and referred in other parts of the code

- One or more attributes

```
type { 'title':
  argument  => value,
  other_arg => value,
}
```

Inside a catalog, for a given type, there can be only one title; otherwise, we get an error as follows:

```
Error: Duplicate declaration: <Type>[<name>] is already declared in file
<manifest_file> at line <line_number>; cannot redeclare on node <node_
name>.
```

Resources can be native (written in Ruby), or defined by users in Puppet DSL.

These are examples of common native resources; what they do should be quite obvious:

```
file { 'motd':
  path    => '/etc/motd',
  content => "Tomorrow is another day\n",
}

package { 'openssh':
  ensure => present,
}

service { 'httpd':
  ensure => running, # Service must be running
  enable => true,    # Service must be enabled at boot time
}
```

We can write code of this kind in manifests, which are files with a .pp extension that contain valid Puppet code. It's possible to test the effect of this code on the local system with the puppet apply command, which expects the path of a manifest file as the argument:

```
puppet apply /etc/puppet/manifests/site.pp
```

We can also directly execute Puppet code with the --execute (-e) option:

```
puppet apply -e "package { 'openssh': ensure => present }"
```

In this case, instead of a manifest file, the argument is a fragment of valid Puppet DSL.

For inline documentation about a resource, use the `describe` subcommand, for example:

```
puppet describe file
```

For a complete reference of the native resource types and their arguments, check `http://docs.puppetlabs.com/references/latest/type.html`.

The resource abstraction layer

From the previous resource examples, we can deduce that the Puppet DSL allows us to concentrate on the types of objects (resources) to manage, and it doesn't bother us on how these resources may be applied on different operating systems.

This is one of Puppet's strong points; resources are abstracted from the underlying OS; we don't have to care or specify how, for example, to install a package on Red Hat Linux, Debian, Solaris, or Mac OS; we just have to provide a valid package name.

This is possible thanks to Puppet's **Resource Abstraction Layer (RAL)**, which is engineered around the concept of **types** and **providers**.

Types, as we have seen, map to an object on the system.

There are more than 50 native types in Puppet (some of them are applicable only to a specific OS); the most commonly used ones are `augeas`, `cron`, `exec`, `file`, `group`, `host`, `mount`, `package`, `service`, and `user`.

To have a look at their Ruby code and learn how to create custom types, check this file:

```
ls -l $(facter rubysitedir)/puppet/type
```

For each type, there is at least one provider, which is the component that enables that type on a specific OS. For example, the `package` type is known for having a large number of providers that manage the packages' installations on many OSes, which are `aix`, `appdmg`, `apple`, `aptitude`, `apt`, `aptrpm`, `blastwave`, `dpkg`, `fink`, `freebsd`, `gem`, `hpux`, `macports`, `msi`, `nim`, `openbsd`, `pacman`, `pip`, `pkgdmg`, `pkg`, `pkgutil`, `portage`, `ports`, `rpm`, `rug`, `sunfreeware`, `sun`, `up2date`, `urpmi`, `yum`, and `zypper`.

We can find them with the following command:

```
ls -l $(facter rubysitedir)/puppet/provider/package/
```

The Puppet executable offers a powerful subcommand to interrogate and operate with the RAL `puppet resource`.

For a list of all the users present on the system, type the following:

```
puppet resource user
```

For a specific user, type the following:

```
puppet resource user root
```

Other examples that might show glimpses of the power of RAL to map a system's resources are as follows:

```
puppet resource package
```

```
puppet resource mount
```

```
puppet resource host
```

```
puppet resource file /etc/hosts
```

```
puppet resource service
```

The output is in the Puppet DSL format; we can use it in our manifests to reproduce that resource wherever we want.

The puppet `resource` subcommand can also be used to modify the properties of a resource directly from the command line, and since it uses the Puppet RAL, we don't have to know how to do that on a specific OS, for example, to enable the `httpd` service:

```
puppet resource service httpd ensure=running enable=true
```

Nodes

We can place the above resources in our first manifest file (`/etc/puppet/manifests/site.pp`) or in the one included from there, and they would be applied to all our Puppet-managed nodes. This is okay for quick samples out of books, but in real life, things are much different. We have hundreds of different resources to manage and apply, with different logic and properties to (dozens? hundreds? thousands?) different systems.

To help you organize your Puppet code, there are two different language elements; with `node`, we can confine resources to a given host and apply them only to it; with `class`, we can group different resources (or other classes) that generally have a common function or task.

Whatever is declared in a node definition is included only in the catalog compiled for that node. The general syntax is as follows:

```
node $name [inherits $parent_node] {
  [ Puppet code, resources and classes applied to the node ]
}
```

Here $name is a placeholder for the `certname` of the client (by default, it's FQDN) or a regular expression; it's possible to inherit in a node whatever is defined in the parent node and inside the curly braces; we can place any kind of Puppet code, such as resource declarations, class inclusions, and variable definitions. Here are some examples:

```
node 'mysql.example.com' {
  package { 'mysql-server':
    ensure => present,
  }
  service { 'mysql':
    ensure => 'running',
  }
}
```

However, generally in nodes we just include classes, so a better real-life example would be the following one:

```
node 'mysql.example.com' {
  include common
  include mysql
}
```

The previous `include` statements do what we might expect; they include all the resources declared in the referred class.

Note that there are alternatives to the usage of the node statement; we can use an **External Node Classifier** (ENC) to define which variables and classes are assigned to nodes, or we can have a nodeless setup, where resources applied to nodes are defined in a case statement based on the hostname or a similar fact that identifies a node.

Classes and defines

A class can be defined (the resources provided by the class are defined for later usage, but are not yet included in the catalog) with this syntax:

```
class mysql {
  $mysql_service_name = $::osfamily ? {
    'RedHat' => 'mysqld',
    default  => 'mysql',
  }
  package { 'mysql-server':
    ensure => present,
  }
  service { 'mysql':
```

```
      name => $mysql_service_name,
      ensure => 'running',
    }
    [...]
}
```

Once defined, a class can be declared (the resources provided by the class are actually included in the catalog) in two ways:

- Just by including it (we can include the same class many times, but it is evaluated only once):

  ```
  include mysql
  ```

- Using the parameterized style (available since Puppet 2.6), where we can optionally pass parameters to the class if available (we can declare a class with this syntax only once for each node in our catalog):

  ```
  class { 'mysql': }
  ```

A parameterized class has a syntax similar to the following code:

```
class mysql (
  $root_password,
  $config_file_template = undef,
  ...
) {
  [...]
}
```

In this code, the expected parameters are defined between parentheses, which may or may not have a default value (parameters without default values, such as the $root_password in this sample, must be set explicitly while declaring the class). The declaration of a parameterized class has exactly the same syntax as that of a normal resource:

```
class { 'mysql':
  $root_password => 's3cr3t',
}
```

Puppet 3.0 introduced a feature called data binding; if we don't pass a value for a given parameter, as in the above example, before using the default value if present, Puppet performs an automatic lookup to a Hiera variable with the name $class::$parameter. In this example, it would be mysql::root_password.

This is an important feature that radically changes the approach on how to manage data in Puppet architectures. We will come back to this topic in the following chapters.

Besides classes, Puppet also has defines, which can be considered as classes that can be used multiple times on the same host (with a different title). Defines are also called defined types, since they are types that can be defined using Puppet DSL, contrary to the native types that are written in Ruby.

They have a similar syntax:

```
define mysql::user (
  $password,                # Mandatory parameter, no defaults set
  $host      = 'localhost', # Parameter with a default value
  [...]
) {
  # Here all the resources
}
```

They are also used in a similar way:

```
mysql::user { 'al':
  $password => 'secret',
}
```

Note that defines (also called user-defined types, defined resource types, or definitions), like the one above, even if written in Puppet DSL, have exactly the same usage pattern of native types, that are written in Ruby (packages, services, files, and so on).

In types, besides the parameters that are explicitly exposed, there are two variables that are automatically set: `$title` is the defined title, and `$name`, which defaults to the value of `$title`, can be set to an alternate value.

Since a define can be declared more than once inside a catalog (with different titles), it's important to avoid to declare, inside a define, resources with a static title. For example, this is wrong:

```
define mysql::user ( ...) {
  exec { 'create_mysql_user':
    [ ... ]
  }
}
```

This is because when there are two different `mysql::user` declarations, it will generate an error like the following:

```
Duplicate definition: Exec[create_mysql_user] is already defined in file
/etc/puppet/modules/mysql/manifests/user.pp at line 2; cannot redefine at
/etc/puppet/modules/mysql/manifests/user.pp:2 on node test.example42.com
```

A correct version could use the `$title` variable, which is inherently different each time:

```
define mysql::user ( ...) {
  exec { "create_mysql_user_${title}":
    [ ... ]
  }
}
```

Class inheritance

We have seen that in Puppet, classes are just containers of resources and have nothing to do with Object-oriented Programming classes; so the definition of class inheritance is somehow limited to a few specific cases.

When using class inheritance, the main class (`puppet` in the following sample) is always evaluated first, and all the variables and resource defaults that it sets are available in the scope of the child class (`puppet::server`).

Moreover, the child class can override the arguments of a resource defined in the parent class:

```
class puppet {
  file { '/etc/puppet/puppet.conf':
    content => template('puppet/client/puppet.conf'),
  }
}
class puppet::server inherits puppet {
  File['/etc/puppet/puppet.conf'] {
    content => template('puppet/server/puppet.conf'),
  }
}
```

Note the syntax used when declaring a resource; we use a syntax like `file { '/etc/puppet/puppet.conf': [...] }`. When referring to it, the syntax is `File['/etc/puppet/puppet.conf']`.

Resource defaults

It is possible to set the default argument values for a resource type in order to reduce code duplication. The general syntax to define a resource default is as follows:

```
Type {
  argument => default_value,
}
```

Common examples are as follows:

```
Exec {
  path => '/sbin:/bin:/usr/sbin:/usr/bin',
}
File {
  mode  => 0644,
  owner => 'root',
  group => 'root',
}
```

Resource defaults can be overridden when declaring a specific resource of the same type.

It is worth noting that the area of effect of the resource defaults might bring unexpected results. The general suggestion is as follows:

- Place `global` resource defaults in `/etc/puppet/manifests/site.pp` outside any node definition.
- Place `local` resource defaults at the beginning of a class that uses them (mostly for clarity sake, as they are independent of the parse-order).

We cannot expect a resource default that is defined in a class to be working in another class, unless it is a child class with an inheritance relationship.

Resource references

In Puppet, any resource is uniquely identified by its type and its name. We cannot have two resources of the same type with the same name in a node's catalog.

We have seen that we declare resources with a syntax like the following one:

```
type { 'name':
  arguments => values,
}
```

When we need to reference them (typically when we define dependencies between resources) in our code, the following is the syntax (note the square brackets and the capital letter):

```
Type['name']
```

Some examples are as follows:

```
file { 'motd': ... }
apache::virtualhost { 'example42.com': .... }
exec { 'download_myapp': .... }
```

These examples are referenced, respectively, with the following code:

```
File['motd']
Apache::Virtualhost['example42.com']
Exec['download_myapp']
```

Variables, facts, and scopes

When writing our manifests, we can set and use variables; they help us in organizing which resources we want to apply, how they are parameterized, and how they change according to our logic, infrastructure, and our needs.

They may have different sources:

- Facter (variables, called facts, automatically generated on the Puppet client)
- User-defined variables in Puppet code (variables that are defined using Puppet DSL)
- User-defined variables from an ENC
- User-defined variables on Hiera
- Puppet's built-in variables

System's facts

When we install Puppet on a system, the `facter` package is installed as a dependency. Facter is executed on the client each time Puppet is run, and it collects a large set of key-value pairs that reflect many properties of the system. They are called facts and provide valuable information such as the system's `operatingsystem`, `operatingsystemrelease`, `osfamily`, `ipaddress`, `hostname`, `fqdn`, and `macaddress` to name just some of the most used ones.

All the facts gathered on the client are available as variables to the Puppet Master and can be used inside manifests to provide a catalog that fits the client.

We can see all the facts of our nodes running locally:

```
facter -p
```

(The `-p` argument is the short version of `--puppet` and also shows eventual custom facts that are added to the native ones, via our modules.)

User variables in Puppet DSL

Variable definition inside the Puppet DSL follows the general syntax:
```
$variable = value
```

Let's see some examples. Here, the value is set as `string`, `boolean`, `array`, or `hash` as shown in the following code:

```
$redis_package_name = 'redis'
$install_java = true
$dns_servers = [ '8.8.8.8' , '8.8.4.4' ]
$config_hash = { user => 'joe', group => 'admin' }
```

Here, the value is the result of a function call (which may have values, as arguments, strings, other data types, or other variables):

```
$config_file_content = template('motd/motd.erb')

$dns_servers = hiera(name_servers)
$dns_servers_count = inline_template('<%= @dns_servers.length %>')
```

Here, the value is determined according to the value of another variable (here, the `$::osfamily` fact is used), using the selector construct:

```
$mysql_service_name = $::osfamily ? {
  'RedHat' => 'mysqld',
  default  => 'mysql',
}
```

A special value for a variable is `undef` (similar to Ruby's nil), which basically removes any value to the variable. This can be useful in resources when we want to disable (and make Puppet ignore) an existing attribute:

```
$config_file_source = undef
file { '/etc/motd':
  source  => $config_file_source,
  content => $config_file_content,
}
```

Note that we can't change the value assigned to a variable inside the same class (more precisely, inside the same scope; we will review them later).

```
$counter = '1'
$counter = $counter + 1
```

The preceding code will produce the following error:

Cannot reassign variable counter

User variables in an ENC

When an ENC is used for classifying nodes, it returns the classes to include in the requested node and variables. All the variables provided by an ENC are at the top scope (we can reference them with $::variablename all over our manifests).

User variables in Hiera

Hiera is another very popular and useful place to place user data (yes, variables); we will review it extensively in *Chapter 2*, *Hiera*; here, let's just point out a few basic usage patterns. We can use it to manage any kind of variable whose value can change according to custom logic in a hierarchical way. Inside manifests, we can look up a Hiera variable using the hiera() function. Some examples are as follows:

```
$dns = hiera(dnsservers)
class { 'resolver':
  dns_server => $dns,
}
```

The previous code can also be written as:

```
class { 'resolver':
  dns_server => hiera(dnsservers),
}
```

In our Hiera YAML files, we would have something like the following:

```
dnsservers:
  - 8.8.8.8
  - 8.8.4.4
```

If our Puppet Master uses Puppet Version 3 or greater, then we can benefit from the Hiera automatic lookup for class parameters, which is the ability to define in Hiera values for any parameter exposed by the class. The above example would become something like the following:

```
include resolver
```

and then, in Hiera YAML files:

```
resolver::dns_server:
  - 8.8.8.8
  - 8.8.4.4
```

Puppet's built-in variables

A bunch of other variables is available and can be used in manifests or templates:

Variables set by the client (agent):

- `$clientcert`: This is the name of the node (the `certname` setting in its `puppet.conf`, by default, is the host's FQDN)
- `$clientversion`: This is the Puppet version of the agent

Variables set by the server (Master):

- `$environment`: This is a very important special variable, which defines the Puppet's environment of a node (for different environments, the Puppet Master can serve manifests and modules from different paths)
- `$servername`, `$serverip`: Respectively the Master's FQDN and IP address.
- `$serverversion`: The Puppet version on the Master (is always better to have Masters with Puppet version equal or newer than the clients)
- `$settings::<setting_name>`: Any configuration setting of the Puppet Master's `puppet.conf`

Variables set by the parser during catalog compilation:

- `$module_name`: This is the name of the module that contains the current resource's definition
- `$caller_module_name`: This is the name of the module that contains the current resource's declaration

A variable's scope

One of the parts where Puppet development can be misleading and not so intuitive is how variables are evaluated according to the place in the code where they are used.

Variables have to be declared before they can be used, and this is dependent on the parse-order; so, also for this reason, Puppet language can't be considered completely declarative.

In Puppet, there are different scopes, which are partially isolated areas of code where variables and resource default values can be confined and accessed.

There are four types of scopes, from general to local there are:

- **Top scope**: Any code defined outside nodes and classes, as what is generally placed in `/etc/puppet/manifests/site.pp`
- **Node scope**: Code defined inside the node's definitions
- **Class scope**: Code defined inside a class or define
- **Sub class scope**: Code defined in a class that inherits another class

We always write code within a scope, and we can directly access variables (that is, by just specifying their name without using the fully qualified name) defined only in the same scope or in a parent or containing one. So:

- Top scope variables can be accessed from anywhere
- Node scope variables can be accessed in classes (used by the node) but not at the Top scope
- Class (also called local) variables are directly available, with their plain name, only from within the same class, or define where they are set or in a child class

The variables' value or resources default arguments that are defined at a more general level can be overridden at a local level (Puppet always uses the most local value).

It's possible to refer to variables outside a scope by specifying their fully qualified name, which contains the name of the class where the variables is defined, for example, `$::apache::config_dir` is a variable called `config_dir`, and is defined in the `apache` class.

One important change introduced in Puppet 3.x is the forcing of static scoping for variables; this indicates that the parent scope for a class can only be its parent class.

Earlier, Puppet versions had dynamic scoping, where parent scopes were assigned both by inheritance (like in static scoping) and by simple declaration; that is, any class has as a parent the first scope where it has been declared. This means that since we can include classes multiple times, the order used by Puppet to parse our manifests may change the parent scope, and therefore, how a variable is evaluated.

This can obviously lead to any kind of unexpected problems if we are not particularly careful about how classes are declared, with variables evaluated in different parse-order dependent ways. The solution is Puppet 3's static scoping and the need to reference to out-of-scope variables with their fully qualified name.

Meta parameters

Meta parameters are general-purpose parameters available to any resource type even if not explicitly defined. They can be used for different purposes:

- Manage the ordering of dependencies and resources (more on them in the next section): `before`, `require`, `subscribe`, `notify`, `stage`
- Manage resources' application policies: `audit` (audit the changes done on the attributes of a resource), `noop` (do not apply any real change for a resource), `schedule` (apply the resources only within a given time schedule), and `loglevel` (manage the log verbosity)
- Add information to a resource using `alias` (adds an alias that can be used to reference a resource) and `tag` (adds a tag that can be used to refer to a group resources according to custom needs; we will see a use case later in this chapter in the external resources section)

Managing order and dependencies

Puppet language is declarative and not procedural (*); it defines states. The order in which resources are written in manifests does not affect the order in which they are applied to the desired state.

 (*) This is not entirely true; contrary to resources, variables definitions are parse-order dependent, so the order is important when it is used to define variables. As a general rule, just set variables before using them, which sounds logical but is actually procedural.

There are cases where we need to set some kind of ordering among resources, for example, we want to manage a configuration file only after the relevant package has been installed, or have a service automatically restart when its configuration files changes.

Also, we may want to install packages only after we've configured our packaging systems (apt sources, yum repos, and so on), or install our application only after the whole system and the middleware has been configured.

To manage these cases, there are three different methods, which can coexist, as follows:

1. Use the meta parameters `before`, `require`, `notify`, and `subscribe`
2. Use the chaining arrows operator (respective to the meta parameters: `->`, `<-`, `<~`, and `~>`)
3. Use run stages

In a typical package/service/configuration file example, we want the package to be installed first. Then, configure it and start the service, and eventually manage its restart if the configuration file changes.

This can be expressed with meta parameters:

```
package { 'exim':
  before => File['exim.conf'],
}
file { 'exim.conf':
  notify => Service['exim'],
}
service { 'exim': }
```

This is equivalent to the following chaining arrows syntax:

```
package {'exim': } ->
file {'exim.conf': } ~>
service{'exim': }
```

However, the same ordering can be expressed using the alternate reverse meta parameters:

```
package { 'exim': }
file { 'exim.conf':
  require => Package['exim'],
}
service { 'exim':
  subscribe => File['exim.conf'],
}
```

They can also be expressed as follows:

```
service{'exim': } <~
file{'exim.conf': } <-
package{'exim': }
```

Run stages

Puppet 2.6 introduced the concept of run stages to help users manage the order of dependencies when applying groups of resources.

Puppet provides a default main stage; we can add any number of stages and manage their ordering with the `stage` resource type using the normal syntax for resources declaration as we have seen previously:

```
stage { 'pre':
  before => Stage['main'],
}
```

This is equivalent to:

```
stage { 'pre': }
Stage['pre'] -> Stage['main']
```

We can assign any class to a defined stage with the `stage` meta parameter:

```
class { 'yum':
  stage => 'pre',
}
```

In this way, all the resources provided by the `yum` class , which is included in pre-stage are applied before all the other resources (in the default main stage).

The idea of stages at the beginning seemed a good solution to better handle large sets of dependencies in Puppet. In reality, some drawbacks and the augmented risk of having dependency cycles make them less useful than expected.

As a rule of thumb, it is recommended to use them for simple classes (that don't include other classes) and where really necessary (for example, to set up package management configurations at the beginning of a Puppet run, or deploy our application after all the other resources have been managed).

Reserved names and allowed characters

As with every language, Puppet DSL has some restrictions on the names we can give to its elements and the allowed characters.

As a general rule, for names of resources, variables, parameters, classes, and modules, we can use only lowercase letters, numbers, and the underscore (_). Usage of hyphens (-) should be avoided (in some cases, it is forbidden; in others, it depends on Puppet's version).

We can use uppercase letters in variable names (but not at their beginning), and use any character for resources' titles.

Names are case-sensitive, and there are some reserved words that cannot be used as names for resources, classes or defines, or as unquoted word strings in the code:

```
and, case, class, default, define, else, elsif, false, if, in,
import, inherits, node, or, true, undef, unless, main, settings,
$string.
```

Conditionals

Puppet provides different constructs to manage conditionals inside manifests.

Selectors, as we have seen, let us set the value of a variable or an argument inside a resource declaration according to the value of another variable. Selectors, therefore, just return values and are not used to conditionally manage entire blocks of code.

Here's an example of a selector:

```
$package_name = $::osfamily ? {
  'RedHat' => 'httpd',
  'Debian' => 'apache2',
  default  => undef,
}
```

A `case` statement is used to execute different blocks of code according to the values of a variable. It's recommended to have a default block for unmatched entries. Case statements can't be used inside resource declarations. We can achieve the same result of the previous selector with this `case` sample:

```
case $::osfamily {
  'Debian': { $package_name = 'apache2' }
  'RedHat': { $package_name = 'httpd' }
  default: { fail ("OS $::operatingsystem not supported") }
}
```

The `if`, `elsif`, and `else` conditionals, like `case`, are used to execute different blocks of code, and can't be used inside resources' declarations. We can use any of Puppet's comparison expressions, and we can combine more than one for complex pattern matching.

The previous sample variables assignment can also be expressed in this way:

```
if $::osfamily == 'Debian' {
  $package_name = 'apache2'
} elsif $::osfamily == 'RedHat' {
  $package_name = 'httpd'
} else {
  fail ("OS $::operatingsystem not supported")
}
```

An `unless` statement is the opposite of `if`. It evaluates a Boolean condition, and if it's false, it executes a block of code.

Comparison operators

Puppet supports comparison operators that resolve to true or false. They are as follows:

- **Equal** `==`, returns `true` if the operands are equal. Used with numbers, strings, arrays, hashes, and Booleans, as shown in the following example:

  ```
  if $::osfamily == 'Debian' { [ ... ] }
  ```

- **Not equal** `!=` , returns true if the operands are different:

  ```
  if $::kernel != 'Linux' { [ ... ] }
  ```

- **Less than** `<`, **greater than** `>`, **less than or equal to** `<=` and **greater than or equal to** `>=` can be used to compare numbers:

  ```
  if $::uptime_days > 365 { [ ... ] }
  if $::operatingsystemrelease <= 6 { [ ... ] }
  ```

- **Regex match** `=~` compares a string (the left operator) with a regular expression (the right operator). Resolves true, if it matches. Regular expressions are enclosed between forward slashes and follow the normal Ruby syntax:

  ```
  if $mode =~ /(server|client)/ { [ ... ] }
  if $::ipaddress =~ /^10\./ { [ ... ] }
  ```

- **Regex not match** `!~` , opposite to `=~`, resolves false if the operands match.

The In operator

The in operator checks if a string is present in another string, an array, or in the keys of a hash; it is case-sensitive:

```
if '64' in $::architecture
if $monitor_tool in [ 'nagios' , 'icinga' , 'sensu' ]
```

Expressions combinations

It's possible to combine multiple comparisons with and and or as shown in the following code:

```
if ($::osfamily == 'RedHat') and ($::operatingsystemrelease == '5') {
[ ... ] }
if (operatingsystem == 'Ubuntu') or ($::operatingsystem == 'Mint') { [
...] }
```

Exported resources

When we need to provide a host with information about the resources present in another host, things in Puppet become trickier. The only official solution has been, for a long time, to use exported resources; resources are declared in the catalog of a node (based on its facts and variables) but applied (collected) on another node. Some alternative approaches are now possible with PuppetDB; we will review them in *Chapter 3, PuppetDB*.

Resources are declared with the special @@ notation, which marks them as exported so that they are not applied to the node where they are declared:

```
@@host { $::fqdn:
  ip  => $::ipaddress,
}
@@concat::fragment { "balance-fe-${::hostname}":
  target  => '/etc/haproxy/haproxy.cfg',
  content => "server ${::hostname} ${::ipaddress} maxconn 5000",
  tag     => "balance-fe",
}
```

Once a catalog that contains exported resources has been applied on a node and stored by the Puppet Master, the exported resources can be collected with the <<|
|>> operator, where it is possible to specify search queries:

```
Host <<| |>>
Concat::Fragment <<| tag == "balance-fe" |>>
Sshkey <<| |>>
Nagios_service <<| |>>
```

In order to use exported resources, we need to enable on the Puppet Master the storeconfigs option and specify the backend to use. For a long time, the only available backend was Rails' active records, which typically used MySQL for data persistence. This solution was the best for its time but suffered severe scaling limitations. Luckily, things have changed a lot with the introduction of PuppetDB, which is a fast and reliable storage solution for all the data generated by Puppet, including exported resources.

In order to configure a Puppet Master to enable storeconfigs with PuppetDB, we have to add these lines in the [master] section of puppet.conf (more on this in a later chapter):

```
storeconfigs = true
storeconfigs_backend = puppetdb
```

If we want to use the old ActiveRecord backend, with a SQLite backend (which is useful to test exported resources without the need to install any other component, but definitively not applicable in production environments), the configuration is (we need to have installed the sqlite packages and ruby bindings) shown in the following code:

```
storeconfigs = true
dbadapter = sqlite3
```

To use ActiveRecords with a MySQL backend, we need these configurations:

```
storeconfigs = true
dbadapter = mysql
dbuser = puppet
dbpassword = secretpassword
dbserver = localhost
dbsocket = /var/run/mysqld/mysqld.sock # If server is local
```

Obviously, we will need to grant the relevant credentials on MySQL:

```
# mysql -u root -p
mysql> create database puppet;
mysql> grant all privileges on puppet.* to puppet@localhost
  identified by 'secretpassword';
```

Virtual resources

Virtual resources define a desired state for a resource without adding it to the catalog. Like normal resources, they are applied only on the node where they are declared, but like virtual resources, we can apply only a subset of the ones we have declared; they also have a similar usage syntax; we declare them with a single @ prefix (instead of the @@ prefix used for exported resources), and we collect them with <| |> (instead of <<| |>>).

A useful and rather typical example involves user management.

We can declare all our users in a single class, included by all our nodes:

```
class my_users {
  @user { 'al': [...] tag => 'admins' }
  @user { 'matt': [...] tag => 'developers' }
  @user { 'joe': [... tag => 'admins' }
[ ... ]
}
```

These users are actually not created on the system; we can decide which ones we want on a specific node with a syntax like the following:

```
User <| tag == admins |>
```

This is equivalent to:

```
realize(User['al'] , User['joe'])
```

Note that the `realize` function needs to address resources by their name.

Modules

Modules are self-contained, distributable, and (ideally) reusable recipes to manage specific applications or system's elements.

They are basically just a directory with a predefined and standard structure that enforces configuration over naming conventions for the managed provided classes, extensions, and files.

The `$modulepath` configuration entry defines where modules are searched; this can be a list of colon-separated directories.

The paths of a module and autoloading

Modules have a standard structure, for example, for a MySQL module:

```
mysql/              # Main module directory

mysql/manifests/    # Manifests directory. Puppet code here.
mysql/lib/          # Plugins directory. Ruby code here
mysql/templates/    # ERB Templates directory
mysql/files/        # Static files directory
mysql/spec/         # Puppet-rspec test directory
mysql/tests/        # Tests / Usage examples directory

mysql/Modulefile   # Module's metadata descriptor
```

This layout enables useful conventions that are widely used in the Puppet world; we must know these to understand where to look for files and classes.

For example, when we use modules and write the code:

```
include mysql
```

Puppet automatically looks for a class called `mysql` defined in the file $modulepath/mysql/manifests/init.pp.

The init.pp script is a special case that applies for classes that have the same name of the module. For subclasses there's a similar convention that takes in consideration the subclass name:

```
include mysql::server
```

It autoloads the file $modulepath/mysql/manifests/server.pp.

A similar scheme is followed also for defines or classes at lower levels:

```
mysql::conf { ...}
```

This define is searched in $modulepath/mysql/manifests/conf.pp

```
include mysql::server::ha
```

This class is searched in $modulepath/mysql/manifests/server/ha.pp.

It's generally recommended to follow these naming conventions that allow the autoloading of classes and defines without the need to explicitly import the manifests that contain them.

 Even if this is not considered a good practice, we can currently define more than one class or define inside the same manifest; when Puppet parses a manifest, it parses its whole contents.

A module's naming conventions apply also to the files that Puppet provides to clients.

We have seen that the `file` resource accepts two different and alternative arguments to manage the content of a file: `source` and `content`. Both of them have a naming convention when used inside a module.

ERB templates are typically parsed via the `template` function with a syntax like the following:

```
content => template('mysql/my.cnf.erb'),
```

This template is found in `$modulepath/mysql/templates/my.cnf.erb`.

This also applies for subdirectories, so for example:

```
content => template('apache/vhost/vhost.conf.erb'),
```

uses a template located in `$modulepath/apache/templates/vhost/vhost.conf.erb`.

A similar approach is followed with static files provided via the `source` argument:

```
source => 'puppet:///modules/mysql/my.cnf'
```

serves a file placed in `$modulepath/mysql/files/my.cnf`.

```
source => 'puppet:///modules/site/openssh/sshd_config'
```

serves a file placed in `$modulepath/site/openssh/sshd_config`

Finally, the whole content of the `lib` subdirectory in a module has a standard scheme. Here, we can place Ruby code that extends Puppet's functionality and is automatically redistributed from the Master to all clients (if the `pluginsync` configuration parameter is set to `true`, this is the default value for Puppet 3 and is widely recommended in any setup).

```
mysql/lib/augeas/lenses/              # Custom Augeas lenses.
mysql/lib/facter/                     # Custom facts.
```

```
mysql/lib/puppet/type/                    # Custom types.
mysql/lib/puppet/provider/<type_name>/    # Custom providers.
mysql/lib/puppet/parser/functions/        # Custom functions.
```

ERB templates

Files provisioned by Puppet can be templates written in Ruby's ERB templating language.

An ERB template can contain whatever text we need, and have inside `<% %>` tags an interpolation of variables or Ruby code. We can access in a template, all the Puppet variables (facts or user-assigned) with the `<%=` tag:

```
# File managed by Puppet on <%= @fqdn %>
search <%= @domain %>
```

It is recommended, and will be mandatory in future Puppet versions to refer to variables in a scope using the @ prefix).

To use out of scope variables, we can use the `scope.lookupvar` method:

```
path <%= scope.lookupvar('apache::vhost_dir') %>
```

This uses the variable's fully qualified name. If the variable is at top scope:

```
path <%= scope.lookupvar('::fqdn') %>
```

Since Puppet 3, we can use this alternate syntax:

```
path <%= scope['apache::vhost_dir'] %>
```

In ERB templates, we can also use more elaborate Ruby code inside a `<%` opening tag, for example, to reiterate over an array:

```
<% @dns_servers.each do |ns| %>
nameserver <%= ns %>
<% end %>
```

The `<%` tag is used to place line of text if some conditions are met:

```
<% if scope.lookupvar('puppet::db') == "puppetdb" -%>
  storeconfigs_backend = puppetdb
<% end -%>
```

Noticed the `-%>` ending tag here? When the dash is present, no line is introduced on the generated file as it would happen if we had written `<% end %>`.

Restoring files from a filebucket

Puppet, by default, makes a local copy of all the files that it changes on a system. This functionality is managed with the `filebucket` type, which allows storing a copy of the original files either on a central server or locally on the managed system.

When we run Puppet, we see messages like:

```
info: /Stage[main]/Ntp/File[ntp.conf]: Filebucketed /etc/ntp.conf to
puppet with sum 7fda24f62b1c7ae951db0f746dc6e0cc
```

The checksum of the original file is useful to retrieve it; in fact, files are saved in the directory `/var/lib/puppet/clientbucket` in a series of subdirectories named according to the same checksum. So, given the above example, we can see the original file content with the command:

```
cat /var/lib/puppet/clientbucket/7/f/d/a/2/4/f/6/
7fda24f62b1c7ae951db0f746dc6e0cc/contents
```

We can show the original path with the command:

```
cat /var/lib/puppet/clientbucket/7/f/d/a/2/4/f/6/
7fda24f62b1c7ae951db0f746dc6e0cc/paths
```

A quick way to search for the saved copies of a file, therefore, is to use a command like the following:

```
grep -R /etc/ntp.conf /var/lib/puppet/clientbucket/
```

Puppet provides the filebucket subcommand to retrieve saved files. In the above example, we can recover the original file with a (not particularly handy) command, as follows:

```
puppet filebucket restore -l --bucket /var/lib/puppet/clientbucket /etc/
ntp.conf 7fda24f62b1c7ae951db0f746dc6e0cc
```

It's possible to configure a remote filebucket, typically on the Puppet Master, using the special `filebucket` type:

```
filebucket { 'central':
  path   => false,    # This is required for remote filebuckets.
  server => 'my.s.com', # Optional, by default is the puppetmaster
}
```

Once `filebucket` is declared, we can assign it to a file with the `backup` argument:

```
file { '/etc/ntp.conf':
  backup => 'central',
}
```

This is generally done using a resource default defined at top scope (typically in our `/etc/puppet/manifests/site.pp`):

```
File { backup => 'central', }
```

Summary

In this chapter, we have reviewed and summarized the basic Puppet principles that are a prerequisite to better understand the contents of the book. We have seen how Puppet is configured and what its main components are: manifests, resources, nodes, and classes, and the power of the Resource Abstraction Layer.

The most useful language elements have been described: variables, references, resources defaults and ordering, conditionals, and comparison operators. We have taken a look at exported and virtual resources and analyzed the structure of a module. We also learned how to work with ERB templates. Finally, we have seen how Puppet's filebucket works and how to recover files modified by Puppet.

We are now ready to face a very important component of the Puppet ecosystem: Hiera, and see how it can be used to separate our data from Puppet code.

2
Hiera

The history of Puppet is an interesting example of how best practices have evolved with time, following new usage patterns and contributions from the community.

Once people started to write manifests and express the desired state of their systems with Puppet's DSL, they found themselves placing custom variables and parameters that expressed various resources of their infrastructures (IP addresses, hostnames, paths, URLs, names, properties, lists of objects, and so on) inside the code used to create the needed resource types.

At times, variables were used to classify and categorize nodes (systems' roles, operational environments, and so on); at other times, facts (such as `$::operatingsystem`) were used to provide resources with the right names and paths according to the underlying OS.

Variables could be defined in different places; they could be set via an ENC, inside node declarations, or inside classes.

There wasn't (and actually, still there isn't) any strict rule on how and where the user's data could be placed, but the general outcome was that we often found ourselves having our custom data defined inside our manifests.

Now, in my very personal and definitely non-orthodox opinion, this is not necessarily or inherently a bad thing; seeing the data we provide when we define our resources gives us a clearer visibility on how things are done and doesn't compel us to look in different places in order to understand what our code is doing.

Nevertheless, such an approach may be fit for relatively simple setups where we don't need to cope with large chunks of data that might come from different sources and change a lot according to different factors.

Also, we might need to have different people working on Puppet who write the code and design its logic and who need to apply configurations, mostly dealing with data.

More generally, the concept of separating data from code is a well-established and sane development practice, which also makes sense in the Puppet world.

The person who faced this issue in the most resolutive way is R.I. Pienaar. First, he developed the `extlookup` function (included in Puppet core for a long time), which allows users to read data from external CSV files. Then, he took a further step and developed **Hiera**, a key-value lookup tool, where data used by our manifests can be placed and evaluated differently according to a custom hierarchy from different data sources.

One of the greatest features of Hiera is its modular pluggable design that allows the usage of different backends that may retrieve data from different sources, such as YAML or JSON files, Puppet classes, MySQL, Redis, REST services, and more.

In this chapter, we will cover the following topics:

- Installing and configuring Hiera
- Defining custom hierarchies and backends
- Using the Hiera command-line tool
- Using the `hiera()`, `hiera_array()`, and `hiera_hash()` functions inside our Puppet manifests
- Integrating Hiera in Puppet 3
- Providing files via Hiera with the `hiera-file` backend
- Encrypting our data with the `hiera-gpg` and `hiera-eyaml` backends
- Using Hiera as an External Node Classifier with `hiera_include()`

Installing and configuring Hiera

From Puppet 3.x, Hiera has been officially integrated, and it is installed as a dependency when we install Puppet.

On Puppet 2.x, we need to install Hiera separately on the node where the Puppet Master resides: we need both the `hiera` and `hiera-puppet` packages, either via the OS native packaging system or via `gem`.

Hiera is not required on the clients unless they operate in a Masterless setup.

Its configuration file is `hiera.yaml`, and its path depends on how it is invoked, which can be either of the following ways:

- When invoked from Puppet, the path will be `/etc/puppet/hiera.yaml` (`/etc/puppetlabs/puppet/hiera.yaml` for Puppet Enterprise)

- When invoked from the CLI or when used within Ruby code, the path is `/etc/hiera.yaml`

It makes sense to create a symlink, and be sure to always use and edit the same file using the following command:

```
ln -s /etc/hiera.yaml /etc/puppet/hiera.yaml
```

The file is a YAML hash, where the top-level keys are Ruby symbols with a colon (:) prefix, which may either be global or backend-specific settings.

Global settings

Global settings are general configurations that are independent of the used backend. They are listed as follows:

- `:hierarchy`: This is a string or an array that describes the data sources to be looked for. Data sources are checked from the top to bottom and may be dynamic, that is, contain variables (we reference them with `%{variablename}`). The default value is `common`.

- `:backends`: This is a string or an array that defines the backends to be used. The default value is `yaml`.

- `:logger`: This is a string of a logger where messages are sent. The default value is `console`.

- `:merge_behavior`: This is a string that describes how hash values are merged across different data sources. The default value is `native`; the first key found in the hierarchy is returned. Alternative values such as `deep` and `deeper` require the `deep_merge` Ruby Gem.

Backend-specific settings

Any backend may have its specific settings; the following are used by the native YAML, JSON, and Puppet ones:

- `:datadir`: This is a string. It is used by the JSON and YAML backends, and it is the directory where the data sources that are defined in the hierarchy can be found. We can place variables (`%{variablename}`) here for a dynamic lookup.

- `:datasource`: This is a string. It is used by the Puppet backend. This is the name of the Puppet class where we need to look for variables.

The hiera.yaml examples

The default content for the `hiera.yaml` configuration file is as follows:

```
---
:backends: yaml
:yaml:
  :datadir: /var/lib/hiera
:hierarchy: common
:logger: console
```

Using these settings, Hiera key-values are read from a YAML file with the path `/var/lib/hiera/common.yaml`.

A real-world configuration that uses the extra GPG backend may look like the following YAML:

```
---
:backends:
  - yaml
  - gpg

:hierarchy:
  - "%{::environment}/nodes/%{::fqdn}"
  - "%{::environment}/roles/%{::role}"
  - "%{::environment}/zones/%{::zone}"
  - "%{::environment}/common"

:yaml:
  :datadir: /etc/puppet/hieradata
:gpg:
  :datadir: /etc/puppet/gpgdata
  :key_dir: /etc/puppet/gpgkeys
```

The previous example uses custom $::role$ and $::zone$ variables that identify the function of the node and its data center, zone, or location. They are not native facts, so we should define them as custom facts or as top scope variables.

Also, an example like the previous one expects to have modules that fully manage the differences in operating systems so that we don't have to manage in our hierarchy different settings for a different OS.

Beware of the hierarchy array. If the individual values begin with a variable to interpolate, we need to quote them with double quotes (").

The following is an example with the usage of the file backend to manage not only key-value entries but also whole files:

```
---
:backends:
  - yaml
  - file
  - gpg

:hierarchy:
  - "%{::env}/fqdn/%{::fqdn}"
  - "%{::env}/role/%{::role}"
  - "%{::env}/zone/%{::zone}"
  - "%{::env}/common"
:yaml:
  :datadir: /etc/puppet/data

:file:
  :datadir: /etc/puppet/data

:gpg:
  :key_dir: /etc/puppet/gpgkeys
  :datadir: /etc/puppet/gpgdata
```

Besides the added backend with its configuration, an alternate approach is used to manage different environments (intended as the operational environments of the nodes, for example, Production, Staging, Test, and Development).

Here, to identify the node's operational environment, we use a custom top scope variable or fact called $::env and not Puppet's internal variable $::environment. The difference is important since it can lead to confusion.

The $::environment variable is used to map different Puppet environments to different directories for modules and manifests. This is useful, for example, to test our Puppet code on some servers.

Our custom $::env variable (we could call it in any other way, such as $::tier or $::stage) identifies the operational environment of the node, whether it's used for development or testing, or provides production services. We can use such a variable to manage our configuration logic accordingly.

Working with the command line on a YAML backend

When we use a backend based on files such as JSON or YAML, which are the most commonly used, we have to recreate on the filesystem the hierarchy defined in our hiera.yaml file; the files that contain Hiera data must be placed in these directories.

Let's see Hiera in action. Provide a sample hierarchy configuration as follows:

```
:hierarchy:
  - "nodes/%{::fqdn}"
  - "env/%{::env}"
  - common

:yaml:
  :datadir: /etc/puppet/hieradata
```

We have to create a directory structure as follows:

```
mkdir -p /etc/puppet/hieradata/nodes
mkdir -p /etc/puppet/hieradata/env
```

Then, work on the YAML files as shown:

vi /etc/puppet/hieradata/nodes/web01.example42.com.yaml

vi /etc/puppet/hieradata/env/production.yaml

vi /etc/puppet/hieradata/env/test.yaml

vi /etc/puppet/hieradata/common.yaml

The previous files are plain YAML files where we can specify the values for any Hiera-managed variable. These values can be strings, arrays, or hashes.

We can place our default settings in /etc/puppet/hieradata/common.yaml as follows:

```
---
# A simple string assigned to a key
timezone: 'Europe/Rome'

# A string with variable interpolation
nagios_server: "nagios.%{::domain}"

# A string with another variable defined in Hiera (!)
dns_nameservers: "%{hiera('dns_servers')}"

# A string assigned to a key that maps to the
# template parameter of the openssh class (on Puppet3)
openssh::template: 'site/common/openssh/sshd_config.erb'

# An array of values
ldap_servers:
  - 10.42.10.31
    10.42.10.32

# An array with a single value
ntp::ntp_servers:
  - 10.42.10.71

# A hash of values
users:
  al:
    home: '/home/al'
    comment: 'Al'
  jenkins:
    password: '!'
    comment: 'Jenkins'
```

Given the previous example, execute a Hiera invocation as follows:

```
hiera ldap_servers
```

It will return the following array:

```
["10.42.10.31", "10.42.10.32"]
```

If we define a different value for a key in a data source that is higher in the hierarchy, that value is returned. Let's create a data source for the test environment by editing the file /etc/puppet/hieradata/env/test.yaml as follows:

```
---
ldap_servers:
- 192.168.0.31
users:
  qa:
    home: '/home/qa'
    comment: 'QA Tester'
```

Consider a normal Hiera lookup for the ldap_servers key as follows:

```
hiera ldap_servers
```

It will still return the common value ["10.42.10.31", "10.42.10.32"].

However, we can explicitly pass the env variable as follows:

```
hiera ldap_servers env=test
```

The returned value is the one for the test env as follows:

```
["192.168.0.31"]
```

If we have a more specific setting for a given node, that value is returned. Suppose we edit the file ldap.example42.com.yaml in /etc/puppet/hieradata/ nodes/ with the following code:

```
---
ldap_servers:
- 127.0.0.1
```

When we query Hiera and refer to a specific node's FQDN using the following command:

```
hiera ldap_servers fqdn=ldap.example42.com
```

The result is the one from the higher source in the hierarchy:

```
["127.0.0.1"]
```

We have seen that by default, Hiera returns the first value found while traversing the data sources' hierarchy, from the first to the last. When more backends are specified, the whole hierarchy of the first backend is fully traversed, and then the same is done for the second and so on.

Hiera also provides some alternate lookup options. When we deal with arrays, for example, we can decide to merge all the values found in the hierarchy instead of returning the first one found. We make our query to specify the `-a` or `--array` option as follows:

```
hiera -a ldap_servers fqdn=ldap.example42.com
```

The result contains all the entries for the `ldap_servers` key in all the data sources of our hierarchy as follows:

```
["127.0.0.1", "10.42.10.31", "10.42.10.32"]
```

Note that the value defined for the `env=test` case is not returned unless we specify it using the following command:

```
hiera -a ldap_servers fqdn=ldap.example42.com env=test
```

In this case, the output would be as follows:

```
["127.0.0.1", "192.168.0.31", "10.42.10.31", "10.42.10.32"]
```

When working with hashes, interesting things can be done.

Let's see what's the value of the `users` key for the test environment:

```
hiera users env=test
```

The output is the hash we configured in `test.yaml`:

```
{"qa"=>{"home"=>"/home/qa", "comment"=>"QA Tester"}}
```

As it normally does, Hiera returns the first value it encounters while traversing the hierarchy, but in this case, we might prefer to have a hash that contains all the values found. Similar to the `-a` option for arrays, we have at our disposal the `-h` (`--hash`) option for hashes:

```
hiera -h users env=test
```

The result is a hash that contains all the users defined in different data sources:

```
{"al"=>{"home"=>"/home/al", "comment"=>"Al"},
 "jenkins"=>{"password"=>"!", "comment"=>"Jenkins"},
 "qa"=>{"home"=>"/home/qa", "comment"=>"QA Tester"}}
```

Note that hashes are not ordered according to the matching order as arrays are.

Let's perform one more experiment. Let's add a new user specific to our `ldap.example42.com` node and give different values to a parameter that is already defined in the common data source. We edit the file `ldap.example42.com.yaml` in `vi /etc/puppet/hieradata/nodes/` with the following code:

```
users:
  openldap:
    groups: 'apps'
  jenkins:
    ensure: absent
```

Consider a hash lookup as follows:

```
hiera -h users fqdn=ldap.example42.com env=test
```

As expected, this would return all the users found in all the hierarchy levels:

```
{"al"=>{"home"=>"/home/al", "comment"=>"Al"},
 "jenkins"=>{"ensure"=>"absent"},
 "qa"=>{"home"=>"/home/qa", "comment"=>"QA Tester"},
 "openldap"=>{"groups"=>"apps"}}
```

Let's take a look at the parameters of the `jenkins` user; being defined both at the node level and in the common data source, the returned value is the one for the higher data source in the hierarchy.

Hiera's management of hashes can be quite powerful, and we can make optimal use of it. For example, we can use them inside Puppet manifests with the `create_resources` function, with the hash of `users` data and a single line of code as follows:

```
create_resources(user, hiera_hash($users))
```

Based on highly customizable Hiera data, we can manage all the users of our nodes.

> We can tune how Hiera manages the merging of hashes with the `merge_behavior` global setting, which allows deeper merging at a single-key levels. Read the official documentation at `http://docs.puppetlabs.com/hiera/1/lookup_types.html#hash-merge` for more details.

Quite often, we need to understand where a given key is set in our hierarchy and what values will be computed for it. The -d (debug) option is rather useful for this. The previous line will return an output as follows:

```
hiera -d -h users fqdn=ldap.example42.com env=test
DEBUG: 2013-12-07 13:11:07 +0100: Hiera YAML backend starting
DEBUG: <datetime>: Looking up users in YAML backend
DEBUG: <datetime>: Looking for data source nodes/ldap.example42.com
DEBUG: <datetime>: Found users in nodes/ldap.example42.com
DEBUG: <datetime>: Looking for data source env/test
DEBUG: <datetime>: Found users in env/test
DEBUG: <datetime>: Looking for data source common
DEBUG: <datetime>: Found users in common
{"al"=>{"home"=>"/home/al", "comment"=>"Al"},
  "jenkins"=>{"ensure"=>"absent"},
  "qa"=>{"home"=>"/home/qa", "comment"=>"QA Tester"},
  "openldap"=>{"groups"=>"apps"}}
```

This output also tells us where Hiera is actually looking for data sources.

In a real Puppet environment, it is quite useful to use the --yaml option, which, when used with a real facts file of a node, allows us to evaluate exactly how Hiera computes its keys for real servers.

On the Puppet Master, the facts of all the managed clients are collected in $vardir/yaml/facts, so this is the best place to see how Hiera evaluates keys for different clients:

```
hiera --yaml /var/lib/puppet/yaml/facts/<node>.yaml ldap_servers
```

Hiera can use other sources to retrieve the facts of a node and return its key values accordingly. We can interrogate the Puppet Master's inventory service with the following command:

```
hiera -i ldap.example42.com ldap_servers
```

As an alternative, we can query mcollective (from a machine where the mco client is installed):

```
hiera -m ldap.example42.com ldap_servers
```

Using Hiera in Puppet

Using the Hiera functions, the data stored in Hiera can be retrieved by the Puppet Master while compiling the catalog. In our manifests, we can have something like the following:

```
$dns_servers = hiera("dns_servers")
```

Note that the name of the Puppet variable need not be the same as that of the Hiera one, so the previous code can also be as follows:

```
$my_dns_servers = hiera("dns_servers")
```

This assigns to the variable `$my_dns_servers` the top value (the first one found while crossing the hierarchy of data sources) retrieved by Hiera for the key `dns_servers`.

We can also merge arrays and hashes here; so in order to retrieve an array of all the values in the hierarchy's data sources of a given key and not just the first one, we can use `hiera_array()` as follows:

```
$my_dns_servers = hiera_array("dns_servers")
```

If we expect a hash value for a given key, we can use the `hiera()` function to retrieve the top value found, or we can use `hiera_hash()` to merge all the found values in a single hash:

```
$openssh_settings = hiera_hash("openssh_settings")
```

All these Hiera functions may receive additional parameters, which are as follows:

- **Second argument**: If present and not blank, then this is the default value to use if no value is found for the given key.
- **Third argument**: This overrides the configured hierarchy by adding a custom data source at the top of it. This might be useful in cases where we need to evaluate data using a logic that is not contemplated by the current hierarchy and for which it isn't worth the effort to add an extra layer in the global configuration.

The following code shows the usage of additional parameters:

```
$my_dns_servers = hiera("dns_servers","8.8.8.8","$country")
```

Dealing with hashes in the Puppet code

With a hash, it is possible to express complex and structured data that has to be managed inside the Puppet code.

Remember that Hiera always returns the value of the first defined level keys, for example, we have a hash with nested hashes as shown in the following code:

```
network::interfaces_hash:
  eth0:
    ipaddress: 10.0.0.193
    netmask: 255.255.255.0
    network: 10.0.0.0
    broadcast: 10.0.0.255
    gateway: 10.0.0.1
    post_up:
      - '/sbin/ifconfig eth3 up'
      - '/sbin/ifconfig eth4 up'
  eth2:
    enable_dhcp: true
  eth3:
    auto: false
    method: manual
  eth4:
    auto: false
    method: manual
```

We can create a variable as follows inside our Puppet code that loads it:

```
$int_hash=hiera('network::interfaces_hash')
```

Then, refer to single values inside its data structure with the following code:

```
$ip_eth0=$int_hash['eth0']['ipaddress']
```

Otherwise, if we need to access this value from a template, we can directly write it in our erb file:

```
ipaddress <%= @int_hash['eth0']['ipaddress'] %>
```

> A complex hash like the previous one is typically used with a create_resources function as follows:
>
> **create_resources('network::interface', $interfaces_hash)**
>
> Here, the custom network::interface define is expected to accept as an argument a hash to configure one or more network interfaces.

Puppet 3 automatic parameter lookup

With Puppet 3, Hiera is shipped directly with the core code, but the integration goes far beyond; an automatic Hiera lookup is done for each class' parameter using the key `$class::$argument`; this functionality is called **data bindings** or **automatic parameter** lookup.

For example, consider the following class definition:

```
class openssh (
  $template = 'openssh/sshd.config.erb',
) { . . . }
```

The value of `$template` will be evaluated according to the following logic:

1. If the user directly and explicitly passes the template argument, then its value is used:

   ```
   class { 'openssh':
     template => 'site/openssh/sshd_config.erb',
   }
   ```

2. If no value is explicitly set, Puppet 3 automatically looks for the Hiera key `openssh::template`.

3. Finally, if no value is found in Hiera, then the default `'openssh/sshd. config.erb'` value is used.

To emulate a similar behavior on Puppet versions earlier than Version 3, we should write something like the following:

```
class openssh (
 $template = hiera("openssh::template",'openssh/sshd.config.erb'),
) { . . . }
```

Evolving usage patterns for class parameters

This strong integration has definitely boosted the adoption of Hiera and is changing the way Puppet code is organized and classes are declared.

Before Puppet 2.6, we could declare classes by just including them, optionally, more than once in our catalog, using the following code line:

```
include openssh
```

We could also manage the behavior of the class just by setting variables and having them dynamically evaluated inside the class, with something like the following code:

```
class openssh {
  file { 'sshd_config':
    content => template($openssh_template),
  }
}
```

This approach suffered the risks of having inconsistent values due to dynamic scoping of variables and parse ordering. Also, when using variables inside the module's code, it wasn't easy to understand what were the variables that could affect the class's behavior, and there was no public API that was easily accessible.

The introduction of parameterized classes in Puppet 2.6 allowed classes to expose their arguments in a clear way using the following code:

```
class openssh (
  $template = 'openssh/sshd.config.erb',
) { . . . }
```

Now, we can pass them explicitly and consistently in a class declaration as shown:

```
class { 'openssh':
  template => 'site/openssh/sshd_config.erb',
}
```

But the fact that we can declare a specific class using parameters only once in a node's catalog presented new challenges on how our custom code had to be organized; we could not include classes wherever needed, but we had to reorganize our manifests in order to avoid duplicate declarations.

From Puppet 3 onwards, it is possible to have the best of both worlds, as we can use the original way to include classes:

```
include openssh
```

We can use this statement in different parts of our manifests and be sure that the value of the `template` parameter is always looked up on the Hiera key `openssh::template`.

Additional Hiera backends

The possibility of creating and adding different backends where data is to be stored is one of the strong points of Hiera as it allows storing Puppet data in any possible source.

This allows integrations with existing tools and gives more options to provide data in a safe and controlled way, for example, a custom web frontend or a CMDB.

Let's review some of the most interesting backends that exist.

The hiera-file backend

The `hiera-file` backend (`https://github.com/adrienthebo/hiera-file`) conceived by Adrien Thebo to manage a type of data that previously couldn't be stored in a sane way in Hiera, that is, plain files.

To install it, just clone the previous git repository in `modulepath` or use its `gem` as follows:

```
gem install hiera-file
```

We configure it by specifying the `file` backend, the `hierarchy` setting we want, and the `datadir` path where our files are placed:

```
---
:backends:
  - file
:hierarchy:
  - "fqdn/%{fqdn}"
  - "role/%{role}"
  - "common"
:file:
  :datadir: /etc/puppet/data
```

Here, the key used for Hiera lookups is actually the name of a file present in the `.d` subdirectories inside `datadir` according to our hierarchy.

For example, consider the following Puppet code:

```
file { '/etc/ssh/sshd_config':
  ensure  => present,
  content => hiera('sshd_config'),
}
```

Given the previous hierarchy (the first file found is returned), the previous code will create a `sshd_config` file at `/etc/ssh/` with the content taken from files searched in these places.

```
/etc/puppet/data/fqdn/<fqdn>.d/sshd_config
/etc/puppet/data/role/<role>.d/sshd_config
/etc/puppet/data/common.d/sshd_config
```

In the previous example, `<fqdn>` and `<role>` have to be substituted with the actual FQDN and the role of our nodes.

If we want to provide an ERB template using `hiera-file`, we can use the following syntax:

```
file { '/etc/ssh/sshd_config':
  ensure  => present,
  content => inline_template(hiera('sshd_config.erb')),
}
```

This will look for and parse an `erb` template in the following places:

```
/etc/puppet/data/fqdn/<fqdn>.d/sshd_config.erb
/etc/puppet/data/role/<role>.d/sshd_config.erb
/etc/puppet/data/common.d/sshd_config.erb
```

The `hiera-file` backend is quite simple to use and very powerful because it allows us to move to Hiera what is generally placed in (site) modules, that is, plain files with which we manage and configure our applications.

The hiera-gpg backend

Here's another plugin that makes a lot of sense; a backend that allows us to encrypt sensitive data, `hiera-gpg` (`https://github.com/crayfishx/hiera-gpg`). It's written by Craig Dunn, who is the author of other very interesting plugins that we are going to review later.

Puppet code and data are generally versioned with an SCM and are distributed accordingly; it has always been an issue to decide how and where to store reserved data such as passwords, private keys, and credentials. They generally were the values assigned to variables either in clear text or as MD5/SHA hashes, but the possibility to expose them has always been a concern for Puppeteers, and various more or less imaginative solutions have been attempted (sometimes, the solution has been to simply ignore the problem and have no solution).

Backends such as `hiera-gpg` are a good solution for these cases. We can install it via its gem (we also need to have the `gpg` executable in our PATH, `gcc`, and the Ruby development libraries package (`ruby-devel`)):

```
gem install hiera-gpg
```

A sample `hiera.yaml` code is as follows:

```
---
:backends:
  - gpg
:hierarchy:
  - %{env}
  - common
:gpg:
  :datadir: /etc/puppet/gpgdata
#   :key_dir: /etc/puppet/gpg
```

The `key_dir` declaration is where our `gpg` keys are searched for; if we don't specify it, by default they are searched for in `~/.gnupg`; so on our Puppet Master, this would be the `.gnupg` directory in the home of the `puppet` user.

First of all, we must create a GPG key with the following command:

```
gpg --gen-key
```

We will be asked for the kind of key, its size and duration (the default settings are acceptable), a name, an e-mail, and a passphrase (even if `gpg` will complain, do not specify a passphrase because `hiera-gpg` doesn't support them).

Once the key is created, we can show it with:

```
gpg --list-key
```

The output is something like the following:

```
/root/.gnupg/pubring.gpg
-----------------------
pub   2048R/C96EECCF 2013-12-08
uid                  Puppet Master (Puppet) <al@lab42.it>
sub   2048R/0AFB6B1F 2013-12-08
```

Now, we can encrypt files, move into our gpg datadir, and create normal YAML files that contain our secrets, for example:

```
---
mysql::root_password: 'V3rys3cr3T!'
```

Note that this is a temporary file that we will probably want to delete because we'll use its encrypted version, which has to be created with the following command:

```
gpg --encrypt -o common.gpg -r C96EECCF common.yaml
```

The -r argument expects our key ID (as seen via gpg -list-key), and -o expects the output file, which must have the same name/path of our datasource with a .gpg suffix.

Then, we can finally use Hiera to get the key's value from the encrypted files, shown as follows:

```
hiera mysql::root_password -d
```

The output text contains debug information and the decrypted value as follows:

```
DEBUG: <datetime>: Hiera YAML backend starting
DEBUG: <datetime>: Looking up mysql::root_password in YAML backend
DEBUG: <datetime>: Looking for data source common
DEBUG: <datetime>: [gpg_backend]: Loaded gpg_backend
DEBUG: <datetime>: [gpg_backend]: Lookup called, key mysql::root_
password resolution type is priority
DEBUG: <datetime>: [gpg_backend]: GNUPGHOME is /root/.gnupg
DEBUG: <datetime>: [gpg_backend]: loaded cipher: /etc/puppet/gpgdata/
common.gpg
DEBUG: <datetime>: [gpg_backend]: result is a String ctx
#<GPGME::Ctx:0x7fb6aaa2f810> txt ---
mysql::root_password: 'V3rys3cr3T!'
DEBUG: <datetime>: [gpg_backend]: GPG decrypt returned valid data
DEBUG: <datetime>: [gpg_backend]: Data contains valid YAML
DEBUG: <datetime>: [gpg_backend]: Key mysql::root_password found in
YAML document, Passing answer to hiera
DEBUG: <datetime>: [gpg_backend]: Assigning answer variable
```

Now, we can delete the cleartext common.yaml file and safely commit in our repository the encrypted GPG file and use our public key for further edits.

When we need to edit our file, we can decrypt it with the following command:

```
gpg -o common.yaml -d common.gpg
```

Note that we'll need the `gpg` private key to decrypt a file; this is required on the Puppet Master, and we need it on any system where we intend to edit these files.

The `hiera-gpg` backend is a neat solution that is used to manage sensitive data, but it has some drawbacks. The most relevant one is that we have to work with full files and we don't have a clear control over who makes changes to it unless we distribute the `gpg` private key to each member of our team.

Other projects have tried to address these limitations: `hiera-eyaml` by Tom Poulton (`https://github.com/TomPoulton/hiera-eyaml`), `hiera_yamlgpg` (`https://github.com/compete/hiera_yamlgpg`), and Raziel (`https://github.com/jbraeuer/raziel`). All of them allow us to work on plain YAML files and encrypt only single values. Therefore, they allow editing of single key entries by any user who has the `gpg` public key (no private key is required to be shared in order to decrypt and edit a whole file).

The hiera-eyaml backend

Let's see how `hiera-eyaml` works as it seems to be the most used and most maintained of the mentioned projects. We install its gem using the following command:

```
gem install hiera-eyaml
```

We edit the `hiera.yaml` file to configure it as follows:

```
---
:backends:
  - eyaml
:hierarchy:
  - "nodes/%{fqdn}"
  - "env/%{env}"
  - common
:eyaml:
  :datadir: /etc/puppet/hieradata
  :pkcs7_private_key: /etc/puppet/keys/private_key.pkcs7.pem
  :pkcs7_public_key:  /etc/puppet/keys/public_key.pkcs7.pem
```

Now, we have at our disposal the powerful `eyaml` command, which makes the whole experience pretty easy and straightforward. We can use it to create our keys, encrypt and decrypt files or single strings, and directly edit on the fly files with encrypted values.

First, let's create our keys using the following command:

```
eyaml createkeys
```

They are placed in the `./keys` directory. Make sure that the user under which the Puppet Master runs (usually `puppet`) has read access to the private key.

Now, we can generate the encrypted value of any Hiera key with the following command:

```
eyaml encrypt -l 'mysql::root_password' -s 'V3ryS3cr3T!'
```

This will print on `stdout` both the plain encrypted string and a block of configuration that we can directly copy in our `.eyaml` files, as follows:

```
---
mysql::root_password: >
    ENC[PKCS7,MIIBeQYJKoZIhvcNAQcDoIIBajCCAWYCAQAxggEhMII   [...]
    +oefgBBdAJ60kXMMh/RHpaXQYX3T]
```

Note that the value is in the format ENC[PKCS7,Encrypted_Value].

Since we have the password stored in plain text in our bash history, we should clean it using the following command:

```
history | grep encrypt
  572   eyaml encrypt -l 'mysql::root_password' -s 'V3ryS3cr3T!'
history -d 572
```

Luckily, we have to generate the keys in a similar fashion only once, since great things happen when we have to change our encrypted values in our eyaml files. We can directly edit them with the following command:

```
eyaml edit /etc/puppet/hieradata/common.eyaml
```

Our editor will open the file and decrypt the encrypted values on the fly so that we can edit our secrets in clear text and save the file again (of course, we can do this only on a machine where we have access to the private key). This particularly makes the management and maintenance of our secrets handy.

To view the decrypted content of an eyaml file, we can use the following command:

```
eyaml decrypt -f /etc/puppet/hieradata/common.eyaml
```

Since `hiera-eyaml` manages both clear text and encrypted values, we can use it as our only backend if we want to work only on YAML files.

The hiera-http and hiera-mysql backends

The `hiera-http` (https://github.com/crayfishx/hiera-http) and `hiera-mysql` (https://github.com/crayfishx/hiera-mysql) backends are other powerful Hiera backends written by Craig Dunn. They perfectly interpret Hiera's modular and extendable design and allow us to retrieve our data either via a REST interface or via MySQL queries on a database.

A quick view of how they could be configured might give you an idea of how they can fit in different cases. To configure `hiera-http` in `hiera.yaml`, we can use settings like the one shown in the following code:

```
:backends:
  - http
:http:
  :host: 127.0.0.1
  :port: 5984
  :output: json
  :failure: graceful
  :paths:
    - /configuration/%{fqdn}
    - /configuration/%{env}
    - /configuration/common
```

To configure `hiera-mysql`, we might have settings like the following:

```
---
:backends:
  - mysql
:mysql:
  :host: localhost
  :user: root
  :pass: examplepassword
  :database: config
  :query: SELECT val FROM configdata WHERE var='%{key}' AND
environment='%{env}'
```

We will not get into the details of these; you can refer to the official documentation to know the implementation and usage details.

However, note how easy and intuitive the syntax to configure them is, and what powerful possibilities they open to let users manage Puppet data from, for example, a web interface, without touching Puppet code or even logging to a server and working with a SCM such as git.

Using Hiera as an ENC

Hiera provides an interesting function called `hiera_include`, which allows users to include all the classes defined for a given key.

This, in practice, exploits the Hiera flexibility to provide classes to nodes as an External Node Classifier does.

It's enough to place the following line in our `site.pp` file at `/etc/puppet/manifests/`:

```
hiera_include('classes')
```

Define in our data sources a `classes` key with an array of the classes to be included.

In a YAML-based backend, it would look like the following:

```
---
classes:
  - apache
  - mysql
  - php
```

This is exactly the same as having some declarations in our `site.pp` as follows:

```
include apache
include mysql
include php
```

The `classes` key (can have any name, but `classes` is a standard de facto) contains an array that is merged along the hierarchy. So we can define in a `common.yaml` file the classes that we want to include in all our nodes, and include specific classes for specific servers, adding them to the different layers of our hierarchy.

Along with the `hiera-file` backend, this function can help us have a fully Hiera-driven configuration on our Puppet architecture. It is one of the many options we have that will help us glue together the pieces that define and build our infrastructure.

Summary

Hiera is a powerful and integrated solution to manage Puppet data outside our code. It requires some extra knowledge and abstraction, but it brings with it a lot of flexibility and extendibility, thanks to its backend plugins.

In this chapter, we have seen how it works and how to use it, especially when coupled with Puppet 3's data bindings. We have also reviewed the most used plugins and grasped the power that comes with them.

Now, it is time to explore another relatively new and great component of a Puppet infrastructure that is going to change how we use and write Puppet code: PuppetDB.

3
PuppetDB

A model based on agents that receive and apply a catalog received from the Puppet Master has an intrinsic limitation. The client has no visibility and direct awareness about the state of resources of the other nodes.

It is not possible, for example, to execute functions that do different things according to different external conditions, during the catalog application. There are many cases where information about other nodes and services could be useful to manage local configurations. For example, we might have to perform the following actions:

- Start a service only when we are sure that the database, the queues, or any external resource it relies upon are already available in some external nodes
- Configure a load balancer that dynamically adds new servers, if they exist
- Manage the setup of a cluster; this setup involves specific sequences of commands to be executed in a certain order on different nodes

The declarative nature of Puppet's DSL might look inappropriate to manage setups or operations where activities have to be done in a procedural way whose sequence might be based on the availability of external resources.

Part of the problem can be solved using facts that are being executed on the client; they provide direct information about its environment.

In the following chapters, we will see how to write custom facts, but the basic concept is that they can contain the output of any command we may want to execute, which can check the state of applications, the availability of remote services, and the system's conditions.

We can use these facts in our manifests to define the resources to apply on the client and manage some of the previous cases. Still, we cannot have direct information on a node about resources on other nodes, besides what can be checked remotely.

The challenge, or at least a part of it, was tackled several years ago with the introduction of exported resources, as we have seen in *Chapter 1, Puppet Essentials*. They are special resources declared on one node but applied on another one.

Exported resources need the activation of the `storeconfigs` option, which used Rails' ActiveRecord libraries for data persistence.

The stored configurations based on ActiveRecord have served the Puppet users for years, but they suffered from performance issues, which could be almost unbearable on large installations with many exported resources.

In 2011, Deepak Giridharagopal, a Puppet Labs Lead Engineer, tackled the whole problem from a totally detached point of view and developed PuppetDB, a marvelous piece of software that copes not only with stored configurations but also with all Puppet-generated data.

In this chapter, we will cover the following topics:

- How to install and configure PuppetDB
- An overview of the available dashboards
- A detailed analysis of the PuppetDB API
- How to use the `puppetdbquery` module
- How PuppetDB can influence our future Puppet code

Installation and configuration

PuppetDB is an open source Closure application complementary to Puppet. It does exactly what the name suggests; it stores Puppet data that comprises the following:

- All the facts of the managed nodes
- A copy of the catalog compiled by the Master and sent to each node
- The reports of the subsequent Puppet runs with all the events that have occurred

What is stored must be queried, and for this, PuppetDB exposes a REST-like API that allows access to all its data.

Out of the box, it can act as an alternative for the following two functions done earlier using the ActiveRecord libraries:

- The backend for stored configurations, where we can store our exported resources
- A replacement of the Inventory Service (an API we can use to query the facts of all the managed nodes)

While read operations are based on a REST-like API, data is written by commands sent by the Puppet Master and queued asynchronously by PuppetDB to a pool of internal workers. These workers deliver data to the persistence layer that is based either on the embedded HSQLDB (usable mostly for testing or for small environments) or on PostgreSQL.

On medium and large sites, PuppetDB should be installed on dedicated machines (eventually, with PostgreSQL on separated nodes); on a small scale, it can be placed on the same server where the Puppet Master resides.

A complete setup involves the following:

- The configuration of the `init` scripts, the main configuration files, and logging on the PuppetDB server
- The connection settings to PuppetDB in the `/etc/puppet/puppetdb.conf` and `/etc/puppet/routes.yaml` files on our Puppet Master

Generally, communication is always between the Puppet Master and PuppetDB, based on certificates signed by the CA on the Master. However, we can have a Masterless setup, where each node communicates directly with PuppetDB.

Masterless PuppetDB setups won't be discussed in this book; for details, refer to `http://docs.puppetlabs.com/puppetdb/1.5/connect_puppet_apply.html`.

PuppetDB configurations

The configuration of PuppetDB involves the following operations on different files:

- The configuration file sourced by the `init` script, which affects how the service is started
- The main configuration settings placed in one or more files
- The logging configuration

The init script configuration

In the configuration file for the `init` script (`/etc/sysconfig/puppetdb` on RedHat or `/etc/default/puppetdb` on Debian), we can manage Java settings such as `JAVA_ARGS` or `JAVA_BIN` or PuppetDB settings such as `USER` (the user with which the PuppetDB process will run), `INSTALL_DIR` (the installation directory), or `CONFIG` (the configuration file path or the path of the directory containing the `.ini` files).

> To configure the maximum Java heap size, we can set `JAVA_ARGS="-Xmx512m"` (the recommended settings are `128m` + `1m` for each managed node if we use PostgreSQL, or `1g` if we use the embedded HSQLDB. Raise this value if we see `OutOfMemoryError` exceptions in logs).
>
> To expose the JMX interface, we can set `JAVA_ARGS="-Dcom.sun.management.jmxremote -Dcom.sun.management.jmxremote.port=1099"`.
>
> This will open a JMX socket on port 1099. Note, anyway, that all the JMX metrics are exposed also via the REST interface using the `/metric` namespace.

Configuration settings

On Puppet Labs packages, configurations are placed in various `.ini` files in the `/etc/puppetdb/conf.d/` directory.

The settings are managed in different `[sections]`; let's see the most important ones.

Application wide settings are placed under the following section:

```
[global]
```

Here are defined the paths where PuppetDB stores its files (`vardir`), configures Log4j (`logging-config`), and some limits on the maximum number of results that a resource or event query may return. If these limits are exceeded, the query returns an error:

```
vardir = /var/lib/puppetdb # Must be writable by Puppetdb user
logging-config = /etc/puppetdb/log4j.properties
resource-query-limit = 20000
event-query-limit = 20000
```

All settings related to the commands used to store data on PuppetDB are placed under the following section:

```
[command-processing]
```

Of particular interest is the `threads` setting that defines how many concurrent command processing threads to use (the default value is CPUs / 2). We can raise this value if our command queue (visible from the performance dashboard that we will analyze later) is constantly larger than zero. In such cases, we should also evaluate if the bottleneck may be on the database's performance.

Other settings are related to the maximum disk space (in MB) that can be dedicated to persistent (`store-usage`) and temporary (`temp-usage`) ActiveMQ message storage. The settings are also dedicated to how long the messages that are not delivered have to be kept in a Dead Letter Office before being archived and compressed (`dlo-compression-threshold`). The valid units here, as in some other settings, are days, hours, minutes, seconds, and milliseconds as we can see in the following example:

```
threads = 4
store-usage = 102400
temp-usage = 51200
dlo-compression-threshold = 1d # Same of 24h, 1440m, 86400s
```

All the settings related to database persistence are under the following section:

```
[database]
```

Here, we define what database to use, how to connect to it, and some important parameters about data retention.

If we use the (default) HSQLDB backend, our settings will be as follows:

```
classname = org.hsqldb.jdbcDriver
subprotocol = hsqldb
subname = file./var/lib/puppetdb/db/db;hsqldb.tx=mvcc;sql.syntax_
pgs=true
```

For a (recommended) PostgreSQL backend, we need something like the following settings:

```
classname = org.postgresql.Driver
subprotocol = postgresql
subname = //<HOST>:<PORT>/<DATABASE>
username = <USERNAME>
password = <PASSWORD>
```

On our PostgreSQL server, we need to create a database and a user for PuppetDB as follows:

```
sudo -u postgres sh
createuser -DRSP puppetdb
createdb -E UTF8 -O puppetdb puppetdb
```

Also, we have to edit pg_hba.conf on the PostgreSQL server to allow access from our PuppetDB host (here, it is 10.42.42.30; it can be 127.0.0.1 if PostgreSQL and PuppetDB are on the same host), as shown in the following configuration:

```
# TYPE  DATABASE    USER    CIDR-ADDRESS    METHOD
host    all         all     10.42.42.30/32  md5
```

Given the above examples and a PostgreSQL server with the IP, 10.42.42.35, the connection settings would be as follows:

```
subname = //10.42.42.35:5432/puppetdb
username = puppetdb
password = <the password entered with the createuser command>
```

If PuppetDB and PostgreSQL server are on separated hosts, we may prefer to encrypt the traffic between them. To do so, we have to enable SSL/TLS on both sides. For a complete overview of the steps required, refer to the official documentation: http://docs.puppetlabs.com/puppetdb/latest/postgres_ssl.html

Other interesting settings manage how often, in minutes, the database is compacted to free up space and remove unused rows (gc-interval) when to autodeactivate nodes that are not reporting (node-ttl), when to completely remove the deactivated nodes (node-purge-ttl), and what is the retention time for reports (report-ttl, default 14d). Values for these settings can be expressed in d, h, m, s, and ms:

```
gc-interval = 60
node-ttl = 15d # Nodes not reporting for 15 days are deactivated
node-purge-ttl = 10d # Nodes purged 10 days after deactivation
report-ttl = 14d # Event reports are kept for 14 days
```

The node-ttl and node-purge-ttl settings are particularly useful in dynamic and elastic environments where nodes are frequently added and decommissioned. Setting them allows us to automatically remove old nodes from our PuppetDB, and if we use exported resources for monitoring or load balancing, these settings definitely help in keeping PuppetDB data clean and relevant. Obviously, node-ttl must be higher than our nodes' Puppet-run interval.

Be aware, though, that if we have the (questionable) habit of disabling regular Puppet execution for manual maintenance, tests, or whatever reason, we may risk deactivating the nodes that are still working.

Finally, note that the nodes' automatic deactivation or purging is done when there is database compaction, so the gc-interval parameter must always be set with smaller intervals.

Another useful parameter is log-slow-statements that defines the number of seconds after any SQL query is considered slow. Slow queries are logged but still executed:

```
log-slow-statements = 10
```

Finally, some settings can be used to fine-tune the database's connection pool; we won't probably need to change the default values (in minutes):

```
conn-max-age = 60 # Maximum idle time
conn-keep-alive = 45 # Client-side keep-alive interval
conn-lifetime = 60 # The maximum lifetime of a connection
```

We can manage the HTTP settings (used for the web performance dashboard, the REST interface, and the commands) under the following section:

```
[jetty]
```

To manage HTTP's unencrypted traffic, we just have to define the listening IP (host; the default is localhost) and port as follows:

```
host = 0.0.0.0 # Listen on any interface (Read Note below)
port = 8080    # If not set, unencrypted HTTP access is disabled
```

Generally, the communication between Puppet Master and PuppetDB is via HTTPS (using certificates signed by the Puppet Master's CA). However, if we enable HTTP to view the web dashboard (that just shows usage metrics, which are not particularly sensible), be aware that the HTTP port can be used also to query and issue commands to PuppetDB (so, it definitively should not be accessed by unauthorized users). Therefore, if we open HTTP access to hosts other than the local host, we should either proxy or firewall the HTTP port to allow access to authorized clients/users only.

This is not an uncommon case, since the HTTPS connection requires a client host's SSL authentication, so it is not usable (in a comfortable way) to access the web dashboard from a browser.

For HTTPS access, some more settings are available to manage the listening address (ssl-host) and port (ssl-port), the path to the PuppetDB server certificate's PEM file (ssl-cert), its private key PEM file (ssl-key), and the path of the CA certificate's PEM file (ssl-ca-cert) used for client authentication. In the following example, the paths used are the ones of Puppet's certificates that leverage on the PuppetMaster's CA:

```
ssl-host = 0.0.0.0
ssl-port = 8081
ssl-key = /var/lib/puppet/ssl/private_keys/puppetdb.site.com.pem
ssl-cert = /var/lib/puppet/ssl/public_keys/puppetdb.site.com.pem
ssl-ca-cert = /var/lib/puppet/ssl/certs/ca.pem
```

The previous settings have been introduced in PuppetDB 1.4, and if present, they are preferred to the earlier (and now deprecated) parameters that managed SSL via the Java keystore files.

Here, we report a sample configuration that uses the Java keystore files as reference; we may find them on older installations:

```
keystore = /etc/puppetdb/ssl/keystore.jks
truststore = /etc/puppetdb/ssl/truststore.jks
key-password = s3cr3t # Passphrase to unlock the keystore file
trust-password = s3cr3t # Passphrase to unlock the truststore file
```

To set up SSL configurations, PuppetDB provides a very handy script that does the right thing according to the PuppetDB version and, eventually, according to the current configurations. Use it and follow the onscreen instructions:

`/usr/sbin/puppetdb-ssl-setup`.

Other optional settings define the cipher suites (`cipher-suites`) that are allowed, SSL protocols (`ssl-protocols`), and the path of a file that contains a list of certificate names (one per line) of the hosts allowed to communicate (via HTTPS) with PuppetDB (`certificate-whitelist`). If these are not set, any host can contact the PuppetDB, given that its client certificate is signed by the configured CA.

Finally, in our configuration file(s), we can enable real-time debugging in the `[repl]` section. This can be enabled to modify the behavior of PuppetDB at runtime and is used for debugging purposes mostly by developers, so it is disabled by default.

For more information, refer to `http://docs.puppetlabs.com/puppetdb/latest/repl.html`.

Logging configuration

Logging is done via Log4j and is configured in the `log4j.properties` file under the `logging-config` settings. By default, informational logs are placed in `/var/log/puppetdb/puppetdb.log`. Log settings can be changed at runtime and be applied without restarting the service.

Configurations on the Puppet Master

To configure the Puppet Master to use PuppetDB, various settings are involved. These settings are as follows:

- On `/etc/puppet/puppet.conf`, the PuppetDB backend has to be enabled for `storeconfigs` and, optionally, for reports:

```
[main]
storeconfigs = true
storeconfigs_backend = puppetdb
report = true
reports = puppetdb
```

```
# The following settings are already disabled by default
# and should remain disabled or absent with puppetdb
thin_storeconfigs = false
async_storeconfigs = false
```

- On `/etc/puppet/puppetdb.conf`, the `server` name and `port` of PuppetDB are configured. We can also define if the Puppet Master should serve the catalog to clients also when PuppetDB is unavailable by setting `soft_write_failure = true`. In this case, a catalog is created without the exported resources and facts, the catalog, and reports are not stored. This option should not be enabled when the exported resources are used. The default values are as follows:

```
server = puppetdb
port = 8081
soft_write_failure = false
```

- In `/etc/puppet/routes.yaml`, the facts' terminus has to be configured to make PuppetDB the authoritative source for the inventory service (create the file if it doesn't exist, and run `puppet config print route_file` to verify its path):

```
---
master:
  facts:
    terminus: puppetdb
    cache: yaml
```

Dashboards

The PuppetDB ecosystem provides web dashboards that definitively help user interaction:

- PuppetDB comes with an integrated performance dashboard
- Puppetboard is a web frontend that allows easy and direct access to PuppetDB data

PuppetDB performance dashboard

PuppetDB integrates a performance dashboard out of the box; we can use it to check how the software is working in real time. It can be accessed via HTTP at `http://puppetdb.server:8080/dashboard/` (if we've set `host = 0.0.0.0` on the PuppetDB configuration). Remember that we should limit HTTP access to authorized clients only, either by firewalling the host's port or setting `host = localhost` and having a local reverse proxy where you can manage access lists or authentication.

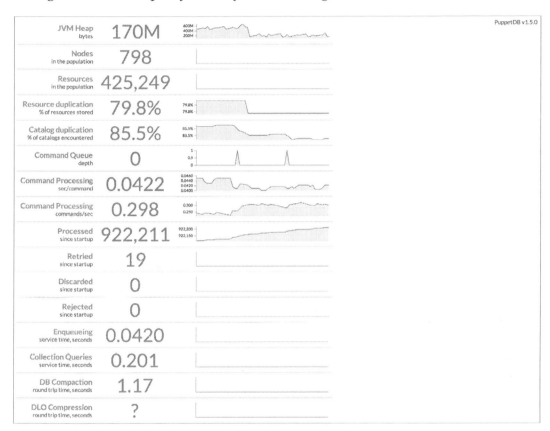

The PuppetDB performance dashboard

From the previous screenshot, the most interesting metrics are as follows:

- **JVM Heap memory usage**: This metric drops when the JVM runs a garbage collection.
- **Nodes**: The total number of nodes whose information is stored on PuppetDB.
- **Resources**: The total number of resources present in all the catalogs that are stored.
- **Catalog duplication**: How much the stored catalogs have in common.
- **Command queue**: How many commands are currently in queue; this value should not be constantly greater than a few units.
- **Command processing**: How many commands are delivered per second.
- **Processed**: How many commands have been processed since the service started.
- **Retried**: How many times the commands' submission has been retried since startup. A retry can be due to temporary reasons. A relatively low figure here is physiological; if we see it growing, we are having ongoing problems.
- **Discarded**: How many commands have been discarded since startup after all the retry attempts. It should not be more than zero.
- **Rejected**: How many commands were rejected and how many deliveries failed since startup. It should not be more than zero.

Puppetboard – query PuppetDB from the Web

The amount of information stored on PuppetDB is huge and precious, and while it can be queried from the command line, a visual interface can help users explore Puppet's data.

Daniele Sluijters, a community member, started a project that has quickly become the visual interface of reference for PuppetDB. This project is Puppetboard, a web frontend written in Python that allows easy browsing of nodes' facts, reports, events, and PuppetDB metrics.

It also allows us to directly query PuppetDB, so all the example queries from the command line, which we'll see in this chapter, can be issued directly from the web interface.

This is a relatively young and quite dynamic project that follows the evolution of PuppetDB's APIs; refer to its GitHub project for the latest installation and usage instructions at https://github.com/nedap/puppetboard.

The PuppetDB API

PuppetDB uses a **Command/Query Responsibility Separation (CQRS)** pattern:

- **Read**: These activities are done for queries on the available REST-like endpoints
- **Write**: These commands update catalog, facts, and reports and deactivate nodes

APIs are versioned (v1, v2, v3, and so on), and the most recent ones add functionalities and try to keep backward compatibility.

Querying PuppetDB (Read)

The URL for queries is structured as follows:

```
http[s]://<server>:<port>/<version>/<endpoint>?query=<query>
```

The available endpoints for queries are `metrics`, `fact-names`, `facts`, `nodes`, `resources`, `reports`, `events`, `event-counts`, `aggregate-event-counts`, and `server-time`.

Query strings are URL-encoded JSON arrays in prefix notation, which makes them look a bit unusual. The general format is as follows:

```
[ "<operator>" , "<field>" , "<value>" ]
```

The comparison operators are =, >=, >, < , <=, and ~ (`regexp` matching). Some examples are as follows:

```
["=", "type", "Service"]
[">=", "timestamp", "2013-12-18T14:00:00"]
["~", "certname", "www\\d+\\.example\\.com"]
```

The expressions can be combined with `and`, `not`, and `or`. An example (here, split into multiple lines for clarity) is as follows:

```
[ "and",
  ["=", "type", "File"],
  ["=", "title", "/etc/hosts" ]
]
```

It's possible to build complex subqueries using the `in` operator, the `extract` statement, and subqueries such as `select-resources` or `select-facts`. An example usable on the `/facts` endpoint to return the IPs of all the nodes that have an apache service is as follows:

```
["and",
  ["=", "name", "ipaddress"],
  ["in", "certname",
    ["extract", "certname",
      ["select-resources",
        ["and",
          ["=", "type", "Service"],
          ["=", "title", "apache"] ] ] ] ] ]
```

Since Version 3 of API, it is possible to paginate and sort the result of queries. Each endpoint may support one or more query parameters, such as `order-by`, `limit`, `include-total`, and `offset`.

It's quite easy to query PuppetDB directly with `curl`; here is the simplest example, with `curl` executed on HTTP on the same PuppetDB host:

```
curl 'http://localhost:8080/v3/facts/web01.example.com'
```

Note the URL to a specific endpoint (`facts`), the API version (`v3`), and the specific client `certname`.

When we have to use queries, we must URL encode chars such as `[` and `]`, and for this, we can use curl's `-data-urlencode` option. When we use it, we have to specify to use the `-X GET` option (otherwise, a post will be done):

```
curl -X GET 'http://localhost:8080/v3/events' --data-urlencode
  'query=["=", "certname" , "puppet.example.com"]'
```

The response, in the JSON array format (note the starting and ending square brackets `[ ]`) contains one or more entries as follows:

```
[ {
  "status" : "noop",
  "timestamp" : "2013-12-18T09:20:54.856Z",
  "certname" : "puppet.example.com",
  "containing-class" : null,
  "containment-path" : null,
  "report" : "3df0ea2301842c647f7cc6920eaf9148750b6ba1",
  "run-start-time" : "2013-12-18T09:20:26.930Z",
  "resource-title" : "/etc/puppet/puppetdb.conf",
  "configuration-version" : "1387358430",
```

```
"run-end-time" : "2013-12-18T09:20:50.643Z",
"property" : "content",
"message" : "current_value {md5}f4b9b4bf9565e0803e0115f4048d006,
  should be {md5}dc6af7f008160afc29afe4bbdada55a (noop)",
"new-value" : "{md5}dc6af7f008160afc29afe4bbdada55a",
"old-value" : "{md5}f4b9b4bf9565e0803e0115f4048d006",
"line" : 25,
"file" : "/etc/puppet/modules/puppet/manifests/server/puppetdb.pp",
"report-receive-time" : "2013-12-18T09:20:56.940Z",
"resource-type" : "File"
} ]
```

> Look at some of the most interesting fields: timestamp, certname, resource-title, resource-type, property, file, and line. Note that the name and kind of fields may vary according to the endpoint used (for example, on other endpoints, we have title and type, instead of resource-title and resource-type).
>
> We can experiment with test queries on various endpoints, as the ones listed later in this chapter, to have a better idea of the kind and name of the fields returned.

When we make requests over HTTPS, we have to reference the certificates' files to use:

```
curl 'https://puppetdb:8081/v3/facts/web01.example.com' \
  --cacert /var/lib/puppet/ssl/certs/ca.pem \
  --cert  /var/lib/puppet/ssl/certs/<node>.pem \
  --key /var/lib/puppet/ssl/private_keys/<node>.pem
```

The PuppetDB commands (Write)

Explicit commands are used (via HTTP's URL-encoded POST to the /commands URL) to populate and modify data.

The commands available on the current PuppetDB version (1.6 at the time of writing this book) are as follows:

- replace catalog: This replaces the stored catalog of a node. Currently, PuppetDB stores only the last catalog compiled by Puppet Master for each node.

- replace facts: This replaces the stored facts of a node. Also, in this case, only the ones received from the latest Puppet run are kept.

- `store report`: This saves the last report of a node's Puppet run. The `report-ttl` configuration parameter manages report retention (14 days by default).

- `deactivate node`: This deactivates a decommissioned node so that its exported resources can't be collected anywhere. A node is reactivated if a new Puppet run is done on it.

 This PuppetDB command is invoked whenever we execute on the Puppet Master the shell command `puppet node deactivate <certname>`. An automatic deactivation of the nodes that do not report can also be done via the `node-ttl` configuration option.

On `/var/log/puppetdb/puppetdb.log`, all the executed commands are shown.

When the Puppet Master receives a client's facts, it immediately submits them to PuppetDB:

```
2013-12-18 10:20:28,387 INFO  [command-proc-48] [puppetdb.command]
[1773a546-993e-479d-bf29-616d6369cc41] [replace facts] web01.example.
com
```

Then, the catalog is compiled, sent to the client, and stored on PuppetDB:

```
2013-12-18 10:20:43,847 INFO  [command-proc-49] [puppetdb.command]
[72cafd22-2281-422a-bab3-4623dd343891] [replace catalog] web01.
example.com
```

Finally, when the report of the Puppet run is received from the client, the Puppet Master submits it to PuppetDB:

```
2013-12-18 10:20:57,279 INFO  [command-proc-49] [puppetdb.command]
[b0c22f66-1796-45d7-8ed0-17a1ecac3e1e] [store report] puppet v2.7.23 -
web01.example.com
```

Querying PuppetDB for fun and profit

PuppetDB stores and exposes a large amount of information. What we can do with it? Probably, much more than what we might guess now. In this section, we explore the REST endpoints that are available, in detail.

Diving into such details might be useful to better understand what can be queried and may trigger new ideas on what we can do with such information.

In these samples, we use `curl` with HTTP directly from the server where PuppetDB is installed.

The /facts endpoint

Show all the facts of all our nodes (be careful, there may be a lot!):

```
curl 'http://localhost:8080/v3/facts'
```

Show the IP addresses of all our nodes (a similar search can be done for any fact):

```
curl 'http://localhost:8080/v3/facts/ipaddress'
```

Show the node that has a specific IP address:

```
curl 'http://localhost:8080/v3/facts/ipaddress/10.42.42.27'
```

Show all the facts of a specific node:

```
curl -X GET http://localhost:8080/v3/facts --data-urlencode \
  'query=["=", "certname", "web01.example.com"]'
```

The response is always a JSON array with an entry per fact; each entry is as follows:

```
{ "certname": <node name>, (IE: www01.example.com)
  "name": <fact name>, (IE: operatingsystem)
  "value": <fact value> (IE: ubuntu) }
```

The /resources endpoint

Show all the resources of the Mount type for all the nodes:

```
curl 'http://localhost:8080/v3/resources/Mount'
```

Show all the resources of a given node:

```
curl -X GET http://localhost:8080/v3/resources --data-urlencode \
  'query=["=", "certname", "web01.example.com"]'
```

Show all nodes that have Service['apache'] with ensure = running:

```
curl -X GET http://localhost:8080/v3/resources/Service \
--data-urlencode 'query=[ "and" , ["=", "title", "apache" ],
                [ "=", ["parameter", "ensure"], "running"] ]'
```

Same procedure as mentioned earlier using a different approach:

```
curl -X GET http://localhost:8080/v3/resources/Service/apache \
--data-urlencode 'query=["=", ["parameter", "ensure"], "running"]'
```

Show all the resources managed for a given node in a given manifest:

```
curl -X GET http://localhost:8080/v3/resources/ --data-urlencode \
  'query=["and" ["=", "file", "/etc/puppet/manifests/apache.pp"], \
            ["=", "certname", "web01.example.com"]]'
```

The response format of the resource's endpoint shows how we can query everything about the resources managed by Puppet and defined in our manifests:

```
{"certname":    "<node name>", (IE: www01.example.com)
 "resource":    "<the resource's unique hash>", (IE: f3h34ds...)
 "type":        "<resource type>", (IE: Service)
 "title":       "<resource title>", (IE: apache)
 "exported":    "<true|false>", (IE: false)
 "tags":        ["<tag>", "<tag>"], (IE: "apache", "class" ...)
 "file": "<manifest path>", (IE: "/etc/puppet/manifests/site.pp")
 "line": "<manifest line>", (IE: "3")
 "parameters": {<parameter>: <value>, (IE: "enable" : true,)
                <parameter>: <value>,
                ...}}
```

The /nodes endpoint

Show all the (not deactivated) nodes:

```
curl 'http://localhost:8080/v3/nodes'
```

Show all the facts of a specific node (a better alternative to the earlier example):

```
curl 'http://localhost:8080/v3/nodes/www01.example.com/facts'
```

Show all the resources of a specific node (a better alternative to the earlier example):

```
curl 'http://localhost:8080/v3/nodes/www01.example.com/resources'
```

Show all the nodes with the CentOS operating system:

```
curl -X GET http://localhost:8080/v3/nodes --data-urlencode \
  'query=["=", ["fact","operatingsystem"], "CentOS"]'
```

The response format is as follows:

```
{"name": <string>,
 "deactivated": <timestamp>,
 "catalog_timestamp": <timestamp>,
 "facts_timestamp": <timestamp>,
 "report_timestamp": <timestamp>}
```

When using the sub URLs of facts and resources, we get replies in the same format as the relative endpoint.

The /catalogs endpoint

Get the whole catalog (the one that was generated more recently) of a node (all the resources and edges):

```
curl 'http://localhost:8080/v3/catalogs/www01.example.com'
```

The /facts-names endpoint

Get the names (just the names, not the values) of all the stored facts:

```
curl 'http://localhost:8080/v3/facts-names'
```

The /metrics endpoint

These are mostly useful to check PuppetDB's performances and operational statistics. Some of them are visible from the performance dashboard.

Get the names of all the metrics available:

```
curl 'http://localhost:8080/v3/metrics/mbeans'
```

The result shows a remarkable list of items in the JMX Mbean ObjectName style:

```
<Mbean-doman>:type=<Type>[,name:<Name>]
```

An example, in URL encoded format:

```
"com.jolbox.bonecp:type=BoneCP" : "/metrics/mbean/com.jolbox.
bonecp%3Atype%3DBoneCP"
```

The metrics that are available are about the nodes' population, database connection, delivery status of the processed commands, HTTP access hits, the processing of commands, HTTP access, storage operations, JVM statistics, and the Message Queue system.

Let's see some examples. To view the total number of nodes registered on PuppetDB we can run the following command:

```
curl http://localhost:8080/v3/metrics/mbean/com.puppetlabs.puppetdb.
query.population%3Atype%3Ddefault%2Cname%3Dnum-nodes
```

The average number of resources per node is obtained with the command:

```
curl http://localhost:8080/v3/metrics/mbean/com.puppetlabs.puppetdb.
query.population%3Atype%3Ddefault%2Cname%3Davg-resources-per-node
```

Statistics about the time used for the `replace-catalog` command:

```
curl http://localhost:8080/v3/metrics/mbean/com.puppetlabs.puppetdb.
scf.storage%3Atype%3Ddefault%2Cname%3Dreplace-catalog-time
```

The /reports endpoint

Show the summaries of all the saved reports of a given node:

```
curl -X GET http://localhost:8080/v3/reports --data-urlencode \
  'query=["=", "certname", "db.example.com"]'
```

The /events endpoint

Search all the reports for failures:

```
curl -X GET 'http://localhost:8080/v3/events' --data-urlencode \
  'query=["=", "status" , "failure"]'
```

Search all the reports for failures on the `Service` type:

```
curl -X GET 'http://localhost:8080/v3/events' --data-urlencode \
  'query=[ "and", ["=", "status" , "failure"], \
                  ["=", "resource-type", "Service"] ]'
```

Search all the reports for any change to the file with the title `"hosts"`:

```
curl -X GET 'http://localhost:8080/v3/events' --data-urlencode \
  'query=[ "and", ["=", "resource-type", "File"], \
                  ["=", "resource-title", "hosts" ] ]'
```

Search all the reports for changes in the content of the file with the title `"hosts"`:

```
curl -X GET 'http://localhost:8080/v3/events' --data-urlencode \
  'query=[ "and", ["=", "resource-type", "File"], \
                  ["=", "resource-title", "hosts" ], \
                  ["=", "property", "content"] ]'
```

Show the changes on the specified file only after a given timestamp:

```
curl -X GET 'http://localhost:8080/v3/events' --data-urlencode \
  'query=[ "and", ["=", "resource-type", "File"], \
                  ["=", "resource-title", "hosts" ], \
                  [">", "timestamp", "2013-12-18T14:00:00"] ]'
```

Show all the changes in a timestamp range:

```
curl -X GET 'http://localhost:8080/v3/events' --data-urlencode \
  'query=[ "and", [">", "timestamp", "2013-12-18T14:00:00"] , \
                  ["<", "timestamp","2013-12-18T15:00:00"] ]'
```

Show all the changes related to resources provided by a specific manifest file:

```
curl -X GET 'http://localhost:8080/v3/events' --data-urlencode \
'query=["=","file","/etc/puppet/modules/hosts/manifests/init.pp"]'
```

The /event-counts endpoint

Show the count of resources of the `Service` type, summarized per resource:

```
curl -X GET 'http://localhost:8080/v3/event-counts' \
  --data-urlencode 'query=["=", "resource-type", "Service" ]' \
  --data-urlencode 'summarize-by=resource'
```

Show the count of resources of the `Package` type, summarized per node name:

```
curl -X GET 'http://localhost:8080/v3/event-counts' \
  --data-urlencode 'query=["=", "resource-type", "Package" ]' \
  --data-urlencode 'summarize-by=certname'
```

The /aggregated-event-counts endpoint

Show the aggregated count of events for a node:

```
curl -G 'http://localhost:8080/v3/aggregate-event-counts' \
  --data-urlencode 'query=["=", "certname", "db.example.com"]' \
  --data-urlencode 'summarize-by=containing-class'
```

Show the aggregated count for all the events on the services on any node:

```
curl -G 'http://localhost:8080/v3/aggregate-event-counts' \
  --data-urlencode 'query=["=", "resource-type", "Service"]' \
  --data-urlencode 'summarize-by=certname'
```

The /server-time endpoint

Show PuppetDB server's time in the ISO-8601 format (this is the format that we'll deal with when querying timestamps):

```
curl http://localhost:8080/v3/server-time
```

The /version endpoint

Show PuppetDB's version:

```
curl http://localhost:8080/v3/version
```

The puppetdbquery module

By now, we have realized how comprehensive the amount of information stored on PuppetDB is, as it provides a complete view of all our nodes' facts, catalogs, and reports. This is useful for a review of what happens on our infrastructure and for the metrics we can extract via queries on all the resources managed by Puppet, but this is not enough.

One of historical Puppet's limitations is the fact that a node basically has knowledge only about itself via its catalog and can interact with other nodes only via exported resources.

This is going to change. With Eric Dalén's puppetdbquery module we can access all PuppetDB data, and use it from different places:

- On the CLI, with a new a Puppet face
- In our manifests, with dedicated functions
- On Hiera, with a dedicated backend

We can install it from the Forge:

```
puppet module install dalen-puppetdbquery
```

Query format

The puppetdbquery module uses a custom format for queries. This format is different (and easier to use) from the native one. All the queries that we can execute with this module are in the following format:

```
Type[Name]{attribute1=foo and attribute2=bar}
```

By default, they are made on normal resources and use the @@ prefix to query the exported resources. The comparison operators are =, !=, >, <, and ~ (regexp matching). The expressions can be combined with and, not, and or.

Query from the command line

The module introduces the query command (as a Puppet face) that allows direct interaction with PuppetDB from the command line for inline help:

```
puppet help query
```

To search for all the RedHat family nodes with version 6, we can type the following:

```
puppet query nodes '(osfamily=RedHat and lsbmajdistrelease=6)'
```

The same query, when executed on facts, shows all the facts for the resulting nodes:

```
puppet query facts '(osfamily=RedHat and lsbmajdistrelease=6)'
```

To show only the IP address of the queried nodes:

```
puppet query facts --facts ipaddress '(osfamily=RedHat and
lsbmajdistrelease=6)'
```

Query from Puppet manifests

The functions provided by the module can be used inside manifests to populate the catalog with data retrieved from PuppetDB.

query_nodes has two arguments: the query to use and, optionally, the fact to return (by default, it provides the certname). The output is an array. Here are some usage samples:

```
$webservers = query_nodes('osfamily=Debian and Class[Apache]')
$webserver_ip = query_nodes('osfamily=Debian and Class[Apache]',
ipaddress)
```

query_facts requires two arguments too: the query to use to discover nodes and the list of facts to return for them. It returns a nested hash in the JSON format. Here is a sample use case:

```
query_facts('Class[Apache]{port=443}', ['osfamily', 'ipaddress'])
```

These functions are dramatically useful to retrieve data from PuppetDB and provide resources on a node according to the resources in catalogs compiled for other nodes.

The PuppetDB Hiera backend

Another powerful feature of the puppetdbquery module is the presence of a Hiera backend that allows us to use PuppetDB data for our Hiera keys. It requires at least one other backend, so it's configured as follows:

```
---
:backends:
  - yaml
  - puppetdb

:hierarchy:
  - nodes/%{fqdn}
  - common
```

The fun begins when we can use a query in our keys, instead of something like the following code:

```
ntp::servers:
  - 'ntp1.example.com'
  - 'ntp2.example.com'
```

We can have a dynamic query as follows:

```
ntp::servers::_nodequery: 'Class[Ntp::Server]'
```

This returns an array with the certname of all the nodes that have the `ntp::server` class in our infrastructure. If we want their IP addresses instead (the same applies for any other fact), use:

```
ntp::servers::_nodequery: ['Class[Ntp::Server]', 'ipaddress']
```

The preceding code can also be written with the following format (the result is the same):

```
ntp::servers::_nodequery:
  query: 'Class[Ntp::Server]'
  fact:  'ipaddress'
```

How Puppet code may change in the future

Now, hold on, stop to read, and think again about what we've seen in this chapter and particularly in the last section. Variables that define our infrastructure can be dynamically populated according to the number of hosts that have specific classes or resources. If we add hosts with these services, they can be automatically used by the other hosts.

This is what we need to configure with Puppet dynamic and elastic environments, where new services are made available to other nodes that are consequently configured.

For example, we can set a variable that returns all the IP addresses of the nodes that have Apache installed:

```
$web_servers_ip = query_nodes('Class[apache]', ipaddress)
```

This variable can be used in an ERB template that configures a load balancer. This is a simple case that probably doesn't fit real scenarios where we probably have different Apache web servers doing different tasks on different servers, but it can give us an idea.

In other cases, we might need to know the value of a fact of a given node and use it on another node. In the following example, `cluster_id` might be a custom fact that returns an ID generated on the `db01` host; its value might be used on another host (a cluster member) to configure it accordingly:

```
$shared_cluster_id = query_facts('hostname=db01', cluster_id)
```

It's important to understand the kind of data we find and query on PuppetDB. What we find with the `puppetdbquery` module, for example, are resources contained in the last catalog generated by the Puppet Master and stored for each node. We are not sure whether these resources have been applied successfully (we should query the event's endpoint for this, but currently, this is not possible with this module), and we are not sure that the services expected are available.

Also, consider how frequently Puppet runs on our nodes, as its convergence time may vary. If the interval is too large, the infrastructure may adapt slowly to new changes, and if it's too small, we may have more risks of some race conditions where a catalog that exposes a new service for a node has not yet been applied. In the meantime, it is already used to configure other nodes to use a service that might not be already configured.

These are probably hypothetical edge cases that we can tackle and manage in the same way in which we would manage a temporarily faulty service, for example, excluding nonresponsive servers from a load balancing pool. Just be aware of them.

Summary

In this chapter, the word PuppetDB has been used zillions of times as an obsessive mantra. While we can use Puppet without it, as we have done for years, it's important to realize that PuppetDB is going to be present in every relevant Puppet infrastructure, and we can bet that more and more applications and tools will emerge around it.

The fact that it's a robust piece of software that is engineered in a brilliant way makes us feel comfortable about the idea that Puppet Labs has decided to use it as the central point of consolidation and gathering for all the data generated by Puppet.

We have seen how to configure PuppetDB and its integration with the Puppet Master and how to interpret its performance dashboard. We have explored the principles of the PuppetDB CQRS API with REST-like endpoints for queries and commands for writing. We have also explored, in some detail, the list of available endpoints with various sample queries.

Finally, we have seen how most of the information gathered by PuppetDB can be queried from our manifests using the `puppetdbquery` module, and how this can dramatically influence how we manage interactions among different nodes.

Now that we have firmly grasped the principles of Puppet, Hiera, and PuppetDB, we can explore how they can be glued together to build different architectures.

4
Designing Puppet Architectures

Puppet is an extensible automation framework, a tool, and a language. We can do great things with it, and we can do them in many different ways. Besides the technicalities of learning the basics of its DSL, one of the biggest challenges for new and not-so-new users of Puppet is to organize code and put things together in a manageable and appropriate way.

It's hard to find a comprehensive documentation on how to use public code (modules) with our custom modules and data, where to place our logic, how to maintain and scale it, and generally, how to manage the resources that we want in our nodes and the data that defines them safely and effectively.

There's not really a single answer that fits all these cases. There are best practices, recommendations, and many debates in the community, but ultimately, it all depends on our own needs and infrastructure, which vary according to multiple factors, such as the following:

- The number and variety of nodes and application stacks to manage
- The infrastructure design and number of data centers or separate networks to manage
- The number and skills of people who work with Puppet
- The number of teams who work with Puppet
- Puppet's presence and integration with other tools
- Policies for change in production

In this chapter, we will outline the elements needed to design a Puppet architecture, reviewing the following elements in particular:

- The tasks to deal with (manage nodes, data, code, files, and so on) and the available components to manage them
- Foreman, which is probably the most used ENC around, with Puppet Enterprise
- The pattern of roles and profiles
- Data separation challenges and issues
- How the various components can be used together in different ways with some sample setups

The components of Puppet architecture

With Puppet, we manage our systems via the catalog that the Puppet Master compiles for each node. This is the total of the resources we have declared in our code, based on the parameters and variables whose values reflect our logic and needs.

Most of the time, we also provide configuration files either as static files or via ERB templates, populated according to the variables we have set.

We can identify the following major tasks when we have to manage what we want to configure on our nodes:

- Definition of the classes to be included in each node
- Definition of the parameters to use for each node
- Definition of the configuration files provided to the nodes

These tasks can be provided by different, partly interchangeable components, which are as follows:

- `site.pp` is the first file parsed by the Puppet Master (by default, its path is `/etc/puppet/manifests/site.pp`) and eventually, all the files that are imported from there (`import nodes/*.pp` would import and parse all the code defined in the files with the `.pp` suffix in the `/etc/puppet/manifests/nodes/` directory). Here, we have code in the Puppet language.
- An **ENC (External Node Classifier)** is an alternative source that can be used to define classes and parameters to apply to nodes. It's enabled with the following lines on the Puppet Master's `puppet.conf`:

```
[master]
  node_terminus = exec
  external_nodes = /etc/puppet/node.rb
```

What's referred by the `external_nodes` parameter can be any script that uses any backend; it's invoked with the client's `certname` as the first argument (`/etc/puppet/node.rb web01.example.com`) and should return a YAML formatted output that defines the classes to include for that node, the parameters, and the Puppet environment to use.

Besides the well-known Puppet-specific ENCs such as The Foreman and Puppet Dashboard (a former Puppet Labs project now maintained by the community members), it's not uncommon to write new custom ones that leverage on existing tools and infrastructure-management solutions.

- **LDAP** can be used to store nodes' information (classes, environment, and variables) as an alternative to the usage of an ENC. To enable LDAP integration, add the following lines to the Master's `puppet.conf`:

```
[master]
  node_terminus = ldap
  ldapserver = ldap.example.com
  ldapbase = ou=Hosts,dc=example,dc=com
```

  Then, we have to add Puppet's schema to our LDAP server. For more information and details, refer to `http://docs.puppetlabs.com/guides/ldap_nodes.html`.

- **Hiera** is the hierarchical key-value datastore we have discussed in *Chapter 2, Hiera*. It is is embedded in Puppet 3 and available as an add-on for previous versions. Here, we can set parameters but also include classes and eventually provide content for files.

- **Public modules** can be retrieved from Puppet Forge, GitHub, or other sources; they typically manage applications and systems' settings. Being public, they might not fit all our custom needs, but they are supposed to be reusable, support different OSes, and adapt to different usage cases. We are supposed to be able to use them without any modification, as if they were public libraries, committing our fixes and enhancements back to the upstream repository. A common but less-recommended alternative is to fork a public module and adapt it to our needs. This might seem a quicker solution, but doesn't definitively help the open source ecosystem and would prevent us from having benefits from updates on the original repository.

- **Site module(s)** are custom modules with local resources and files where we can place all the logic we need or the resources we can't manage with public modules. They may be one or more and may be called `site` or have the name of our company, customer, or project. Site modules have particular sense as a companion to public modules when they are used without local modifications. On site modules, we can place local settings, files, custom logic, and resources.

The distinction between public reusable modules and site modules is purely formal; they are both Puppet modules with a standard structure. It might make sense to place the ones we develop internally in a dedicated directory (module paths), which is different from the one where we place shared modules downloaded from public sources.

Let's see how these components might fit our Puppet tasks.

Defining the classes to include in each node

This is typically done when we talk about node classification in Puppet. This is the task that the Puppet Master accomplishes when it receives a request from a client node and has to determine the classes and parameters to use for that specific node.

Node classification can be done in the following different ways:

- We can use the node declaration in site.pp and other manifests eventually imported from there. In this way, we identify each node by certname and declare all the resources and classes we want for it, as shown in the following code:

```
node 'web01.example.com' {
  include ::general
  include ::apache
}
```

  Here, we may even decide to follow a nodeless layout, where we don't use the node declaration at all and rely on facts to manage the classes and parameters to be assigned to our nodes. An example of this approach is examined later in this chapter.

- On an ENC, we can define the classes (and parameters) that each node should have. The returned YAML for our simple case would be something like the following lines of code:

```
---
classes:
  - general:
  - apache:
parameters:
  dns_servers:
```

```
   - 8.8.8.8
   - 8.8.4.4
  smtp_server: smtp.example.com
environment: production
```

- Via **LDAP**, where we can have a hierarchical structure where a node can inherit the classes (referenced with the `puppetClass` attribute) set in a parent node (`parentNode`).

- Via **Hiera**, using the `hiera_include` function just add in `site.pp` as follows:

  `hiera_include('classes')`.

  Then, define our hierarchy under the key named `classes`, what to include for each node. For example, with a YAML backend, our case would be represented with the following lines of code:

  ```
  ---
  classes:
    - general
    - apache
  ```

- In site module(s), any custom logic can be placed as, for example, the classes and resources to include for all the nodes or for specific groups of nodes.

Defining the parameters to use for each node

This is another crucial part, as with parameters, we can characterize our nodes and define the resources we want for them.

Generally, to identify and characterize a node in order to differentiate it from the others and provide the specific resources we want for it, we need very few key parameters, such as the following (the names used here may be common but are arbitrary and are not Puppet's internal ones):

- `role` is almost a standard de facto name to identify the kind of server. A node is supposed to have just one role, which might be something like `webserver`, `app_be`, `db`, or anything that identifies the function of the node. Note that web servers that serve different web applications should have different roles (that is, `webserver_site`, `webserver_blog`, and so on). We can have one or more nodes with the same role.

- env or any name that identifies the operational environment of the node (if it is a development, test, qa, or production server).

 Note that this doesn't necessarily match Puppet's internal environment variable. Someone prefers to merge the env information inside role, having roles such as webserver_prod and webserver_devel.

- Zone, site, data center, country, or any parameter that might identify the network, country, availability zone, or datacenter where the node is placed. A node is supposed to belong to only one of this. We might not require this in our infrastructure.

- Tenant, component, application, project, and cluster might be the other kind of variables that characterize our node. There's not a real standard on their naming, and their usage and necessity strictly depend on the underlying infrastructure.

With parameters such as these, any node can be fully identified and be served with any specific configuration. It makes sense to provide them, where possible, as facts.

The parameters we use in our manifests may have a different nature:

- role/env/zone as defined earlier are used to identify the nodes; they typically are used to determine the values of other parameters

- OS-related parameters such as package names and file paths

- Parameters that define the services of our infrastructure (DNS servers, NTP servers, and so on)

- Username and passwords, which should be reserved, used to manage credentials

- Parameters that express any further custom logic and classifying need (master, slave, host_number, and so on)

- Parameters exposed by the parameterized classes or defines we use

Often, the value of some parameters depend on the value of other ones. For example, the DNS or NTP server may change according to the zone or region on a node. When we start to design our Puppet architecture, it's important to have a general idea of the variations involved and the possible exceptions, as we will probably define our logic according to them. As a general rule, we will use the identifying parameters (role/env/zone) to define most of the other parameters most of the time, so we'll probably need to use them in our Hiera hierarchy or in Puppet selectors. This also means that we probably will need to set them as top scope variables (for example, via an ENC) or facts.

As with the classes that have to be included, parameters may be set by various components; some of them are actually the same, as in Puppet, a node's classification involves both classes to include and parameters to apply. These components are:

- In `site.pp`, we can set variables. If they are outside nodes' definitions, they are at top scope; if they are inside, they are at node scope. Top scope variables should be referenced with a `::` prefix, for example, `$::role`. Node scope variables are available inside the node's classes with their plain name, for example, `$role`.

- An ENC returns parameters, treated as top scope variables, alongside classes, and the logic of how they can be set depends entirely on its structure. Popular ENCs such as The Foreman, Puppet Dashboard, and the Puppet Enterprise Console allow users to set variables for single nodes or for groups, often in a hierarchical fashion. The kind and amount of parameters set here depend on how much information we want to manage on the ENC and how much to manage somewhere else.

- LDAP, when used as a node's classifier, returns variables for each node as defined with the `puppetVar` attribute. They are all set at top scope.

- In Hiera, we set keys that we can map to Puppet variables with the `hiera()`, `hiera_array()` and `hiera_hash()` functions inside our Puppet code. Puppet 3's data bindings automatically map class' parameters to Hiera keys, so for these cases, we don't have to explicitly use `hiera*` functions. The defined hierarchy determines how the keys' values change according to the values of other variables. On Hiera, ideally, we should place variables related to our infrastructure and credentials but not OS-related variables (they should stay in modules if we want them to be reusable).

> A lot of documentation about Hiera shows sample hierarchies with facts such as `osfamily` and `operatingsystem`. In my very personal opinion, such variables should not stay there (weighting the hierarchy size), as OS differences should be managed in the classes and modules used and not in Hiera.

- On public shared modules, we typically deal with OS-specific parameters. Modules should be considered as reusable components that know all about how to manage an application on different OS but nothing about custom logic. They should expose parameters and defines that allow users to determine their behavior and fit their own needs.

- On site module(s), we may place infrastructural parameters, credentials, and any custom logic, more or less based on other variables.

- Finally, it's possible and generally recommended to create custom facts that identify the node directly from the agent. An example of this approach is a totally facts-driven infrastructure, where all the node-identifying variables, upon which all the other parameters are defined, are set as facts.

Defining the configuration files provided to the nodes

It's almost certain that we will need to manage configuration files with Puppet and that we need to store them somewhere, either as plain static files to serve via Puppet's fileserver functionality using the `source` argument of the `File` type or via `.erb` templates.

While it's possible to configure custom fileserver shares for static files and absolute paths for templates, it's definitely recommended to rely on the modules' autoloading conventions and place such files inside custom or public modules, unless we decide to use Hiera for them.

Configuration files, therefore, are typically placed in:

- **Public modules**: These may provide default templates that use variables exposed as parameters by the modules' classes and defines. As users, we don't directly manage the module's template but the variables used inside it. A good and reusable module should allow us to override the default template with a custom one. In this case, our custom template should be placed in a site module. If we've forked a public shared module and maintain a custom version we might be tempted to place there all our custom files and templates. Doing so, we lose in reusability and gain, maybe, in short term usage simplicity.

- **Site module(s)**: These are, instead, a more correct place for custom files and templates, if we want to maintain a setup based on public shared modules, which are not forked, and custom site ones where all our stuff stays confined in a single or few modules. This allows us to recreate similar setups just by copying and modifying our site modules, as all our logic, files and resources are concentrated there.

- **Hiera**: Thanks to the smart hiera-file backend, Hiera can be an interesting alternative place where to store configuration files, both static ones or templates. We can benefit of the hierarchy logic that works for us and can manage any kind of file without touching modules.

- Custom **fileserver** mounts can be used to serve any kind of static files from any directory of the Puppet Master. They can be useful if we need to provide via Puppet files generated/managed by third-party scripts or tools. An entry in /etc/puppet/fileserver.conf like:

```
[data]
path /etc/puppet/static_files
allow *.example.com
```

Allows serving a file like /etc/puppet/static_files/generated/file. txt with the argument:

```
source => 'puppet:///data/generated/file.txt',
```

Defining custom resources and classes

We'll probably need to provide custom resources, which are not declared in the shared modules, to our nodes, because these resources are too specific. We'll probably want to create some grouping classes, for example, to manage the common baseline of resources and classes we want applied to all our nodes.

This is typically a bunch of custom code and logic that we have to place somewhere. The usual locations are as follows:

- **Shared modules**: These are forked and modified to including custom resources; as already outlined, this approach doesn't pay in the long term.
- **Site module(s)**: These are preferred place-to-place custom stuff, included some classes where we can manage common baselines, role classes, and other containers' classes.
- **Hiera**, partially, if we are fond of the create_resources function fed by hashes provided in Hiera. In this case, somewhere (in a site or shared module or maybe, even in site.pp), we have to place the create_ resources statements.

The Foreman

The Foreman is definitely the biggest open source software product related to Puppet and not directly developed by Puppet Labs.

The project was started by Ohad Levy, who now works at Red Hat and leads its development, supported by a great team of internal employees and community members.

The Foreman can work as a Puppet ENC and reporting tool; it presents an alternative to the Inventory System, and most of all, it can manage the whole lifecycle of the system, from provisioning to configuration and decommissioning.

Some of its features have been quite ahead of their times. For example, the `foreman()` function made possible for a long time what is done now with the `puppetdbquery` module.

It allows direct query of all the data gathered by The Foreman: facts, nodes classification, and Puppet-run reports.

Let's look at this example that assigns to the `$web_servers` variable the list of hosts that belong to the `web` hostgroup, which have reported successfully in the last hour:

```
$web_servers = foreman("hosts", "hostgroup ~ web and status.failed = 0
and last_report < \"1 hour ago\"")
```

This was possible long before PuppetDB was even conceived.

The Foreman really deserves at least a book by itself, so here, we will just summarize its features and explore how it can fit in a Puppet architecture.

We can decide which components to use:

- Systems provisioning and life-cycle management
- Nodes IP addressing and naming
- The Puppet ENC function based on a complete web interface
- Management of client certificates on the Puppet Master
- The Puppet reporting function with a powerful query interface
- The Facts querying function, equivalent to the Puppet Inventory system

For some of these features, we may need to install Foreman's Smart Proxies on some infrastructural servers. The proxies are registered on the central Foreman server and provide a way to remotely control relevant services (DHCP, PXE, DNS, Puppet Master, and so on).

The Web GUI based on Rails is quite complete and appealing, but it might prove cumbersome when we have to deal with a large number of nodes. For this reason, we can also manage Foreman via the CLI.

The original `foreman-cli` command has been around for years but is now deprecated for the new `hammer` (https://github.com/theforeman/hammer-cli) with the Foreman plugin, which is very versatile and powerful as it allows us to manage, via the command line, most of what we can do on the web interface.

Roles and profiles

In 2012, Craig Dunn wrote a blog post (`http://www.craigdunn.org/2012/05/239/`) that quickly became a point of reference on how to organize Puppet code. He discussed his concept of roles and profiles. The role describes what the server represents, a live web server, a development web server, a mail server, and so on. Each node can have one and only one role. Note that in his post, he manages environments inside roles (two web servers on two different environments have two different roles):

```
node www1 {
   include ::role::www::dev
}
node www2 {
   include ::role::www::live
}
node smtp1 {
   include ::role::mailserver
}
```

Then, he introduces the concept of profiles, which include and manage modules to define a logical technical stack. A role can include one or more profiles:

```
class role {
   include profile::base
}
class role::www inherits role {
   include ::profile::tomcat
}
```

In environment-related subroles, we can manage the exceptions we need (here, for example, the `www::dev` role includes both the `database` and `webserver::dev` profiles):

```
class role::www::dev inherits role::www {
   include ::profile::webserver::dev
   include ::profile::database
}
class role::www::live inherits role::www {
   include ::profile::webserver::live
}
```

Usage of class inheritance here is not mandatory, but it is useful to minimize code duplication.

This model expects modules to be the only components where resources are actually defined and managed; they are supposed to be reusable (we use them without modifying them) and manage only the components they are written for.

In profiles, we can manage resources and the ordering of classes; we can initialize variables and use them as values for arguments in the declared classes, and we can generally benefit from having an extra layer of abstraction:

```
Class profile::base {
  include ::networking
  include ::users
}
class profile::tomcat {
  class { '::jdk': }
  class { '::tomcat': }
}
class profile::webserver {
  class { '::httpd': }
  class { '::php': }
  class { '::memcache': }
}
```

In profiles subclasses, we can manage exceptions or particular cases:

```
class profile::webserver::dev inherits profile::webserver {
  Class['::php'] {
    loglevel   => "debug"
  }
}
```

This model is quite flexible and has gained a lot of attention and endorsement from Puppet Labs. It's not the only approach that we can follow to organize the resources we need for our nodes in a sane way, but it's the current best practice and a good point of reference, as it formalizes the concept of role and exposes how we can organize and add layers of abstraction between our nodes and the used modules.

The data and the code

Hiera's crusade and possibly main reason to exist is data separation. In practical terms, this means to convert Puppet code like the following one:

```
$dns_server = $zone ? {
  'it'    => '1.2.3.4',
  default => '8.8.8.8',
}
```

```
class { '::resolver':
  server => $dns_servers,
}
```

Into something where there's no trace of local settings like:

```
$dns_server = hiera('dns_server')
class { '::resolver':
  server => $dns_servers,
}
```

With Puppet 3, the preceding code can be even more simplified with just the following line:

```
include ::resolver
```

This expects the `resolver::server` key evaluated as needed in our Hiera data sources.

The advantages of having data (in this case, the IP of the DNS server, whatever is the logic to elaborate it) in a separated place are clear:

- We can manage and modify data without changing our code
- Different people can work on data and code
- Hiera's pluggable backend system dramatically enhances how and where data can be managed, allowing seamless integration with third-party tools and data sources
- Code layout is simpler and more error proof
- The lookup hierarchy is configurable

Nevertheless, there are a few little drawbacks or maybe, just the necessary side effects or needed evolutionary steps. They are as follows:

- What we've learned about Puppet and used to do without Hiera is obsolete
- We don't see, directly in our code, the values we are using
- We have two different places where we can look to understand what code does
- We need to set the variables we use in our hierarchy as top scope variables or facts, or anyway, we need to refer to them with a fixed fully qualified name
- We might have to refactor a lot of existing code to move our data and logic into Hiera

A personal note: I've been quite a late jumper on the Hiera wagon. While developing modules with the ambition that they can be reusable, I decided I couldn't exclude users who weren't using this additional component. So, until Puppet 3 with Hiera integrated in it became mainstream, I didn't want to force the usage of Hiera in my code.

Now things are different. Puppet 3's data bindings change the whole scene, Hiera is deeply integrated and is here to stay, and so, even if we can happily live without using it, I would definitively recommend its usage in most of the cases.

Sample architectures

We have outlined the main tasks and components we can use to put things together in a Puppet architecture; we have looked at Foreman, Hiera, and the roles and profiles pattern. Now, let's see some real examples based on them.

The default approach

By default, Puppet doesn't use an ENC and lets us classify nodes directly in /etc/ puppet/manifests/site.pp (or in files imported from there) with the node statement. So, a very basic setup would have site.pp with a content like the following:

```
node www01 {
  # Place here resources to apply to this node in Puppet DSL:
  # file, package service, mount...
}
node lb01 {
  # Resources for this node: file, package service...
}
```

This is all we basically need; no modules with their classes, no Hiera, no ENC. We just need good old plain Puppet code as they teach us in schools, so to speak.

This basic approach, useful just for the first tests, obviously does not scale well and would quickly become a huge mess of duplicated code.

The next step is to use classes that group resources, and if these classes are placed inside modules, we can include them directly without the need to explicitly import the containing files:

```
node www01 {
  include ::apache
  include ::php
}
```

Also, this approach, even if definitively cleaner, will quickly be overwhelmed by redundant code. So, we will probably want to introduce grouping classes that group other classes and resources according to the desired logic.

One common example is a `general` class, which includes all the modules, classes, and resources we want to apply to all our nodes.

Another example is a `role` class, which includes all the extra resources needed by a particular kind of node:

```
node www01 {
  include ::general
  include ::role::www
}
```

We can then have other grouping classes to better organize and reuse our resources, such as the profiles we have just discussed.

> Note that with the names mentioned earlier, we would need two different local (site) modules: `general` and `role`. I personally prefer to place all the local, custom resources in a single module, to be called `site`, or even better, with the name of the project, customer, or company. Given this, the previous example could be:
>
> ```
> node www01 {
>   include ::site
>   include ::site::role::www
> }
> ```
>
> These are only naming matters that have consequences on directories' layout and eventually on permissions management on our SCM, but the principle of grouping resources according to custom logic is the same.

Until now, we have just included classes, and often, the same classes are included by nodes that need different effects from them, for example, slightly different configuration files, or specific resources, or any kind of variation we have in the real world when configuring the same application on different systems.

Here is where we need to use variables and parameters to alter the behavior of a class according to custom needs.

Here is where the complexity begins, because there are various elements to consider, such as:

- What are the variables that identify our node
- If they are sufficient to manage all the variations in our nodes
- Where we want to place our logic that copes with them

- Where configurations should be provided as plain static files, where it is better to use templates, and where we could just modify single lines inside files

- How these choices may affect the risk of doing a change that affects unexpected nodes

> The most frequent and dangerous mistakes with Puppet are due to people making changes in code (or data) that are supposed to be made for a specific node but affect other nodes as well. Most of the time, this happens when people don't know the structure and logic of the Puppet codebase they are working on well enough. There are no easy rules to prevent such problems; just some general suggestions such as the following:
>
> - Promote code peer review and communication among the Puppeteers
> - Test code changes on canary nodes
> - Use naming conventions and coherent code organization to maximize the principle of least surprise
> - Embrace code simplicity, readability, and documentation
> - Be wary of the scope and extent of our abstraction layers

We also need classes that actually allow things to be changed via parameters or variables if we want to avoid placing our logic directly inside them.

Patterns on how to manage variables and their effect on the applied resources have changed a lot with the evolution of Puppet and the introduction of new tools and functionalities.

We won't indulge in how things were done in the good old times; in a modern and currently recommended Puppet setup, we expect to have:

- At least Puppet 3 on the Puppet Master to eventually enjoy data bindings
- Classes that expose parameters that allow us to manage them
- Reusable public modules that allow us to adapt them to our use case without modifications

In this case, we can basically follow two different approaches. We can keep on including classes and set the values we want for the parameters we need to modify on Hiera. So, in our example, we could have something as follows in `site/manifests/role/www.pp`:

```
class site::role::www {
  include ::apache
  include ::php
}
```

On Hiera, we can have a file such as `hieradata/env/devel.yaml`, where we set parameters like the following:

```
---
  apache::port: 8080
```

Alternatively, we might use explicit class declarations like:

```
class site::role::www {
  $apache_port = $env ? {
    devel   => '8080',
    default => '80',
  }
  class { '::apache':
    port => $apache_port,
  }
  include ::php
}
```

In such a declaration, the data and logic on how to determine it is definitively inside the code.

Basic ENC, logic in the site module, and Hiera backend

ENC and Hiera can be alternative or complementary; this approach gets advantages from both and uses the `site` module for most of the logic for class inclusion, the configuration files, and the custom resources.

In Hiera, all the class parameters are placed.

In ENC, when it's not possible to set variables via facts, we set the variables that identify our nodes and can be used on our Hiera's hierarchy.

In `site.pp` or in the same ENC, we include just a single `site` class, and here, we manage our grouping logic. For example, with general `baseline` and `role` classes:

```
class site {
  include ::site::general
  if $::role {
    include "::site::roles::${::role}"
  }
}
```

In our `role` classes, which are included if the `$role` variable is set on the ENC, we can manage all the role-specific resources, eventually dealing with differences according to the environment, other identifying variables directly in the role class, or using profiles.

 Note that in this chapter, we've always referred to class names with their full name, so a class such as `mysql` is referred with `::mysql`. This is useful to avoid name collisions when, for example, role names may clash with existing modules. If we don't use the leading `::` chars, we will have problems, for example, with a class called `site::role::mysql`, which may mess with the main class, `mysql`.

The Foreman and Hiera

The Foreman can act as a Puppet ENC; it's probably the most common ENC around, and we can use both Foreman and Hiera in our architecture.

In this case, we should strictly separate responsibilities and scopes even if they might be overlapping; let's review our components and how they might fit in a scenario based on The Foreman, Hiera, and the usual site module(s):

- Classes to be included in nodes can be done in The Foreman, the site module, or both. It mostly depends on how much logic we want in The Foreman, and how many activities have to be done via its interface and how many are moved into site module(s). We can decide to define roles and profiles in the site module and use The Foreman just to define top scope variables and the inclusion of a single basic class, as in the previous example. Alternatively, we may prefer to use The Foreman's HostGroups to classify and group nodes, moving most of the classes' grouping logic into The Foreman.

- Variables to be assigned to nodes can be done in both The Foreman and Hiera. It probably makes sense to set only the variables we need to identify nodes (if they are not provided by facts), in The Foreman, and generally, the ones we might need to use in Hiera's hierarchy. All the other variables and the logic on how to derive them should stay in Hiera.

- Files should stay in our site module, or eventually, in Hiera (with the `hiera-file` plugin).

The Hiera-based setup

A common scenario involves the usage of Hiera to manage both the classes to include them in nodes and their parameters and eventually few handy resource defaults.

No ENC is used; site.pp just needs the following:

```
hiera_include('classes')
```

Classes and parameters can be assigned to nodes enjoying the flexibility of our hierarchy, so in a common.yaml we can have:

```
---
# Common classes on all nodes
classes:
  - puppet
  - openssh
  - timezone
  - resolver
# Common Class Parameters
timezone::timezone: 'Europe/Rome'
resolver::dns_servers:
  - 8.8.8.8
  - 8.8.4.4
```

In a specific datasource file such as role/web.yaml, we can add the classes and the parameters we want to apply to that group of nodes:

```
---
classes:
  - stack_lamp
stack_lamp::apache_include: true
stack_lamp::php_include: true
stack_lamp::mysql_include: false
```

The modules we use (here, an example is stack_lamp; however, it could be something like profile::webserver or apache and php) should expose as parameters anything that is needed to configure things as expected.

Configuration files and templates can be placed in a site module.

The Hiera-only setup

The Hiera-only setup is a somewhat extreme approach. Everything is managed by Hiera: the classes to include in nodes, their parameters, and also the configuration files to serve to the clients. Configuration files are delivered via the `hiera-file` plugin; also, in this scenario, we need modules and relevant classes that expose parameters to manage the content of files.

Secrets, credentials, and sensitive data may be encrypted via `hiera-eyaml` or `hiera-gpg`.

We may wonder whether a site module is still needed, as most of its common functions (provide custom files, manage logic, define and manage variables) can be moved into Hiera.

The answer is probably yes: even in a similar, strongly Hiera-oriented scenario, a site module is usually needed. We might, for example, use custom classes to manage edge cases or exceptions that could be difficult to replicate with Hiera without adding a specific entry in the hierarchy.

One important point to consider when moving most of our logic in Hiera is how much this costs in terms of the length of the hierarchy. Sometimes, a simple, even if not elegant, custom class that deals with a particular edge case may save us from adding a layer in the hierarchy.

Foreman smart variables

Smart variables are The Foreman's alternative approach to Hiera for the full management of the variables used by nodes.

The Foreman can automatically detect the parameters exposed by classes and allows us to set values for them according to custom logic, providing them via the ENC functionality (support for parameterized classes via ENC has been available since Puppet 2.6.5).

To each class, we can map one or more smart variables, which may have different values according to customizable conditions and hierarchies.

The logic is somewhat similar to Hiera, with the notable difference that we can have a different hierarchy for each variable and have other ways to define its content according to custom queries and conditions.

User's experience benefits from the web interface and may result in being easier than editing directly Hiera files. The Foreman's auditing features allows us to track changes as an SCM would do on plain files.

We don't have the multiple backends flexibility as we have with Hiera, and we'll be completely tied to The Foreman for the management on our nodes.

Personally, I have no idea of how many people are extensively using smart variables in their setups; just be aware that there exists this alternative for data management.

Fact-driven truths

A fact-driven approach was theorized by Jordan Sissel, the Logstash's author, in a 2010's blog post (`http://www.semicomplete.com/blog/geekery/puppet-nodeless-configuration`). The most authoritative information we can have about a node comes from its own facts.

We may decide to use facts in various places, such as in our hierarchy, in our site code, in templates, and if our facts permit us to identify the nodes' role, environment, zone, or any identifying variable, we might not even need nodes classification and manage everything in our site module or via Hiera.

It is now very easy to add custom facts by placing a file in the node's `/etc/facter/facts.d` directory. This can be done, for instance, by a cloud provisioning script.

Alternatively, if our node names are standardized and informative, we can easily define our identifying variables in custom facts, which might be provided by our site module.

If all the variables that identify our node come from facts, we can have `site.pp` as simple as:

```
include site
```

In our `site/manifests/init.pp`, we have something like the following code:

```
class site {
  if $::role {
    include "site::roles::role_${::role}"
  }
}
```

The top scope `$::role` variable would be, obviously, a fact.

Logic for data and classes to include can be managed where we prefer in site modules, Hiera or the ENC.

The principle here is that as much data as possible and especially the nodes' identifying variables, should come from facts.

Also, in this case, common sense applies and extreme usage deviations should be avoided; in particular; a custom Ruby fact should compute its output without any local data. If we start placing data inside the fact in order to return data, we are probably doing something wrong.

Nodeless site.pp

We have seen that site.pp does not necessarily need to have node definitions in its content in imported files. We don't need them when we drive everything via facts, where we manage class inclusion in Hiera, and we don't need them with an approach where conditionals based on host names are used to set the top scope variables that identify nodes:

```
# nodeless site.pp

# Roles are based on hostnames
case $::hostname {
  /^web/: { $role = 'web' }
  /^puppet$/: { $role = 'puppet' }
  /^lb/: { $role = 'lb' }
  /^log/: { $role = 'log' }
  /^db/: { $role = 'db' }
  /^el/: { $role = 'el' }
  /^monitor/: { $role = 'monitor' }
  default: { $role = 'default' }
}

# Env is based on hostname or (sub) domain
if 'devel' in $::fqdn { $env = 'devel' }
elsif 'test' in $::fqdn { $env = 'test' }
elsif 'qa' in $::fqdn { $env = 'qa' }
else { $env = 'prod' }

include site
# hiera_include('classes')
```

Here, the $role and $env variables are set at the top scope according to hostnames named in a way that we can parse them with Puppet code.

At the end, we just include our site class or use hiera_include to manage the grouping logic for what classes to include in our nodes.

Such an approach makes sense only where we don't have to manage many different hostnames or roles and where the names of our nodes follow a naming pattern that lets us derive identifying variables.

 Note that the $::hostname or $clientcert variables might be forged and return untrusted values. Since Puppet 3.4, if we set trusted_node_data = true in puppet.conf, we have the special variable, $trusted['certname'] to identify a verified hostname, at our disposal.

Node inheritance done right

Node inheritance has a bad reputation. All the Puppet books around, even the ones of a giant like James Turnbull, and the official Puppet Labs documentation describe it as a bad practice, and this puzzles me, as I had successfully used this approach for years.

The main problem, I think, has been a documentation issue, as it's not well explained to users that node inheritance makes sense when used to assign variables, but it is dangerous when used to manage class grouping.

Let's see an example of a wrong approach to node inheritance:

```
node default {
  include general
}
node 'it' inherits default {
  $zone = 'it'
}
node 'web01.it.example.com' inherits 'it' {
  $role = 'web'
  include role::web
}
```

The issue in this extremely simplified example is that when Puppet parses general, it hasn't set the $role and $zone values, and the result for the resources declared in general, depending on them, would probably not be what was expected.

When node inheritance is used only to set and eventually override variables and not to include classes, none of these problems are present:

```
node basenode {
  dns_server = '8.8.8.8'
}
node 'it' inherits basenode {
  $zone = 'it'
```

```
    $dns_server = '1.2.3.4'
}
node 'web01.it.example.com' inherits 'it' {
  $role = 'web'
  include site
}
```

Downloading the example code

You can download the example code files for all Packt books you have purchased from your account at http://www.packtpub.com. If you purchased this book elsewhere, you can visit http://www.packtpub.com/support and register to have the files e-mailed directly to you.

The upstream git repository is available at https://github.com/example42/puppet-architectures.

Now, I would not use this approach anymore, as it requires an include line for each node, and it sets variables at node scope. This implies that while they can be used in the node's classes, we cannot refer to them with a fully qualified name, and so, for example, we cannot use them on a Hiera hierarchy.

Still, in situations where an ENC and Hiera are not used and the node names are not descriptive, this is a working and effective way to identify nodes using the benefits of a hierarchical structure, based on inheritance.

Summary

This has been a hard chapter, probably to read, surely to write, because there is a wide spectrum of available alternatives when we deal with the challenges we have when we design Puppet architectures.

We have examined the tasks we have to deal with: how to manage nodes, how to group them, how to set the parameters of the classes we use, and where to place the configuration files we use. We have reviewed several tools at our disposal: The Foreman, Hiera, and our custom site modules.

We have seen some examples on how these elements can be managed in different combinations. Now, it is time to explore modules, an important component of a Puppet setup, more deeply and see how to write really reusable ones.

5
Using and Writing Reusable Modules

The members of the Puppet community have always wondered how to write code that could be reused. In the early days, this was done with recipes collected on the old Wiki, where people shared fragments of code for specific tasks. Then, we were introduced to **modules**, which allowed users to present all the configuration files, Puppet, and Ruby code needed to manage a specific application in a unique directory.

People started writing modules, someone even made a full collection of them (the father of all the modules' collections is David Schmitt; then, others followed), and at the European Puppet Camp in 2010, Luke Kanies announced the launch of the **Puppet Forge**, a central repository of modules that can be installed and managed directly from the command line.

It seemed to be the solution to the already growing mess of unstructured, sparse, uninteroperable, and incompatible modules, but to be realistic, it took some time before becoming the powerful resource that it is now.

In this chapter, we will review the following:

- The evolution of modules' layouts
- The parameters dilemma – what class parameters have to be exposed and where
- The principles for the reusability of modules

The evolution of modules' layouts

Over the years, different modules' layouts have been explored, following the evolution of Puppet's features and the refinement of usage patterns.

There has never been a unique way of writing a module, but patterns and best practices have emerged, and we are going to review the most relevant ones.

Class parameters – from zero to data bindings

The introduction of parameterized classes with Puppet 2.6 has been a crucial step in standardizing the interfaces of classes. In the earlier versions, there wasn't a unique way to pass data to a class, and variables defined anywhere could be dynamically used inside Puppet code or in templates to manage the module's behavior; there was no standard API to access or set them. We used to define parameterless classes in a similar fashion:

```
class apache {
  # Variables used in DSL or in templates were dynamically scoped
  # and referenced without using their fully qualified name.
  # IE: $port, not $apache::port or $::apache_port
}
```

Such classes were declared always and only with the following line:

```
include apache
```

The introduction of parameters in classes has been important, because it allowed a single entry point for class' data as in this example:

```
class apache (
  $port = 80  ) {
}
```

The default value of the parameter can be overridden with an explicit declaration, as shown in the following code:

```
class { 'apache':
  port => 8080,
}
```

Such a solution has not been completely decisive. The usage of parameterized classes introduced new challenges such as the need to declare them only once in our catalog for each node. This forced people to rethink some of their assumptions on how and where to make class inclusion in their code.

We could still use `include apache` as many times as we wanted in our manifests, but we didn't have any method to set specific parameters if the class didn't explicitly manage a way to look up for external variables, for example, with the following syntax:

```
class apache (
  $port = hiera('apache::port','80') {
}
```

This obviously would have required all the module's users to use Hiera.

I would dare to say that the circle has been closed with Puppet 3's data bindings. The automatic Hiera lookup of class parameters allows us to set parameters via either the explicit declaration or plain inclusion with the values of parameters set in Hiera.

After years of pain, alternative solutions, creative and unorthodox approaches, and evolution of the tool, I'd say that now the mainstream and recommended way to use classes is to just include them and manage their parameters via Hiera using Puppet 3's data-binding feature.

In a manifest, we can declare classes with the following simple line:

```
include apache
```

We can be sure that whatever parse order is followed by Puppet, its data can be defined in Hiera files. So, with a YAML backend, we'll use a syntax that is as simple as:

```
---
  apache::port: '8080'
```

The params pattern

When people had to cope with different OS in a module, they typically started using selectors or conditionals to assign the correct values based on facts such as `operatingsystem` and `operatingsystemrelease` and the more recent `osfamily` to variables or parameters.

A typical case with a selector is as follows:

```
class apache {
  $apache_name = $::operatingsystem ? {
    /(?i:Debian|Ubuntu|Mint)/        => 'apache2',
    /(?i:RedHat|CentOS|Scientific)/ => 'httpd',
    default                          => 'apache'
  }
```

```
    package { $apache_name:
      ensure => present,
    }
  }
```

Having this mix of variables' definitions and resource declarations was far from elegant, and in some time, people started placing the management of the module's variables in a dedicated class, which was usually called `params`.

They can be set with selectors, as in the previous example, or more commonly, inside the `case` statements, which are always based on facts related to the underlying OS:

```
class apache::params {
  case $::osfamily {
    'RedHat': {
      $apache_name = 'httpd'
    }
    'Debian': {
      $apache_name = 'apache2'
    }
    default: {
      fail("Operating system ${::operatingsystem} not supported")
    }
  }
}
```

The main class only has to include the `params` class and refer to internal variables using their fully qualified name as follows:

```
class apache {
  include apache::params
  package { $apache::params::apache_name:
    ensure => present,
  }
}
```

This is a basic implementation of the so-called params pattern, and it has the advantage of having a single place where we define all the internal variables of a module or the default values for its parameters.

In the next example, the package name is also exposed as a parameter (this can be considered a reusability feature, as it allows users to override the default package name for the application that is going to be installed). As the default value is defined in `params.pp`, the main `apache` class has to inherit it, as shown in the following code:

```
class apache (
  $package_name = $apache::params::package_name,
) inherits apache::params {
  package { $apache::params::package_name:
    ensure => present,
  }
}
```

The params pattern has been widely used, and it works well. Still, it mixes code and data, even if this is done only in a dedicated subclass.

Data in modules

The first proposals about a way to separate modules' data from their code date back to 2010 with a blog post from Dan Bode titled *Proposal: Managing Puppet's configuration data* at `http://bodepd.com/wordpress/?p=64`.

In those times, Hiera was not yet available (the post refers to its ancestor, **extlookup**). However, most of the principles described in the blog post have been considered when a solution was implemented.

When Hiera was introduced, it seemed a good solution to manage OS-related variations via its hierarchy. It soon became clear that global site-related data, as it can be the one we place on our data sources, is not an appropriate backend for modules' internal data if we want them to be reusable and distributable.

Possible solutions inspired or derived from Dan's post have been identified for some time. One such solution was released on Puppet 3.3.0 as an experimental feature, an implementation of what's generally summarized by the term **data in modules**. It featured a module's local `hiera.yaml` and the relevant Hiera data to manage the module's variables.

It finally seemed the long sought-after solution to have data separation also for a module's internal data, but it failed to pass Puppet Labs' user acceptance tests.

It was not so easy for modules' authors to manage, and this implementation has been removed in the following Puppet versions; however, the issue is too important to be ignored. So, R.I. Pienaar proposed an implementation based on an independent module, which is given at `https://github.com/ripienaar/puppet-module-data`.

This approach is much simpler to use and doesn't require big changes to the existing code. Being implemented as a module, this solution can be used on most Puppet installations (Version 3.x is required) and does exactly what we can expect.

We will come back to this in *Chapter 12, Future Puppet*, as the topic is hot and its evolution is ongoing. For a more detailed (and better-written) overview of the evolution of data in modules, check out this excellent blog post by Puppet Labs' Gary Larizza at `http://garylarizza.com/blog/2013/12/08/when-to-hiera/`.

Files and class names

Besides the `init.pp` file, with the main class, all the other classes and defines in the manifests' directory of a module can have any name; still, some names are more common than the others. We have seen that `params.pp` is a sort of standard de facto pattern and is not the only one; it's common, for example, to have files such as `server.pp` and `client.pp` with subclasses to manage the server/client components of an application.

R.I. Pienaar (definitely one of the most influential contributors to Puppet's evolution) recommended a module layout in a blog post. This module layout involves splitting the main module's resources in three different classes and relevant files: `install.pp` to manage the installation of the application, `config.pp` to manage its configuration, and `service.pp` to manage its service(s). So, a typical package-service-configuration module can have the following code in its `init.pp` file:

```
class postgresql [...] { [...]
  class{'postgresql::install': } ->
  class{'postgresql::config': } ~>
  class{'postgresql::service': }
}
```

In the referred subclasses, the module can have the relevant resources to manage. This pattern has pros and cons. Its advantages are as follows:

- Clear separation of the components provided by the module

- Easier to manage relationships and dependencies that are based not on single resources that may vary, but on whole subclasses that are always the same

- More compact and easier to read `init.pp`

- Naming standardization for common components

Some drawbacks, in my very personal opinion, are as follows:

- Various extra objects are added to the catalog to do the same things. This might have performance implications at a large scale even if the reduced number of relationships might balance the final count.

- It is more cumbersome to manage the relationship logic via users' parameters (for example, when we want to provide a parameter that defines whether to restart a service or not after a change in the configurations).

- For simple package-service-configuration modules, it looks redundant to have three extra classes with just one resource for each.

In any case, beware that such an approach requires the `contain` function (available from Puppet 3.4.0) or the **anchor pattern** to work correctly.

The anchor pattern

Puppet has had a long-standing issue that affected and confused many users for years (`https://tickets.puppetlabs.com/browse/PUP-99`): one of its effects is that when we define a dependency on a class, Puppet extends this dependency to the resources declared in that class, as we may expect, but not to other classes eventually declared (included) there.

This may create problems and lead to unexpected behaviors (dependencies not managed in the order expected) when referring to a class such as `postgresql`, which we have seen, where the main class includes other subclasses.

A widely used workaround is the anchor pattern defined by Puppet Lab's Jeff McCune. It is based on the `anchor` type included in Puppet Labs' `stdlib` module. The `anchor` type can be declared as a normal resource in the following way:

```
anchor { 'postgresql::start': }
anchor { 'postgresql::end': }
```

It can then be used to contain the declared classes in a dependency chain as follows:

```
anchor { 'postgresql::start': } ->
class{'postgresql::install': } ->
class{'postgresql::config': } ~>
class{'postgresql::service': } ->
anchor { 'postgresql::end': }
```

In this way, we can create a relationship that involves a whole class with a chaining arrow as follows:

```
class { 'postgresql': } -> class { 'wordpress': }
```

By doing so, we are sure that all the resources provided in the `postgresql` class are applied before the `wordpress` class' declarations, because they are explicitly contained in the anchor resource type.

The parameters dilemma

In modules, we typically set up applications. Most of the time, this is done by installing packages, configuring files, and managing services.

We can write a module that does exactly what we need for our working scenario, or we can try to design it keeping in mind people with different needs and infrastructures who may use it.

These people might be us in the future when we'll have to manage a Puppet setup for another project or cope with different kinds of servers or manage unexpected or nonstandard requirements. While facing these new challenges, we might regret not having written our code in an abstract enough and reusable way.

Parameters are our APIs to the module's functionality; their values affect the module's behavior and how users can adapt it to fulfill their needs.

Hypothetically, we could enforce exactly what we need inside our code and forgo the need to have any parameter. Maybe, our code could be simpler to use and read in the beginning, but this would be a technical debt we will have to pay sooner or later.

We need parameters, and we need them to allow a user's customization of what the module does in order to adapt it to different use cases.

Still, it is not so obvious to define what parameters to use and where to place them; let's review some possible cases.

There might be different kinds of parameters, and they can perform the following tasks:

- Manage variables that provide the main configuration settings for an application (for example, `ntp_server`, `munin_server`, or similar)
- Manage most or all configuration settings for an application (for a sample `ntp.conf` file, they would be `driftfile`, `statistics`, `server`, `restrict`, and so on)

- Manage triggers that define which components of the module should be used (`install_server`, `enable_passenger`, and similar parameters)

- Manage the attributes of the resources declared inside a class or define (`config_file_source`, `package_name`, and whatever attribute we value as important enough to be exposed for customization)

- Manage the behavior of the module or some of its components (`service_autorestart`, `debug` and `ensure`)

- Manage external parameters related to applications, references, or classes (such as `db_server` and `db_user`) that are not directly managed by the module but are needed to configure its application

There are also various places where these parameters can be exposed and can act as entry points where we can feed our configuration data. They are as follows:

- The main module's class, which is defined in the `init.pp` file

- Single subclasses that may act as single responsibility points for specific features (class names such as `modulename::server` or `modulename::db::mysql` with their own parameters that can be directly set)

- Configuration classes, which are used as entry points for various settings, to override a module's defaults (`modulename::settings`, `modulename::globals`)

- Normal defines provided by the module

There is no established and common structure or agreement regarding the kind of parameters and where to expose them.

They depend on several factors. However, the main design decision that the module's author has to take, which heavily affects the kind of parameters to expose, is how the configurations are provided: are they file-based or setting-based? These configurations are explained as follows:

- **File-based**: They expect the module to manage the application's configuration via complete files, which are generally provided as ERB templates whose content is derived from the parameters exposed by the classes or defines that use it

- **Setting-based**: They have a more granular approach; the application's configuration files are managed as single configuration entries, typically single lines, which compose the final file

In the first case, where files are managed as a whole, the module's classes should do the following:

- Expose parameters that define at least the application's main settings and optionally most or all the other settings, as long as they are managed in the default template

- Allow users to provide a custom ERB template that overrides the module's default one and can be used to manage custom settings that are not manageable via parameters

- Allow users to provide configurations as plain static files to serve via the `source` argument, as some users may prefer to manage the configuration files the way they are

In the second case, the module should do the following:

- Provide native or defined types that allow the manipulation of single lines inside a configuration file

- Eventually provide classes (either a single main one or many subclasses) that expose all the possible configuration settings for the managed application (thre might be many and hard to keep updated) as parameters

 I don't have a clear answer to what would be the preferred approach; I suppose it depends on the kind of the managed application, the users' preference, and the complexity and structure of the configuration files. The good news is that a module's author can accommodate both the approaches and leave the choice to the user.

Naming standards

The module's ecosystem has grown erratically, with many people redoing modules for the same application, either forking the existing ones or developing them from scratch.

In this case, quantity is not a plus; there's really no advantage for Puppet users to have dozens of different modules for a single application, written with different layouts, parameters names, entry points, OS coverage, and feature sets.

Even worse, when we use modules that have dependencies on other modules (as described in `Modulefile`), we may quickly end up having conflicts that may prevent us from installing a module with the `puppet module` command and force us to fork and fix it just for our case.

Modules' interoperability is a wider issue that has not yet been solved, but there is something that can be done if there is a common will: an attempt to standardize the naming conventions for modules' classes and parameters' names.

The various benefits are as follows:

- Saner and simpler user experience
- Easier modules' interoperability
- Suggested reusability patterns
- Predictability in usage and development

It's common sense that such an effort should be driven by Puppet Labs, but for the moment, it remains a community effort under the label `stdmod`, and can be found at `https://github.com/stdmod`.

The naming conventions defined there embrace some standard de facto naming and try to define general rules for parameters and class names. For the ones that affect the resources' arguments, the pattern is `[prefix_]resource_attribute`, so this implies the following parameters' names:

```
config_file_path , config_file_content, package_name,
    init_config_file_path, client_package_name
```

Many other names are defined; the basic principle is that a `stdmod` compliant module is not expected to have them all, but if it exposes parameters that have the same functions, it should call them as defined by the standard.

Reusability patterns

Modules' reusability is a topic that has got more and more attention during the last few years; as more people started using Puppet, the need of having some common and shared code to manage common things became more evident.

The following are the reusable modules' main characteristics:

- They can be used by different people without the need to modify their content
- They support different operating systems and allow easy extension to new ones
- They allow users to override the default files provided by the module
- They might have an opinionated approach to the managed resources but don't force it
- They follow a single responsibility principle and should manage only the application they are made for

Reusability, we must underline, is not an all or nothing feature; we might have different levels of reusability to fulfill the needs of a variant percentage of users. For example, a module might support Red Hat and Debian derivatives but not Solaris or AIX; is it reusable? If we use the latter OS, definitely not; if we don't use them, then yes, it is reusable for us.

I am personally a bit extreme about reusability, and according to me, a module should also be able to do the following:

- Allow users to provide alternative classes for eventual dependencies from other modules to ease interoperability

- Allow any kind of treatment of the managed configuration files, be it file or setting based

- Allow alternative installation methods

- Allow users to provide their own classes for users or other resources, which could be managed in custom and alternative ways

- Allow users to modify the default settings (calculated inside the module according to the underlining OS) for package and service names, file paths, and other more or less internal variables that are not always exposed as parameters

- Expose parameters that allow the removal of resources provided by the module (this is a functionality feature more than a reusability one)

- Abstract monitoring and firewalling features so that they are not directly tied to specific modules or applications

Managing files

Everything is a file in UNIX, and most of the time, Puppet manages files. A module can expose parameters that allow its users to manipulate configuration files, and it can follow one or both of the file/setting approaches, as they are not alternative and can coexist.

To manage the contents of a file, Puppet provides the following alternative solutions:

- Use ERB templates populated with variables that come from parameters, facts, or any scope (argument for `File type: content => template('modulename/path/templatefile.erb')`)

- Use the `source` parameter to retrieve static files from the PuppetMaster's fileserver

- Manage the file content via concat (https://github.com/puppetlabs/ puppetlabs-concat), a module that provides resources, which allow us to build a file joining different fragments
- Manage the file contents via augeas, a native type that interfaces with the **Augeas** configuration editing tool (http://augeas.net/)
- Manage it with an alternative in file-line-editing tools

For the first two cases, we can expose parameters that allow defining the module's main configuration file either directly via the source and content arguments or by specifying the name of the template to be passed to the template() function as follows:

```
class redis (
  $config_file           = $redis::params::file,
  $config_file_source    = undef,
  $config_file_template  = undef,
  $config_file_content   = undef,
  ) {
```

We can manage the configuration file's arguments with the following code:

```
$managed_config_file_content = $config_file_content ? {
  undef   => $config_file_template ? {
    undef   => undef,
    default => template($config_file_template),
  },
  default => $config_file_content,
}
```

The $managed_config_file_content variable computed here takes the value of the $config_file_content variable if present; otherwise, it uses the template define with $config_file_template. Also, if this parameter is unset, the value is undef. These variables are then used as follows:

```
if $redis::config_file {
  file { 'redis.conf':
    path    => $redis::config_file,
    source  => $redis::config_file_source,
    content => $redis::managed_config_file_content,
  }
}
}
```

Users can therefore populate `redis.conf` in the following different ways:

- Via a custom ERB template (placed in the `site` module) as follows:

```
class { 'redis':
  config_file_template => 'site/redis/redis.conf.erb',
}
```

- By directly providing the content attribute as follows:

```
class { 'redis':
  config_file_content =>
    template('site/redis/redis.conf.erb'),
}
```

- Using a static file sourced from a file server as follows:

```
class { 'redis':
  config_file_source => 'puppet:///modules/site/redis/redis.conf',
}
```

In case users prefer to manage the file in other ways (Augeas, concat, and so on), they can just include the main class as follows, which, by default, does not manage the configuration file's contents and uses any method to alter them:

```
class { 'redis': }
```

A good module could also provide custom defines that allow easy and direct ways to alter configuration files' single lines, either using Augeas or other file line-management tools.

Managing configuration hash patterns

If we want a full "infrastructure as data" setup and be able to manage all our configuration settings as data, we can follow these two approaches regarding the number, name, and kind of parameters to expose:

- Provide a parameter for each configuration entry we want to manage
- Provide a single parameter that expects a hash where any configuration entry may be defined

The first approach requires a substantial and ongoing effort, as we have to keep our module's classes updated with all the current and future configuration settings our application may have.

Its benefit is that it allows us to manage them as plain and easily readable data on, for example, Hiera YAML files. Such an approach is followed, for example, by the OpenStack modules (https://github.com/stackforge), where the configurations of the single components of OpenStack are managed on a settings-based approach that is fed by the parameters of various classes and subclasses.

For example, the Nova module (https://github.com/stackforge/puppet-nova) has many subclasses where there are exposed parameters that map to Nova's configuration entries and are applied via the nova_config native type, which is basically a line-editing tool that works line-by-line.

An alternative and quicker approach is to just define a single parameter such as config_file_options_hash that accepts any settings as a hash, as shown in the following code:

```
class openssh (
  $config_file_options_hash   = { },
}
```

Then, users can manage the hash in a custom template via a custom function such as the hash_lookup() provided by the stdmod shared module (https://github.com/stdmod/stdmod) as follows:

```
# File Managed by Puppet
[...]
  Port <%= scope.function_hash_lookup(['Port','22']) %>
  PermitRootLogin <%= scope.function_hash_lookup(['PermitRootLogin','yes']) %>
  UsePAM <%= scope.function_hash_lookup(['UsePAM','yes']) %>
[...]
```

Also, the users can manage the hash by referring directly to a specific key of the config_file_options_hash parameter in the following way:

```
  Port <%= scope.lookupvar('openssh::config_file_options_hash')
['Port'] ||=
  '22' %>
  PermitRootLogin <%=
    scope.lookupvar('openssh::config_file_options_hash')
      ['PermitRootLogin'] ||= 'yes' %>
  UsePAM <%=
    scope.lookupvar('openssh::config_file_options_hash')['UsePAM']
      ||= 'yes' %>
[...]
```

Needless to say that Hiera is a good place to define these parameters; on a YAML-based backend, we can set these parameters with the following settings:

```
---
openssh::config_file_template: 'site/openssh/sshd_config.erb'
openssh::config_file_options_hash:
  Port: '22222'
  PermitRootLogin: 'no'
```

We may also prefer to use an explicit parameterized class declaration as follows:

```
class { 'openssh':
  config_file_template    => 'site/openssh/sshd_config.erb'
  config_file_options_hash => {
    Port            => '22222',
    PermitRootLogin => 'no',
  }
}
```

Managing multiple configuration files

An application may have different configuration files, and our module should provide ways to manage them. In these cases, we may have the following various options to implement in a reusable module:

- Expose parameters that let us configure the whole **configuration directory**
- Expose parameters that let us configure specific **extra files**
- Provide a **general-purpose define** that eases the management of configuration files

To manage the whole configuration directory, the following parameters should be enough:

```
class redis (
  $config_dir_path          = $redis::params::config_dir,
  $config_dir_source        = undef,
  $config_dir_purge         = false,
  $config_dir_recurse       = true,
) {
  $config_dir_ensure = $ensure ? {
    'absent'  => 'absent',
    'present' => 'directory',
  }
```

```
    if $redis::config_dir_source {
      file { 'redis.dir':
        ensure  => $redis::config_dir_ensure,
        path    => $redis::config_dir_path,
        source  => $redis::config_dir_source,
        recurse => $redis::config_dir_recurse,
        purge   => $redis::config_dir_purge,
        force   => $redis::config_dir_purge,
      }
    }
}
```

Such a code would allow us to provide a custom location on the Puppet Master to use as source for the whole configuration directory as follows:

```
class { 'redis':
  config_dir_source => 'puppet:///modules/site/redis/conf/',
}
```

We can also provide a custom source according to specific node names or roles, and purge any config file that is not managed. All the destination files not present on the source directory would be deleted. Use this option only when we want to have complete control over the contents of a directory. This can be done using the following code:

```
class { 'redis':
  config_dir_source => [
                  "puppet:///modules/site/redis/conf--${::fqdn}/",
                  "puppet:///modules/site/redis/conf-${::role}/",
                  'puppet:///modules/site/redis/conf/' ],
  config_dir_purge  => true,
}
```

Consider that the source files placed in the site module in this example, according to a naming hierarchy that allows overrides per node or role name, can only be static and not templates.

If we want to provide parameters that allow direct management of alternative extra files, we can add parameters as shown in the following stdmod compliant code:

```
class postgresql (
  $hba_file_path            = $postgresql::params::hba_file_path,
  $hba_file_template        = undef,
  $hba_file_content         = undef,
  $hba_file_options_hash    = { } ,
) { [...] }
```

Finally, we can place a general-purpose define in our module. This define allows users to provide the content for any file in the configuration directory. An example is given at `https://github.com/example42/puppet-pacemaker/blob/master/manifests/conf.pp`.

The usage of such a define is as easy as follows:

```
pacemaker::conf { 'authkey':
  source => 'site/pacemaker/authkey',
}
```

Managing users and dependencies

Sometimes, a module has to create a system user or have some prerequisite packages installed in order to have its application running correctly.

These are the kind of extra resources that can create conflicts among modules, as we may have them already defined somewhere else in the catalog via other modules.

For example, we may want to manage users in our own way and don't want them to be created by an application module, or we may already have classes that manage the module's prerequisite.

There's not a universally defined way to cope with these cases in Puppet. The principle of a single point of responsibility might conflict with the need to have a full working module when it requires external prerequisite resources (packages, Yum repos, Apt sources, and so on).

My personal approach, which I've not seen used around actually, is to let the users define the name of alternative classes, if any, where such resources can be managed.

On the code side, the implementation is quite easy, as shown in the following example:

```
class elasticsearch (
  $user_class            = 'elasticsearch::user',
  ) { [...]
  if $elasticsearch::user_class {
    require $elasticsearch::user_class
  }
```

Of course, in `elasticsearch/manifests/user.pp`, we define the module's default `elasticsearch::user` class.

The module's users can provide custom classes with the following code:

```
class { 'elasticsearch':
  user_class => 'site::users::elasticsearch',
}
```

Otherwise, the modules' users can decide to manage system users in other ways and unset any class name with the following code:

```
class { 'elasticsearch':
  user_class => '',
}
```

Something similar can be done for a dependency class or an other module's classes.

In an outburst of reusability spree in some cases, I added parameters to let users define alternative classes for the typical module classes using the following code:

```
class postgresql (
  $install_class          = 'postgresql::install',
  $config_class           = 'postgresql::config',
  $setup_class            = 'postgresql::setup',
  $service_class          = 'postgresql::service',
  [... ] ) { [...] }
```

Maybe this is really too much, but, for example, allowing the users the option to define the install class to use and have it integrated in the module's own relationships logic may be useful for cases where we want to manage the installation in a custom way.

Managing the installation options

Generally, it is recommended that we always install applications via packages, which are eventually to be created onsite when we can't find fitting public repositories.

Still, sometimes, we might need, have to, or want to install an application in other ways, for example, just downloading its archive, extracting it, and eventually compiling it.

It may not be a best practice, but still, it can be done and people do it.

Another reusability feature that a module may provide is alternate methods to manage the installation of an application. Its implementation may be as easy as shown in the following code:

```
class elasticsearch (
  $install_class       = 'elasticsearch::install',
```

```
    $install            = 'package',
    $install_base_url   = $elasticsearch::params::install_base_url,
    $install_destination = '/opt',
  ) {
```

These options expose the installation methods to use the name of the installation class (so that it can be overridden), and when the installation is done via an archive, they expose the URL from where to retrieve it and the destination directory where to install it.

In init.pp, we can include the install class using the parameter that sets its name as follows:

```
    include $install_class
```

In the default install class file (here, install.pp), we can manage the install parameter with a case switch as follows:

```
class elasticsearch::install {
  case $elasticsearch::install {
    package: {
      package { $elasticsearch::package:
        ensure   => $elasticsearch::managed_package_ensure,
        provider => $elasticsearch::package_provider,
      }
    }
    upstream: {
      puppi::netinstall { 'netinstall_elasticsearch':
        url             => $elasticsearch::base_url,
        destination_dir => $elasticsearch::install_destination,
        owner           => $elasticsearch::user,
        group           => $elasticsearch::user,
      }
    }
    default: { fail('No valid install method defined') }
  }
}
```

 The puppi::netinstall define in the previous code comes from a module of mine, available at https://github.com/example42/puppi, and it's used to download, extract, and eventually execute custom commands on any kind of archive.

Users can, therefore, define which installation method to use with the install parameter, and they can even provide another class to manage the installation of the application in a custom way.

Managing extra resources

Many times, we have some customizations in our environment that cannot be managed just by setting different parameters or names. Sometimes, we have to create extra resources that no public module may provide, as they are too custom and specific.

While we can place these extra resources in any class we may include in our nodes, it may be useful to link this extra class directly to our module, providing a parameter that lets us specify the name of an extra custom class, which, if present, is included (and contained) by the module. To do this, use the following code:

```
class elasticsearch (
  $my_class            = undef,
  ) { [...]
  if $elasticsearch::my_class {
    include $elasticsearch::my_class
    Class[$elasticsearch::my_class] ->
    Anchor['elasticsearch::end']
  }
}
```

Another method to let users create extra resources by passing a parameter to a class is based on the `create_resources` function. We have already seen it; it creates all the resources of a given type from a nested hash where their names and arguments can be defined. An example, which can be found at `https://github.com/example42/puppet-network`, is as follows:

```
class network (
  $interfaces_hash          = undef,
  [...] ) { [...]
  if $interfaces_hash {
    create_resources('network::interface', $interfaces_hash)
  }
}
```

In this case, the type used is `network::interface` (provided by the same module), and it can be fed with a hash. On Hiera, with the YAML backend, it could look as follows:

```
  ---
    network::interfaces_hash:
      eth0:
        method: manual
        bond_master: 'bond3'
```

```
      allow_hotplug: 'bond3 eth0 eth1 eth2 eth3'
  eth1:
    method: manual
    bond_master: 'bond3'
  bond3:
    ipaddress: '10.10.10.3'
    netmask: '255.255.255.0'
    gateway: '10.10.10.1'
    dns_nameservers: '8.8.8.8 8.8.4.4'
    bond_mode: 'balance-alb'
    bond_miimon: '100'
    bond_slaves: 'none'
```

As we can imagine, the usage patterns that such a function allows are quite wide and interesting. The possibility of providing all the information (as pure data) that we need to create a resource has big implications. It embraces an "infrastructure as data" approach and may definitely shift most of the logic and the implementation that is done inside Puppet manifests and code, on the data backend.

Summary

In this chapter, we have reviewed Puppet modules by exploring various aspects.

We have seen the evolution and layout of modules: how the evolution of Puppet language has influenced the design of modules, in particular, how parameters are exposed and managed, from class parameterization to data in modules. We have also seen common approaches such as the params and anchor patterns.

We have faced the parameters' dilemma; we have analyzed the different kinds of parameters a module can expose and where they can be placed. We have also covered the `stdmod` naming convention initiative.

Finally, we have reviewed the most important reusability patterns. We have studied some of the reusability options we can add to modules to manage configuration files, extra resources, custom classes, and installation options.

Now, it's time to take a further step and examine how we can organize modules at a higher abstraction layer and how people are trying to manage full stacks of applications; this is a relatively unexplored field where different approaches are still trying to find a common consensus and adoption.

6
Higher Abstraction Modules

Most of the modules we find on the Puppet Forge have one thing in common: they typically manage a single application (Apache, JBoss, ElasticSearch, MySQL, and so on) or a system's feature (such as networking, users, limits, or sysctl).

A good thing is that a rigorous approach to a single responsibility principle is important in order to have modules that can better interoperate, do just what they are expected to do, and behave like libraries that offer well-identified and atomic services to their users.

Still, our infrastructures are more complex; they require different applications to be configured to work together, where configurations may change according to the number and topology of the other components and some kind of cross-application dependencies have to be followed to fulfill a complete setup.

This is generally managed by Puppet users when they group and organize classes according to their needs. Most of the time, this is done in local site modules. This is where many traps hide and make Puppet users' lives more difficult.

The roles and profiles pattern described in *Chapter 4, Designing Puppet Architectures*, is a first attempt to formalize an approach to organization of classes that is based on higher abstraction layers. It lets users coordinate the configurations of different modules and makes them composable so that the same elements can adapt to different topologies, application stacks, and infrastructures.

Still, there is much to explore in this field, and I think much is yet to be done about it. In this chapter, we will review the following topics:

- Why we need higher abstraction modules
- The OpenStack example
- A very personal approach to reusable stacks

Understanding the need for higher abstractions

It took some years in Puppet evolution to achieve the remarkable goal of having good and reusable modules that can be used to install applications quickly and easily and configure them as needed in different contexts.

The Puppet Forge offers quality and variety, and even if I think that many standardization efforts are still needed, both beginners and advanced users can now easily manage most of the applications they need to administer with Puppet.

Still, when it comes to organizing modules and configurations for our infrastructures, documentation, public code, and samples are sparse, given the notable exception of the pattern of roles and profiles.

The main reason is quite obvious. Here is where customizations begin and things get 'local'; here is where we use site modules, ENCs, and/or a bunch of Hiera data to configure our army of servers according to our needs with Puppet.

The concept of application stack is obviously not new; we always have to cope with stacks of applications, from simple ones such as the well-known Apache, PHP, and MySQL (the OS is irrelevant here), plus the PHP application to deploy on top of it, to more complex ones where different components of the stack are interconnected in various ways.

In modern times, such stacks are supposed to be composable and elastic; we can have a (L)AMP stack where the web servers can scale horizontally, where eventually, we may have a software load balancer that has to account for the newly added web frontends. We may also have a backend database which we might have to scale as well, for example, by adding new slaves.

We need to manage this on Puppet, and here the complexity begins. It's not difficult to puppetize an existing stack of applications, group the classes as expected for our nodes, and configure the relevant software; this is what we have always done after all.

This is what is done in role classes, for example, where profiles or module applications are included as needed, typically managing the dependencies in the installation order if they refer to resources applied to the same node.

It is more difficult to puppetize a dynamic and composable stack, where cross-node dependencies are automatically managed, and we can change the topology of our architecture easily, add new servers seamlessly, and do this without having to manually review and adapt configuration files. This is because our classes are so smart that they expose parameters to manage different scenarios.

It's more difficult, but definitely more powerful. Once we achieve the ability to define our components and topology, we can start working on a higher level, where users don't have to mess with Puppet code but can manage infrastructures with data.

When we have to deal only with data, things may become more interesting, as we can provide data in different ways, for example, via an external GUI. This can restrain and validate users' input and expose only high-level settings.

The OpenStack example

The Puppet OpenStack modules (search `puppet` in the repository list of `http://github.com/stackforge`) are probably the largest and most remarkable example of how Puppet is used to manage a complex set of applications that have to be interconnected and configured accordingly.

Component (application) modules

There are different modules for each OpenStack component (Nova, Glance, Horizon, Cinder, Ceilometer, Keystone, Swift, Quantum/Neutron, and so on); they can be retrieved from `https://github.com/stackforge/puppet-<component>`; so, for example, Nova's module is `https://github.com/stackforge/puppet-nova`.

These modules manage all the different configurations via a settings-based approach, with native types that set the single lines of each configuration file (there may be more than one for each component) and with different subclasses that expose all the parameters needed to manage different services or features of each component.

For example, in the Nova module, we have native types such as `nova_config` or `nova_paste_api_ini` that are used to manage single lines in the `/etc/nova/nova.conf` and `/etc/nova/api-paste.ini` configuration files, respectively.

These types are used in classes such as `nova::compute` and `nova::vncproxy` (and many others) to set specific configuration settings according to the parameters provided by users.

There is also a `nova::generic_service` define that manages the installation and specific Nova services.

Finally, subclasses such as `nova::rabbitmq` or `nova::db::mysql` manage the integration with third-party modules to create, for example, database users and credentials.

A similar structure is replicated on the modules of the other OpenStack components with the added benefit of having a coherent and predictable structure and usage pattern, which makes users' life definitively more comfortable.

Therefore, the general approach followed for OpenStack's component modules is to have multiple entry points for data, basically one for each subclass, with configuration files managed with a settings-based approach.

These single component modules can be composed in different ways; we will review a few of them. They are as follows:

- The official and original StackForge's `openstack` module
- A Puppet Labs module based on roles and profiles
- A completely data-driven approach based on the scenario node terminus

Raising abstraction – the official openstack module

The official and general `openstack` module (`https://github.com/stackforge/puppet-openstack`) can manage specific roles in an OpenStack infrastructure (compute, controller, and so on) and allow users to quickly and easily define specific (rather limited, I'd say) topologies.

For example, the `openstack::all` class manages an all-in-one installation of all the components on a single node, `openstack::controller` installs the OpenStack Controller components on a node, and `openstack::computer` installs the OpenStack Compute ones.

All these classes expose parameters that allow users to set public and private addresses, users' credentials, network settings, and whatever is needed to configure the whole OpenStack environment at a high level. In many cases, the parameters and part of the code are duplicated. For example, the `openstack::all` and `openstack::controller` classes have many parts in common, and for each parameter added to the main OpenStack classes, there's a need to replicate it on the declared component classes.

This `openstack` module can definitively be considered a module that operates at a higher abstraction layer and uses the classes and defines of application modules but has some severe limitations on flexibility and maintainability.

Raising abstraction – the Puppet Labs OpenStack module

Puppet Labs has published another higher abstraction module to manage OpenStack (probably the one used for their internal infrastructure). This is an alternative to StackForge's `puppet-openstack` module, but it uses the same mainstream component modules.

We can find it at `https://github.com/puppetlabs/puppetlabs-havana` (there's also a version for Grizzly, an earlier OpenStack release), and it's definitively worth a look, as it's also a good real-life example of the application of the pattern of roles and profiles.

On your nodes, we include the relevant role classes as follows:

```
node /^controller/ {
  include ::havana::role::controller
}
node /^network/ {
  include ::havana::role::network
}
node /^compute/ {
  include ::havana::role::compute
}
```

The profile classes are included in the role classes and a high-level dependency order is managed. For example, in `havana::role::controller`, which is the most complex role class, we have the following classes:

```
class havana::role::controller inherits ::havana::role {
  class { '::havana::profile::firewall': }
  class { '::havana::profile::rabbitmq': } ->
  class { '::havana::profile::memcache': } ->
  class { '::havana::profile::mysql': } ->
  class { '::havana::profile::mongodb': } ->
  class { '::havana::profile::keystone': } ->
  class { '::havana::profile::ceilometer::api': } ->
  class { '::havana::profile::glance::auth': } ->
  class { '::havana::profile::cinder::api': } ->
  class { '::havana::profile::nova::api': } ->
  class { '::havana::profile::neutron::server': } ->
  class { '::havana::profile::heat::api': } ->
  class { '::havana::profile::horizon': }
  class { '::havana::profile::auth_file': }
}
```

The needed resources are finally declared in the profile classes using both the official OpenStack components' modules and classes and defines from other modules, such as the Puppet Labs' firewall module to manage firewalling or the MongoDB, MySQL, RabbitMQ, and Memcache modules, which are not part of the OpenStack modules set but are needed for the setup. Here, we can also find spot resources' declarations such as SELinux settings or the usage of `create_resources()` to manage OpenStack's users.

These profiles classes don't expose parameters but access configuration data through explicit `hiera()` function calls. Hiera's namespacing is quite clear and well organized, and users can configure the whole setup with YAML files with the following contents:

```
havana::region: 'openstack'
######## Network
havana::network::api: '192.168.11.0/24'
havana::network::api::device: 'eth1'
havana::network::external: '192.168.22.0/24'
havana::network::external::device: 'eth2'
havana::network::management: '172.16.33.0/24'
havana::network::management::device: 'eth3'
havana::network::data: '172.16.44.0/24'
havana::network::data::device: 'eth4'

######## Fixed IPs (controller)
havana::controller::address::api: '192.168.11.4'
havana::controller::address::management: '172.16.33.4'
havana::storage::address::api: '192.168.11.5'
havana::storage::address::management: '172.16.33.5'

######## Database
havana::mysql::root_password: 'spam-gak'
havana::mysql::allowed_hosts: ['localhost', '127.0.0.1',
   '172.16.33.%']

######## RabbitMQ
havana::rabbitmq::user: 'openstack'
havana::rabbitmq::password: 'pose-vix'
```

The module supports only RedHat-based distributions, and compared to StackForge's official OpenStack module, it looks more organized, with less code duplication and some added flexibility.

Raising abstraction – the scenario-based approach

Both the previous approaches have the remarkable benefit of making the installation of a very complex setup such as an OpenStack infrastructure relatively easy, but they both lack flexibility, the possibility to easily compose components in custom ways, and support for high availability. If we need to manage custom topologies, we have to sweat a lot, and we need to study the module's internal details and their options carefully.

Dan Bode, one of the most active developers of the OpenStack modules, has worked on an alternative approach to manage them at a higher abstraction layer. He has written a Puppet node terminus called **scenario** (`https://github.com/bodepd/scenario_node_terminus`) upon which he has developed a completely data-driven approach (given at `https://github.com/stackforge/puppet_openstack_builder`) to the setup of the OpenStack infrastructure. This system allows to set with data both the OpenStack's configurations (as done in previous alternatives) and the composition of the classes and resources.

Among the interesting features of this project, which might be considered a StackForge official alternative to the `puppet-openstack` module, there is the possibility of composing the classes for use in different class groups (called scenarios here) entirely defined by YAML files.

When it comes to fully data-driven infrastructures, this is definitely a cutting edge approach. But beware; this is also somehow creepy.

We have a whole bunch of data; part of it is used to generate other data and all the logic is managed by Hiera's huge hierarchies, where exceptions and classifying needs have to be managed by an extra layer in Hiera configuration.

To manage parameters, we have a `hiera.yaml` file as follows:

```
---
:backends:
  - data_mapper
:hierarchy:
  - "hostname/%{hostname}"
  - "client/%{clientcert}"
  - user
  - jenkins
  - user.%{scenario}
  - user.common
```

```
        - "osfamily/%{osfamily}"
        - "enable_ha/%{enable_ha}"
        - "install_tempest/%{install_tempest}"
        - "cinder_backend/%{cinder_backend}"
        - "glance_backend/%{glance_backend}"
        - "rpc_type/%{rpc_type}"
        - "db_type/%{db_type}"
        - "tenant_network_type/%{tenant_network_type}"
        - "network_type/%{network_type}"
        - "network_plugin/%{network_plugin}"
        - "password_management/%{password_management}"
        - "scenario/%{scenario}"
        - grizzly_hack
        - common
    :yaml:
        :datadir: /etc/puppet/data/hiera_data
    :data_mapper:
        :datadir: /etc/puppet/data/data_mappings
```

The previous code is definitively not a champion of simplicity. It is a perfect example of what can happen when we move not only the configuration data, but also grouping and compositing logic into Hiera: we need extra layers in our hierarchy to accommodate different cases.

The scenario node terminus, which is an alternative to the classic Puppet nodes' classification options, can be also used for other projects or cases. I suppose only time will tell us if it's an approach that will be embraced by Puppet users.

Taking an alternate approach

Let me tell you a small personal story about Puppet, OpenStack, and choices. I had been asked by a customer to puppetize a multiregion, fully High Availabilty OpenStack infrastructure.

The customer's internal crew had great OpenStack skills and no Puppet experience; they manually configured an internal testing setup, and they wanted to be able to quickly reproduce it on different data centers.

At that time, I had no experience on OpenStack and started to study both OpenStack and its existing Puppet modules.

After some time, I realized that it would have been quite a pain to reproduce the configuration files that already exist with the settings-based OpenStack's official modules. I also realized that it would have been quite hard for the crew to manage their configurations with a pure data-driven approach.

The situation, therefore, was as follows:

- I didn't know much of OpenStack nor of its Puppet modules
- The customer's team used to work and think on a file-based logic
- The OpenStack architecture of the single regions was always the same (given the variable data) and was definitely more complex than the samples in the existing modules
- Internal Puppet skills had to be built on a training-on-the-job basis
- Budget and time were limited

I opted for what can be definitively considered a "bad idea": to write my own OpenStack modules, well aware that I was trying to do it alone in a few days without even knowing the product, part of what many skilled and knowledgeable people had done in months of collaborative work.

Modules are published on GitHub and are based on the reusability and duplicability patterns I've refined over the years; they all have a standard structure that can be quickly cloned to create a new module with a limited effort.

For example, the Nova module (`https://github.com/example42/puppet-nova`) has standard `stdmod` compliant parameters in the Nova class that allow users to freely manage packages, services, and configuration files. OpenStack components such as Nova may have anyway different services to manage, so I copied the idea of a general purpose `nova::generic_service` define to manage them and added an always-useful define called `nova::conf` to manage any configuration file.

Once the basic structure was defined, all the other modules were cloned and adapted to manage the other OpenStack components (most of the time, it was just a matter of few retouches on the module's `params.pp` manifest).

Configurations are delivered via ERB templates; a single site module (not released, as it's tailored around that specific infrastructure) defines all the grouping logic and uses classes and defines of all the classes in a single site module. Data is stored on Hiera, and it is mostly limited to endpoints' addresses, credentials, networking, and other parameters that may change per region or role.

Most of the complexity of an OpenStack configuration is managed as static or dynamic data in templates. The structure is, therefore, not particularly flexible but reproduces the designed and requested layout.

Adaptation to different topologies is not supposed to be frequent and is a matter of changing templates and logic in the site class.

The tuning of configurations, which might be more frequent, is a matter of changing the ERB templates, so it results in an easier way for the local crew to manage them directly.

Frankly, I'd hardly recommend the usage of these modules of mine to set up an OpenStack infrastructure, but they can be useful to replicate an existing one or to manage it in a file-driven way.

The general lesson we can take from this is the usual golden one, especially true in the Puppet world: there's never the best way to do things, but the most fitting one for a specific project.

An approach to reusable stack modules

What we have seen until now are more or less standard and mainstream Puppet documentation and usage patterns, and I have surely forgotten valuable alternatives. I may have left traces of personal opinions on some solutions, but they are all common and existing ones; nothing has been invented.

In this section, I'm going to discuss something that is not mainstream, has not been validated in the field, and is definitely a personal idea on a possible approach to higher abstraction modules.

It's not completely new or revolutionary: I'd rather call it evolutionary in the line of established patterns such as parameterized classes, the growing usage of PuppetDB, and roles and profiles, with a particular focus on reusability.

Here, I call 'stack' a module that has classes with parameters, files, and templates, which allows the configuration of a complete application stack, either on a single all-in-one node or on separate nodes.

It is supposed to be used by all the nodes that concur to define our application stack, each one activating the single components we want to be installed locally.

The components are managed by normal application modules, whose classes and defines are declared inside the stack module according to a somehow opinionated logic that reflects the stack's target.

In my opinion, there's an important difference between application (or component) modules and stack (higher abstraction) modules.

Application modules are supposed to be like reusable libraries: they shouldn't force a specific configuration, unless it is strictly necessary, for the module to work. They should not be opinionated and should expose alternative reusability options (for example, different ways to manage configuration files without forcing only a settings- or file-based approach).

Stack modules have to provide a working setup: they need templates and resources to make the whole stuff work together. They are inherently opinionated as they provide a specific solution, but they can present customization options that allow reusability in similar setups.

The stack's classes expose parameters that allow the following:

- A high-level setting of the stacks main parameters
- Triggers to enable or disable the single components of the stack
- Possibility to provide custom templates as an alternative to the default ones
- Credentials, settings, and parameters for the relevant components

Let's see a sample `stack::logstash` class that manages a logging infrastructure based on LogStash (a log collector and parsing tool), ElasticSearch (a search engine), and Kibana (a web frontend for ElasticSearch). This is obviously an opinionated setup even if it is quite common for LogStash.

The class can have the following parameters:

```
class stack::logstash (
  $syslog_install                = false,
  $syslog_config_template        = 'stack/logstash/syslog.conf.erb',
  $syslog_config_hash            = { },
  $syslog_server                 = false,
  $syslog_files                  = '*.*',
  $syslog_server_port            = '5544',

  $elasticsearch_install         = false,
  $elasticsearch_config_template =
    'stack/logstash/elasticsearch.yml.erb',
  $elasticsearch_config_hash     = { },
  $elasticsearch_protocol        = 'http',
  $elasticsearch_server          = '',
  $elasticsearch_server_port     = '9200',
  $elasticsearch_cluster_name    = 'logs',
  $elasticsearch_java_heap_size  = '1024',
  $elasticsearch_version         = '1.0.1',
```

```
$logstash_install                = false,
$logstash_config_template = 'stack/logstash/logstash.conf.erb',
$logstash_config_hash            = { },

$kibana_install                  = false,
$kibana_config_template          = undef,
$kibana_config_hash              = { },

) {
```

We can see some of the reusability-oriented parameters we have discussed in *Chapter 5, Using and Writing Reusable Modules*; the class' users can provide the following:

- High-level parameters that define hostnames or IP addresses of the infrastructure components (if not explicitly provided, the module tries to calculate them automatically via PuppetDB) such as `syslog_server`, `elasticsearch_server`, and so on

- Custom ERB templates such as `syslog_config_template` and `logstash_config_template` for each managed application that overrides the default ones

- Custom hash of configuration settings such as `logstash_config_hash` if they want a fully data-driven setup (they need to provide templates that use these hashes)

For each of the managed components, there's a Boolean parameter that defines if such component has to be installed (`elasticsearch_install`, `logstash_install`, and so on).

The implementation of the managed components is quite straightforward: if these variables are true, the relevant classes are declared with parameters computed in the stack class:

```
if $elasticsearch_install {
  class { 'elasticsearch':
    version       => $elasticsearch_version,
    java_opts     => $elasticsearch_java_opts,
    template      => $elasticsearch_config_template,
  }
}
if $syslog_server and $syslog_install {
  if $syslog_config_template {
    rsyslog::config { 'logstash_stack':
      content  => template($syslog_config_template),
    }
```

```
    }
    class { '::rsyslog':
      syslog_server => $syslog_server,
    }
  }
```

The resources used for each component can be different and have different parameters that are defined according to the stack class' logic and the modules used.

The choice of which vendors to use for the application modules and how many features, reusability options, and flexibility to expose to the stack's users as class parameters is up to the stack's author.

The stack class(es) are supposed to be the only entry point for user parameters, and they are the place where resources, classes, and defines are declared.

A stack's variables, which are then used to configure the application modules, can be set via parameters or calculated and derived according to the needed logic.

This is a relevant point to underline: the stack works at a higher abstraction layer and can manipulate and manage how interconnected resources are configured.

At the stack level, we can define, for example, how many ElasticSearch servers are available, what the Logstash indexers are, and how to configure them in a coherent way.

We can also query PuppetDB in order to set variables based on our dynamic infrastructure data.

In the following example, the `query_nodes` function from the `puppetdbquery` module (we have seen it in *Chapter 3, PuppetDB*) is used to fetch hostnames and IP addresses of the nodes where the stack class has installed ElasticSearch. The value retrieved from PuppetDB is used if there's not an explicit `$elasticsearch_server` parameter set by users:

```
$real_elasticsearch_server = $elasticsearch_server ? {
  ''      => query_nodes('Class[elasticsearch]',ipaddress),
  default => $elasticsearch_server,
}
```

In this case, the stack manages configurations via a file-based approach, so it uses templates to configure applications.

The stack class has to provide default templates that should be possible to override, where the stack's variables are used. For example, `stack/logstash/syslog.conf.erb` can be something like the following:

```
<%= scope.lookupvar('stack::logstash::syslog_files') %> @@<%=
  scope.lookupvar('stack::logstash::syslog_server') %>:<%=
    scope.lookupvar('stack::logstash::syslog_server_port') %>
```

Here the `scope.lookupvar()` function is used to get variables by their fully qualified name so that they can be consistently used in our classes and templates.

 Note that such a model requires all the used application modules to expose parameters that allow (in this case, the stack's developer) the possibility to provide custom templates to its users.

When using Hiera, the general stack's parameters can be set in `common.yaml` as follows:

```
---
  stack::logstash::syslog_server: '10.42.42.15'
  stack::logstash::elasticsearch_server: '10.42.42.151'
  stack::logstash::syslog_install: true
```

Specific settings or install Booleans can be specified in role-related files such as `el.yaml` as follows:

```
---
  stack::logstash::elasticsearch_install: true
  stack::logstash::elasticsearch_java_opts: '-Xmx1g -Xms512m'
```

Compared to profiles, as commonly described, such stacks have the following differences:

- They expose parameters, so user's data directly refers to the stack's classes
- The stack class is included by all the nodes that concur to the stack, with different components enabled via parameters
- Cross-dependencies, order of executions, and shared variables used for different applications are better managed at the stack level, thanks to there being a unique class that declares all the others
- The stack allows to decouple user data and code from the application modules, allowing to change the application module implementations without touching the exposed parameters and interface to users

A possible limitation of such an approach is when the same node includes different stack classes and has overlapping components (for example, an apache class). In this case, the user should manage the exception.

Summary

Puppet modules are getting better and better: they are more reusable, they better fit just what they are supposed to do, and they offer stable and reliant interfaces to the management of different applications.

They are, therefore, getting nearer to the status where they can be considered as shared libraries that can be used by different users to compose the configurations needed in their environments.

Here is where many people are struggling in order to achieve a sane organization of resources, good patterns to group them, and better approaches to a dynamic, reproducible, structured, and maybe, reusable management of complete stacks of applications.

Using these higher abstraction layer modules, people are experimenting with different practices; some have become common, such as the roles and profiles pattern, but still, few are engineered with the vision to be reusable and eventually allow single components to be composed freely to fit different topologies.

In this chapter, we have focused on reviewing why we need higher abstraction modules and why it would be great to have them reusable and flexible.

We have examined the OpenStack example, which involves many different applications that have to work together in a coherent and integrated way.

Finally, we have explored a personal approach to higher abstraction modules: stacks.

There's still much to do on this topic, and I think much will be done in the future years.

In the next chapter, we move to completely new topics: we are going to explore the practical challenges we face when we have to introduce Puppet, either on a new or existing infrastructure.

7
Deploying and Migrating Puppet

We're probably already working with Puppet, or we are planning to use it in the near future. In any case, we have to face the daunting task of automating the configuration and reproducing the state of a variable number of different servers.

Using Puppet for a server infrastructure involves analysis, planning, and decisions.

In this chapter, we will review the different aspects to be considered in our journey towards infrastructure automation:

- The possible scenarios we might face can involve new setups, migrations, and updates of the existing systems
- How we can manage Puppet migrations with a step–by–step approach divided in reiterated phases such as information gathering, priorities definition, an evaluation on how to proceed, coding, testing, applying the changes, and verifying their reports
- The cultural and procedural changes that configuration management involves

Examining the potential scenarios and approaches

Puppet is a tool that offers a world of order, control, and automation; we have learned it, we know at least the basics of how it works, and we want to install it on our servers.

We might have just a few dozens or several thousands of systems to manage. They might be similar to or very different from one another and have very few things to be configured, or a large number of resources to deal with.

We might manage them manually or maybe already have some automation scripts or tools, Puppet itself included, that help us in installing and maintaining them. We might need to optimize, refactor, and fix solutions that operate in a suboptimal way.

We might have a brand new project to build, and this time, we want to do the right thing and automate it from the beginning.

The number of variables here are many. Every snowflake is unique, but there's a basic and crucial distinction to make; it defines where our work will be done:

- On a brand new server's infrastructure
- On existing systems, either managed manually or already semiautomated
- On an infrastructure already managed by Puppet, to be heavily refactored

This distinction is quite important and can heavily affect how quickly and safely we can work with Puppet.

New infrastructures

If we work on a startup or a new project, we have the opportunity to create our infrastructure from scratch. This is often a preferred, easier, more comfortable, and safer option for the following reasons:

- **More freedom on architectural choices**: Starting from scratch, we are not bound to existing solutions; we can concentrate on the tools and languages that better fit our current and future needs without caring about backward compatibility and existing legacies. This freedom does not strictly relate to just our Puppet activities, and it allows us to evaluate technologies also based on how easily they can be automated.

- **Brand new operating system and application stacks, possibly homogeneous**: We can choose a recent version of our preferred OS, and even better, we can start from a standardized setup where all the servers have the same OS and version. This definitely makes our life with Puppet easier and our infrastructure more coherent and easier to manage.

- **Clean setups**: We don't have to care, reproduce, reverse engineer, and maintain the existing systems, so we exactly know the configurations needed on them. We will always face the risk of messing with them in the future, but introducing a configuration management system at the beginning definitely helps in keeping things tidy and homogeneous for a long time.

- **Sound design**: This can be defined from the foundations. We can set up our servers using all our expertise on how to do things in a good way. We can benefit from the fact that the newer versions of applications generally make their setup easier, for example, it's more and more common, with recent software, to have simplified configuration and installation procedures.

- **No mess with the current production**: Being a new project, we don't have to cope with the existing running systems, and we don't face the risk of introducing disrupting changes while applying or testing our Puppet configurations.

- **Faster and smoother deployment times**: These are the natural consequences of being free from working on the existing setups in production. We don't have to care about maintenance windows, safe runs, double checks, remediation times, and all the burdens that can greatly reduce the pace of our work.

Existing manually managed infrastructures

When we need to automate existing systems, things are quite different, as we have to cope with years of stratifications of many people's work with different skills under variant conditions. They may be the result of a more or less frantic and inorganic growth and evolution of an IT infrastructure, whose design patterns may have changed or evolved with time. This might not be the case for everybody, but it is quite common on infrastructures where a configuration management tool has not been steadily introduced.

We will probably have to manage the following:

- **A heterogeneous mess of different operating systems and versions, deployed over multiple years**. It is indeed very difficult to have OS homogeneity on a mature infrastructure. If we are lucky, we have different versions of the same OS. This is because they were installed in different times, but more likely, we have to manage a forest of variegated systems, from Windows to Unix to almost any conceivable Linux distribution, installed according to the project software needs, commercial choices, or personal preferences of the sys admins in charge at the times.

- **Heterogeneous hardware** from multiple vendors and of different ages is likely to be present in our infrastructure. We have probably already made great progress in the last years, introducing virtualization, and maybe, a large effort of consolidation of the previous hardware mess has already been done. Still, if we haven't moved everything on the cloud, it's very likely that our hardware is based on different models possibly by different vendors.

- **Incoherent setups**, with systems configured by different people who may have used different logic, settings, and approaches also for the same kind of functionality. System admins might be complex and arcane people who like to make great things in many unexpected ways. Order and coherency will not always find a place on their crazy keyboards.

- **Uncertain setup procedures**, whose documentation may be incomplete, obsolete, or just not existing. Sometimes, we have to reverse engineer them; sometimes, the offered functionality is easy to understand and replicate, and at other times, we may have an arcane black box, configured at the dawn of times by people who don't work anymore in the company. Nobody wants to touch this black box because it's too critical, fragile, or simply indecipherable.

- **Production systems**, where it is always delicate and difficult to operate. We might be able to work only on limited maintenance windows, with extra care of the changes introduced by Puppet and their evaluation on operations. We have to make choices and decisions for each change, as the homogeneity that Puppet introduces will probably change and leverage some configurations.

- **Longer Puppet rollout times** are the obvious side effects when we work on existing systems. This has to be accounted with attention, as it might influence our strategy on how to introduce Puppet.

We have two possible approaches to follow when dealing with existing systems; they are not alternative. We can adopt both of them in parallel, evaluating which one is the most fitting for each node:

- **Node migration**: We make new servers managed by Puppet that replace the existing ones

- **Node update**: We install Puppet on the existing machines and start managing them with Puppet

Node migration

A migration approach involves the installation and configuration, via Puppet, of new servers as replacements of the existing ones. We build a system from scratch, we configure it so that it reproduces the current functionalities, and when ready, we promote it to production and decommission the old machine.

The main advantages of such an approach compared to a local update are the following:

- We can operate on new systems that are not (yet) in production, so we can work faster and with lesser risks. There's no need to care about breaking the existing configurations or introducing downtimes to production.

- The setup procedure is done from scratch, so we're validating whether it's fully working and if we have full Puppet coverage of the needed configurations. Once a system has been successfully migrated and fully automated, we can be confident that we can consistently repeat its setup any time.

- We can test our systems before decommissioning the old ones, and a rollback is generally possible if something goes wrong when we make the switch.

- We can use such an occasion to rejuvenate our servers, install newer and patched operating systems, and generally, have a more recent application stack (if our migrated applications can run on it).

There is a critical moment to consider when we follow this approach, that is, when we shift from the old systems to the new ones.

Generally, this can be done with a change of IP on the involved systems (with relevant ARP cache cleanups on peer devices on the same network), a change of DNS entries, or a change in the configurations of load balancers or firewalls; all these approaches are reversible, being mostly done at the network level, and rollback procedures can be automated for a quick recovery in case of problems.

Whatever the approach used, we'll have the new systems doing what was previously done by old and different ones, so we might have untested and unexpected side effects. We may see these side effects with the features of an application that are not commonly used or with scheduled jobs, either local or triggered on remote systems, which might manifest themselves at later and unexpected times.

So, it makes sense to keep the migrated systems under observation for some days and double check if, besides the correct behavior of the main services they provide, other functionalities and interactions with external systems are preserved.

Generally, the shift is easier if no data is involved; much more attention is definitively needed when migrating systems that persist data, such as, databases.

Here, the scenarios might be quite different, and the strategy to follow for data migration depends on the software used, the kind and size of data, if it's stored locally or via network, and other factors that definitively are out of the scope of this book.

Node update

When we prefer or have to install Puppet on existing, running systems, the scenario changes drastically, different variables come into play, and the approaches to follow are definitively alternative.

In these cases, we will have:

- Probably different operating systems to manage; some of them might be rather ancient. Here, we might have problems in installing a recent version of Puppet, so it makes sense to verify whether the version of the client is compatible with the one of the Puppet Master.

- Undetermined setup and configuration procedures that we might have to gradually cover with Puppet with the hope to have managed whatever is needed.

- Puppet deployments on running production systems, so we have to manage the risk of configuration changes delivered by Puppet; this makes your life harder and more dangerous, especially if we don't follow some precautions (more on this later).

- Manual configurations accumulated over time will probably determine systems that are not configured in the same way, and we'll realize this when Puppet will be deployed. What's likely to happen is that many unexpected configurations will be discovered and probably, wrong or suboptimal settings will be fixed.

Existing automated infrastructures

What has been described in the previous paragraphs might have been a common situation some years ago; now, times have definitively changed, and people have been using configuration management tools and cloud computing for years.

Actually, it is likely that we might already have a Puppet setup, and we are looking for ways to reorganize and refactor it.

This is becoming a quite common situation. We learn Puppet while we work on it, and during the years of usage, patterns evolve, the product offers new and better ways to do things, and we understand better what has worked and what hasn't.

So, we might end up in scenarios where our Puppet architecture and code are in different shapes:

- We have some old code that needs fixing and refactoring in a somehow limited and noninvasive way: no revolutions, just evolutions

- Our setup works well but is based on older Puppet versions, and the migration needs a more or less wide refactoring (a typical case here is the upgrade from Version 2.x to 3.x)

- Our setup does its job more or less, but we want to introduce new technologies (for example Hiera) or reorganize our code radically (for example, introducing well-separated and reusable application modules and/or the roles and profiles pattern)

- Our Puppet code is a complete mess; it produces more problems than the ones it solves, and we definitely need a complete rewrite

Upgrading the Puppet Master

Different cases may need different solutions; they can follow some of the patterns we describe for the setup of new infrastructures or the migration or update of existing ones. However, here, the work is mostly done on the Puppet Master rather than the clients, so we might follow different approaches.

One of them implies the refactoring of the code and tools, keeping the same Puppet Master. If there are a few things to be changed, this can be based on simple evolutionary fixes on the existing code base; if the changes are more radical, we can use Puppet's environments to manage the old and new codebase in parallel and have clients switching to the new environment in a gradual and controlled way.

Alternatively, we can consider the creation of a new Puppet Master when the changes are more radical, either for the versions and tools used or for a complete overhaul of the codebase. In these cases, we might prefer keeping the same certificate authority and Puppet Master's certificate or create a new one with the extra effort of having to re-sign our clients' certificates. Such an approach actually may involve the creation of new systems that point directly to the new Puppet Master or the reconfiguration of the existing ones. In both cases, we can follow the same gradual approach described for other scenarios.

When we need to upgrade the Puppet Master, a few rules have to be considered.

The Puppet Master's version should always be newer than the version on the clients. Client-server compatibility between single major releases is generally guaranteed. 2.7 servers are backward compatible with 2.6 clients, and 3.x servers are compatible with 2.7 clients. In most cases, backward compatibility extends for more versions, but this is not guaranteed.

It's recommended that you upgrade from one major version to the next one, avoiding wider jumps. Starting from Version 3, a semantic versioning scheme (earlier major versions can be considered as 2.7, 2.6, 0.25, and 0.24) has been introduced, and a major version change, now expressed by the first digit, can have backward incompatibilities regarding the language syntax and other components that are not related to the client-server communication. Puppet Labs, however, has the good habit of logging deprecation notices for features that are going to be removed or managed in different ways, so we can look at the Puppet Master's logs for any similar notice and fix our code before making the next upgrade step.

Patterns for extending Puppet coverage

Let's analyze in detail what to do when we have to introduce Puppet on an existing infrastructure.

Some of these activities are needed also when working on a brand new project or when we want to refactor our existing Puppet configurations; consider them as a reference that you can adapt to your own needs and scenario.

The obvious assumption is that Puppet deployment on something that is already working and serving services has to be gradual. We have to understand the current situation, the expected goals, what is quick or easy to do, where and what to manage with Puppet, and our operational priorities.

Raising the bar, step by step

A gradual approach involves a step-by-step process that needs informed decisions, reiterations, and verification of what is done, evaluating each case according to its uniqueness.

We can extend our Puppet coverage using the following two axes:

- **Vertically**: Working on all the existing nodes managed by Puppet and adding, step by step, more and more resources under its control. At the end of the process, we can have full coverage both on the common baselines and the role's specific features. In this case, it is better to make a single change at a time and propagate it to the whole infrastructure.

- **Horizontally**: Adding new nodes under Puppet management, either with a migration or with an update approach. Here, the operations are done node by node; they are placed under Puppet control, and the baseline of common resources (plus eventually, what is specific for the node's role) is all applied in a single run.

The delivery process should be iterative and can be divided in the following five phases:

- **Collect info**: We need to know the territory where we operate
- **Set priorities**: We need to define what is more important and urgent
- **Make choices**: We need to evaluate and decide how to proceed
- **Code**: We need to write the needed Puppet manifests and modules
- **Apply changes**: We need to run Puppet and check for reports

The first iterations will probably concentrate on developing the common baseline of resources to apply to all the nodes. These can be propagated both horizontally and vertically, looping on the phases mentioned earlier with emphasis on some of them according to the specific step we are making; they might last for days or a few minutes.

Let's explore more deeply what happens during the phases of each reiteration.

Knowing the territory

Before running Puppet on an existing server's infrastructure, we need to know the territory. It sounds obvious; it is obvious. So obvious that sometimes we forget to do it properly.

We have to know what we want to automate and gather as much info as possible about:

- How many servers are involved
- What are their operating systems and their major versions
- What are the common configuration files and resources to be managed on a basic system (our general baseline)
- How many different kind of servers we have (our Puppet roles)
- What are the main applications' stacks used
- What are the most critical systems
- Which servers are going to be decommissioned soon
- What kind of servers we need to deploy in the future

We may have this information from an existing Inventory System or internal documentation, so it should not be hard to gather it and have a general idea of the numbers involved.

For each application or system resource that we plan to manage with Puppet, we also need to know further details, such as the following:

- How configurations change on different servers according to the infrastructural factors such as the role of the server, operational environment, datacenter, or zone. We will use variables based on these factors to identify nodes and differentiate the configurations according to them.

- How differently the same configuration is managed on our operating systems. We will need to manage these OS differences in our modules and Puppet code.

- If there are unique or special cases, where the configuration is done differently, we will manage these exceptions on a per-node basis.

 It's definitively not necessary to gather all this information from the beginning; some details are useful just when we need to automate the relevant components. What's important at the beginning is the general overview about the systems involved, their operating systems, roles, and life expectancy.

Defining priorities

We said that the automation of an existing infrastructure is a gradual process, where we start from 0 percent of systems and configuration coverage, and we move them step by step in a state where they are managed by Puppet. We might not reach a full 100 percent coverage, and for each step, we might consider what's worth managing with Puppet and what is not.

Ideally, every server of our infrastructure should be fully managed by Puppet; we should be able to provision a system from scratch and have it up and running after a Puppet run. The setup procedure is expected to be fully automated, controlled, replicable, and scalable.

There are cases anyway where this rule is not necessarily recommended. When the setup procedure of an application requires the execution of a few specific commands, with varying arguments that might not be easily predictable or which need users' interactivity, the automation becomes difficult and expensive in terms of the implementation time.

If such setups have to de done only once on a system (during the installation time) and are supposed to be done on very few systems that have a medium-to-long life, we may question whether it makes sense to try to do them with Puppet, spending several hours on what can be quickly done manually in a few minutes.

This becomes even more evident when we have to manage with Puppet an existing system where such a setup is already done, or when the version of our application may change in the future and the setup procedure may be different, rendering all our efforts to fully manage it with Puppet useless.

So, when we face the big task of automating an infrastructure, we definitively have to set priorities and make choices, decide what makes sense to automate first, and what can be postponed or simply ignored.

We have to consider different tasks that cover different needs.

Automate servers deployment

Automating servers deployment is one of the most important things to do, and there are big chances that we're already managing it in some way. The installation of an operating system should be as quick and automated as possible. This actually is not strictly related to configuration management, as it's a step that occurs before we install and run our configuration agent. There are countless ways to automate installations on bare metal, virtual machines, or cloud instances. Whatever we choose, the general rule is that OS provisioning should be quick and essential. We can manage all the specific settings and packages of a given server type via our configuration management tool, which is invoked in a second step and is independent of the method we've used to install our system.

 There's at least one exception for this general rule: if we need to provision new systems very quickly, for example, in an AWS autoscaling infrastructure, we might prefer to use AMIs that have already installed and partially configured the needed applications. This makes the spin up of a cloud instance definitely faster.

Automate common configurations

Here, we enter into the realm of Puppet. We may have many different servers fulfilling different tasks, but it is very likely that we'll need a common baseline of shared configurations for each of them. The specific settings may change according to different conditions, but the configurations to be managed are always the same. They typically involve the configuration of the DNS resolver and network configuration, user authentication, NTP and timezone settings, monitoring agents, log management, routine system tasks, backup setup, configuration of OpenSSH, the same Puppet client setup, and whatever other configuration we may want to manage on all our systems. Our first priority should be to cover these settings; once completed, the benefits are real, as it allows us to quickly rollout changes that, if done manually, would probably involve a lot of wasted time.

Automate the most important roles

The next big step is to automate the most important roles; once we've managed the common ground, it is time to raise the bar and start covering the roles we have in our infrastructure. Here, things may become more difficult as we start directly manipulating the software that delivers the services of our systems. It makes sense to start from the most used ones, also evaluating how quickly and easily they can be managed. An important element to consider is indeed the kind of servers we need to set up in the near future. It's probably better to work first on the automation of roles that we need to deploy from scratch before taking care of the roles that are already in production.

Refine and automate application deployments

We don't need to and actually should not manage the deployment of applications via Puppet, but we can configure with Puppet the environment of our deployment tool, be that Capistrano, Run Deck, Puppi (disclaimer: I wrote it), the native OS package system, or any other. We might manage deployments with custom scripts or maybe manually, executing a sequence of documented commands, and in such a case, this is definitely a thing to fix. Puppet can help, but it is only a part of the solution; we should concentrate on how to manage the delivery of our deployment via the simple execution of a single command, even executed manually from the shell.

Once we achieve this, we can manage this execution with whatever orchestration, remote execution, or continuous integration tool we have in-house or we want to introduce, but this can be considered as a subsequent evolutionary step. The very first prerequisite is that we should be able to deliver the deployment of our applications with a single command (it may be a script that runs a sequence of other commands, of course) that doesn't involve human interaction. Puppet here can help set up and configure things, but, I stress it again, it should not be used to actually trigger the execution of such a command; this is not its tasks and function. Puppet sets and maintains the systems' state, and it is not made to trigger one-shot commands.

Integrate what already works well

Our infrastructure is the result of years of work and efforts and the sweat and blood of many sysadmins. It might be a total chaos or stay in good shape; but probably, there's something (or much) good there. We should consider Puppet as a tool that automates with a formal language what we are already doing, either with other kind of automation procedures or manually. We have to review what is working well in our setup procedures and what is not, what doesn't cause any problems, and what drains a lot of time or fails often. We can start working on what wastes our time and works in a suboptimal way, and keep and integrate what does its job well. For example, if we have custom scripts that install and configure a complex application stack, we might consider using them directly in our manifests (with a plain exec resource) instead of recreating all the configurations and resources that the scripts deliver and build, under Puppet. We can always fix this later when other priorities have been tackled and there's time for wider refactoring.

Automate monitoring

Monitoring is a beast of its own in a complex infrastructure. There are different things to monitor (servers, services, applications, network equipment, hardware and software components, and so on), different kinds of tasks (checking, alerting, and trends graphing), different approaches (on premise, SaaS, via local agents or remote sensors), and definitively different tools that do the job. We probably use different solutions according to what and how we need to monitor, and we are probably managing them in different ways. Maintenance of the checks and the metrics to be monitored can be a time-wasting effort in some cases, and here is where it makes sense to use Puppet to automate long and painful manual operations.

Management and automation of a monitoring infrastructure can be rather complex if the used tool doesn't provide mechanisms of self-discovery. Nagios, for example, probably the most loved, hated, and used monitoring tool, might be a real pain to maintain manually, but at the same time, it is not too easy to manage with Puppet, as it requires external resources and expects us to define all the desired checks with Puppet code. Given its complexity, the automation of monitoring activities might not be at the top of our to-do list. As it's often a quite time-consuming task, we have to face it, sooner or later, especially if we are planning the installation of many new servers for which we want to automate not only their setup, but also their monitoring.

Evaluating solutions

When we know our territory and have set priorities about what to do, we have more elements to make decisions. There are many choices to ponder about, but we don't need to make them all together. Let's start from the priorities we've set and define how to behave case-per-case.

Among the decisions to make, we have to evaluate the following:

- **If Puppet can or should be installed on old or arcane systems**: Here, it's important to understand what is the newest version of Puppet that can be installed (its compatibility with the native Ruby version is important here; refer to `http://docs.puppetlabs.com/guides/platforms.html#ruby-versions` for details), how this can affect the version of Puppet on the Puppet Master according to what we have seen about client-server compatibility.

- **Where it makes sense to install Puppet**: Old servers, which require low maintenance and provide services that are planned to be decommissioned soon and do not have a long expected life, might not deserve our attention and might be skipped or managed with low priority.

- **The strategy to follow for each node — migration or update**: There are no strict rules on this. Both the alternatives are possible and can be evaluated for each host, case by case. Old but needed systems on obsolete hardware based on an OS that is not widely spread in our infrastructure and whose configurations might be easy to automate are good candidates for migration. The alternative update path might be preferred on our most common existing operating systems so that the time spent in implementing configurations with Puppet can be reused multiple times.

- **How easily and quickly configurations can be done**: Activities that we know to be rather quick to implement and present low risks in their deployment can be delivered with precedence, both to reduce our backlog of things to do and to give us the feeling that something is moving. While deploying them, we can also gather confidence on the procedures and know our systems better.

- **Impact and risks have always to be accounted for**: Puppet is going to change the configurations; in some cases, it might just add or remove some new lines or comments, and in other cases, it will actually change the content of configurations. By doing this, it will probably restart the relevant services and in any case have an impact on our systems. Is it safe? Can it be done at any time? What happens if something goes wrong? What kind of side effects can we expect from a change? All of these questions need a more or less comprehensive answer, and this has to be done for each step. Incidentally, this is the reason why each step should be limited and introduce only a single change. It will be easier to control its application and diagnose eventual problems.

- **Current maintenance efforts and the system's stability**: This should be considered when defining how to proceed and what to do first. If we are losing a lot of time doing repetitive tasks that can be automated via Puppet or we keep on firefighting recurring failures on some troublesome systems, we should definitively concentrate on them. In this case, the rule of doing what is easier to do first has to be coupled with another common sense rule: automate and fix first what results in a lot of wasted time.

Coding

We have gathered information about our systems, set priorities, and evaluated solutions; now, it's finally time to write some code. The previous steps may have involved a varying amount of time, from very few minutes to days. If we have spent too much time on them, we have probably done something wrong, or we might have done too much upfront planning too early instead of a step-by-step approach, where the single phases reiterate relatively quickly.

In any case, our first coding task should be to develop the common baseline for all our systems. This is probably the first and most useful thing to do. We can start covering the most important and used operating systems in our infrastructure; we don't need to manage the general baseline of all our servers from the beginning. The common classes and resources can be placed in a grouping class (something like `::site::general`). This is likely to include other classes that might be both from shared modules (`::openssh`, `::ntp`) and custom ones (`::site::users`, `::site::hardening`). It also makes sense to include in `::site::general` a class that includes a subset of common resources, something we can call `::site::minimal`. This can be useful to let us install Puppet with minimal configurations (eventually, just what's needed to manage the same Puppet client and nothing more) on as many servers as possible and then, gradually extend coverage of new systems' configurations just by moving the resources and classes from `::site::general` to `::site::minimal`. These are just samples on how practically a common baseline might be introduced; the mileages may vary.

Once the common baseline is configured, we can concentrate on developing full roles, starting with the most useful, easy-to-manage, and common ones. This might take a varying about of time, but the general idea is that each new node should be fully managed. It doesn't make sense to introduce technical debts also on the brand new nodes we have to deploy that are managed by Puppet. So, if we had to choose between automating the existing or new servers, we should give precedence to the latter ones.

Besides the macro activities that involve a high level of planning, we will face some micro decisions on how to manage the configurations for a given application on our servers, at every step. There are some common-sense rules to consider, and they replicate the phases we have described that involve information gathering and decisions on the approaches to follow.

We must know how the configuration file(s) of an application change on our systems. This is generally affected by two factors: operating system and infrastructure logic.

The differences in operating systems are influenced by the version of the installed application (which might support different configuration options), how it has been packaged, and where the files are placed. Even a configuration file as common as `/etc/ssh/sshd_config` can change in a relevant way on different operating systems.

Infrastructure logic may affect the content of a file in various ways. We may have single parameters whose values change according to the various factors strictly related to our infrastructure (for example, we may have different name servers or domains in `/etc/resolv.conf` according to the region or data center where our server is located). We can also have whole portions of configurations that might be totally different according to factors such as the role of a system (for example, the same Puppet configuration file, `puppet.conf`, is quite different on clients and the Puppet Master).

According to how the configuration files of an application change on our servers, we can use the following different approaches for managing them with Puppet:

- All the configuration files are the same. Simply put, we can provide the same file either via the `source` argument or with `content` based on a ERB template that doesn't have variables interpolation.

- Configuration files are mostly the same; they change only for a few parameters. This is a typical case where we can use ERB templates that interpolate variables that might be set via parameters in the class that provides the template. An important thing to consider here is how these parameters change in our nodes, according to what logic (server's role, zone/ data center/country, or operational environment), and if this logic may be expressed by what we defined as node-identifying variables in *Chapter 4, Designing Puppet Architectures*. This is important because it gives us glimpses of how correct we have been in setting them.

- Configuration files are quite different, and one or a few parameters are not enough to express all the differences that occur on our nodes. Here, things get trickier; we can use completely different ERB templates (or static files) for each major configuration layout, or we might be tempted to manage these differences with an `if` statement inside a unique template.

The latter is a solution I'm not particularly fond of, because, as a general rule, I would avoid placing logic inside files (in this case, ERB templates). However, it might make sense in cases where we want to avoid excessive duplication of files, which differ just for some portions. In some cases, we might prefer a settings-based approach. Instead of managing the whole configuration file, we can just set the single lines that we need.

I find this useful in two main cases: when different operating systems have quite different configuration files and we just need to enable a specific configuration setting or when we manage configuration files of web applications that might not be provided by native packages (that generally don't overwrite existing configuration files and are inherently conservative on applications' versions). A typical example here can be the database connection settings of, for example, a PHP application.

Applying changes

So, we are finally ready to run our Puppet code and apply it to our servers.

Some of the precautions to be taken here can be applied whenever we work with Puppet; some are more specific to the cases where Puppet is introduced on the existing systems, and it changes the running configurations.

The procedure to follow when we have to apply new Puppet code can definitively vary according to the amount of the managed node, their importance for our business, and the maintenance rules we follow in our company.

Still, a few common points can definitively be recommended:

- **Communicate**: This is a primary rule that should be applied every time. We are going to change the way some configurations are managed on systems; whoever might have the permissions and tasks to modify them should be aware that what was managed earlier in a manual or some other way is now managed by Puppet. At least, in the operations teams, the whole Puppet rollout process should be shared.

- **Test with noop**: There's a wonderfully useful option of the Puppet command: `--noop`. It allows us to execute a Puppet run and see its effects without actually making any change to the system. This is extremely useful to see how configuration files would change and spot potential problems before they occur. If we have Puppet running continuously on our servers at regular intervals (being triggered via cron or running as an agent), we should test our code in a dedicated environment before pushing it in the production one. We will review how to manage the code workflow in *Chapter 8, Code Workflow Management* .

- **Test on different systems**: If our configuration changes according to the OS of a system, its role or any other factor, we should verify how it behaves for each different case before propagating the change to all the servers. Also, in this case, we can use Puppet environments to test our code before pushing it to production, and even if it is generally not recommended, if we feel confident, we don't have to test each possible case. A very interesting project that allows us to assess the impact of Puppet changes on our infrastructure is Gonzo by Simon Croome, and it can be found at `https://github.com/croomes/gonzo`.

- **Propagate the change**: Once we have tested with `--noop`, if it doesn't harm the system, and once we've applied it to different kind of servers and we had the expected results, we can be more confident that our change won't disrupt our operations and we can deploy it to production. Propagation of the change may depend on different factors such as the way a Puppet run is triggered, its interval, the topology of our infrastructure, and the possibility to rollout changes in a segmented way.

- **Watch reports**: During the deployment of our change, it's quite important to keep an eye on Puppet reports and spot errors or unexpected changes. Puppet has a multitude of different report options and web frontends such as The Foreman, Puppet Dashboard, or Puppet Enterprise that provide easy-to-access and useful reporting features that we can check to verify how our rollout is proceeding.

- **Don't be surprised of the skeletons in the closet**: When we apply a configuration on many servers that have been managed manually for many years, we are making a major cleanup and standardization activity. We can easily spot old and forgotten parameters that could be incorrect or suboptimal, which might refer to old systems no longer in production or obsolete settings. This is normal and is a beneficial side effect of the introduction of Puppet.

- **Review and patch uncovered configurations**: It may happen that the configuration provided via Puppet doesn't honor some special case that we hadn't considered. No need to panic; we can fix things in a pragmatic and methodic way, giving priority to the urgent cases (eventually rolling back manually the configuration changed by Puppet and disabling its execution run on the involved servers until we fix it). Often in such cases, the exception can be managed on a per-node basis; also, for this reason, it's useful to have the possibility of having configurations to manage special cases per specific nodes, on Hiera hierarchies or anywhere in our code.

Things change

Once we introduce a tool like Puppet in our infrastructure, everything changes and we should be well aware of this.

Infrastructure as code

There's a wonderful term that describes what tools like Puppet or Chef have introduced in IT operations: infrastructure as code. We define our IT infrastructure with formal code, the configurations of our servers, the procedures to set them up, and whatever is needed to turn a piece of bare metal or a blank VM to a system that provides services for our purposes.

When we can use a programming language to configure our systems, a lot of powerful collateral effects take place. These are inherently related to the fact that we are dealing with code.

Versioning

Code can be versioned with an SCM. The history of our commits reflects the history of our infrastructure. We can know who did a change and when and why they did it. There's a huge intrinsic value in this: the power of contextual documentation and communication. Puppet code is inherently the documentation of the infrastructure, and the commits log reflects how this code has been deployed and evolved. It quickly communicates in a single place the rationale and reasons behind some changes that are much better than sparse e-mail, a wiki, phone calls, or direct voice requests. Also, for this reason, it is quite important to be disciplined and exhaustive when doing our commits. Each commit on the Puppet code base should reflect a single change and explain as much as possible about it, possibly referring to relevant ticket numbers.

Reproducibility and predictability

Code can be run as many times as we want. We have already underlined this concept in *Chapter 1, Puppet Essentials,* but it's worth further attention. Once we express how to set up our systems with code, we can be confident that what works once works always. The setup procedure can be repeated and it always delivers the same result (given that we have correctly managed the dependencies of resources). There's a wonderful feeling we gain once we have Puppet on our systems. We are confident that their setup is coherent and done how we expected it. A new server is installed, and all the configurations we expect from it are delivered in a quick and automated way. There is no real need to double check whether some settings are correct and whether all the common configurations are applied as expected in a mature and well-tested Puppet infrastructure they are.

There's more, though, a lot more. Ideally, we just need our Puppet codebase and a backup of our application data to rebuild our whole infrastructure from scratch in a reasonable amount of time. In a perfect world, we can create a disaster recovery site from scratch in few minutes or hours, given that we have quick and automated deployment procedures (in the cloud, this is not difficult), 100 percent Puppet coverage of all the needed configurations, and automated or semiautomated application deployments and restore facilities of our data. A completely automated disaster recovery site setup from scratch is probably not even needed (it's much more probable that during a crisis, we have all our sysadmin working actively on an existing DR site), but whatever can be automated can save time and human errors during the most critical hours.

Testing

In the next chapter, we will review the testing methodologies we have at our disposal when writing the Puppet code. However, here it is important to stress that the possibility of testing our code allows us to preventively verify how our changes may affect the systems where we want to apply them and make them much more controlled and predictable. This is crucial for tools such as Puppet that directly affect how systems operate and can introduce changes (and failures) at scale. Proper testing can help us in being more confident on how to deliver our code to production.

Maintenance

Code can be refactored and refined. The more we develop Puppet code, the more we understand Puppet and how to make it fit better to our infrastructure. This is a learning process that inevitably has to be done on our own and on our infrastructure. We will definitely consider what we wrote a year or just few months ago inaccurate and inappropriate for new technical requirements that have emerged or just badly written. The good news is that as any type of code, this can be refactored and made better. How and what to fix in our code base should depend on how it affects our work. Badly formatted code that works and does its duties has less refactoring priority than code that creates problems, is difficult to maintain, or doesn't fit new requirements.

Evolution of the system administrator

It should be clear by now that such a radical change of how systems are managed also involves a change on how the system administrator works.

The primary and most important point is that the sysadmin has more and more to cope with code. This involves that somehow he has to adopt a developer's approach to his work. He can do this using an SCM and testing and refactoring code, which might be activities that are not familiar to a sysadmin but have to be tackled and embraced because they are simply needed.

The second radical change involves how systems are managed. Ideally, in a Puppet managed infrastructure, we don't even need to SSH to a system and issue commands from the shell; any manual change on the system should be definitively avoided.

This might be frustrating and irritating, as we can quickly do things that require a lot more time on Puppet, manually (write the code, commit, test, apply; for a 5-second trivial change done by hand, we might may take several minutes with a complete Puppet workflow).

The point is that what is done on Puppet remains; it can be applied when the system is reinstalled and is inherently documented. A quick manual fix is easily and quickly forgotten and may make us lose a lot of time when there's the need to replicate it, and there's no trace of how, where, and why it was done.

Many of the most annoying and dangerous issues people have when Puppet is introduced are actually due to the lack of real embracement of the mindset and techniques that the tool requires. People make manual changes and don't implement them in manifests. Then, at the first Puppet run, they are reverted, and if any kind of problem takes place, Puppet gets the blame. In other cases, there's the temptation to simply disable it and leave the system modified manually. This may make sense in exceptional emergency cases, but after the manual fix, the change has to be integrated and Puppet should be re-enabled.

If this doesn't happen, we will soon fill our infrastructure with servers where Puppet is disabled and the drift for the configured baselines gets wider and wider, making the process of re-enabling the service more and more difficult, risky, and time consuming.

Designing a Puppet-friendly infrastructure

We should have realized by now that there are things that Puppet does well and things that are not properly in its chords. Puppet is great for managing files, packages, and services and is less effective in executing plain commands, especially if they have an occasional nature.

Once we start introducing Puppet in our infrastructures, we should begin, where possible, to make things in a way that favors its implementation.

Some time ago, in a conference open space, I remember a discussion with a developer on how to make a Java application better manageable with Puppet. From his point of view, a good API could be a solid approach to make it better configurable. All the sysadmins, and Puppet users replied that actually this was far from being a nice thing to have. Plain configuration files were definitively a preferred approach to manage the application's configuration.

If we can express it with a file, we can easily manage it with Puppet. Whatever requires the execution of commands, even if it is doable, is always considered with skepticism.

The installation of software should definitively be done via the OS-native packages. Even if most of us have done their defines that fetch a tarball, unpack it and compile, nobody really likes such an approach. It involves a procedural and nondeclarative way of performing activities that it makes idempotence more difficult and is definitively worse to express with Puppet DSL.

Services should be managed following the OS-native approach, be that `init`, `systemd`, `upstart`, or whatever. Managing them with the execution of a command in a custom startup script is definitively not Puppet friendly.

Configuration files from common stacks of applications should be leveraged. For example, when we have to manage the Java settings on an application server, it makes sense to manage them always on the same place; standardizing them is a matter of overall coherence and easier management.

Once we gain affinity and expertise with Puppet, we quickly understand the things that can be done quickly and safely and the ones that make our life harder, requiring more resources or quick and dirty patches.

It is our responsibility to discuss this with the developers and the stakeholders of an application to find a shared approach to its setup that makes it easier to be managed with Puppet while preserving the requested implementation needs.

Summary

The introduction of Puppet on an infrastructure is a long and intriguing voyage without return. It requires planning, patience, method, experience, and skills, but it brings great results.

There's definitively no unique way to face it. In this chapter, we have exposed the general scenarios we might face, the possible alternative approaches, and have suggested a step-by-step procedure articulated on different phases: information gathering, priority setting, decision making, code development, testing, and rollout to production.

These phases should be reiterated at each step with emphasis on what matters to make things done.

We have also faced the changes that such a process involves; how we need a new mindset and new processes to sustain a Puppet setup.

Complementary to this is an effective management of our code: how it's versioned, reviewed, tested, and maintained. These are some of the topics we are going to see in the next chapter.

8
Code Workflow Management

All the Puppet manifests, public shared modules, site modules, and (Hiera) data are the code and data we create and use. We need tools and workflows to manage them.

In this chapter, we will review the existing tools and techniques to manage Puppet's code workflow from when it is written to when it is deployed to production.

Most people in the Puppet world use **Git** to version their code, so we will refer mostly to it. However, similar processes can be followed if we manage our code with Subversion, Mercurial, or any other source code-management tool.

In this chapter, we give an overview of the tools that can help us with our Puppet code. We will cover the following topics:

- Writing with Geppetto and Vim
- Managing with Git
- Reviewing with Gerrit
- Testing modules with rspec-puppet
- Testing Puppet runs with rspec-system-puppet and Beaker, using Vagrant
- Deploying with `librarian-puppet` or `r10k`
- Automating with Travis or Jenkins

Writing the Puppet code

Each one of us has a favorite tool for code writing. It may change according to the language we use, our familiarity with the software, or the preference of the moment.

Whatever the tool we use, it should make our experience as smooth, productive, and enjoyable as possible.

I am a Vim guy, without being a Guru. Having a sys admin background, I feel comfortable using the same tool "wherever" I am, whether on the local terminal or on the remote ssh session. We can, more or less, expect to find Vim on any system under our keyboard.

A developer, I guess, feels more comfortable with a tool that runs on his computer and can greatly enhance the writing experience with syntax checks, cross references, and the power of an IDE.

For this, there is **Geppetto**, a full-featured IDE based on Eclipse and dedicated to the Puppet code. Other popular editors, such as TextMate and Sublime Text, have Puppet plugins that can be quite useful.

The good news is that all of them can make our lives easier and more productive when we write the Puppet code.

Geppetto

Geppetto (`http://puppetlabs.github.io/geppetto/`) is the tool of reference for writing the Puppet code. It is an open source software by Puppet Labs and is a result of its acquisition of the startup Cloudsmith that developed it.

We can install Geppetto as a standalone application or as an Eclipse plugin. It has very useful features, which are as follows:

- Code syntax and style checking
- Contextual documentation
- Integration with the Puppet Forge
- Integration with PuppetDB
- All the features inherited from Eclipse

When we launch the tool, we are prompted for a directory where to create our Geppetto workplace. In a workplace, we can create projects that, most times, are modules we can directly import from the Forge or an SCM repository.

 Geppetto may be memory-hungry with large projects; if we bump into an `Internal Error: Java heap space` error, we probably have to enlarge the memory pools for the JVM Geppetto to run in. In `geppetto.ini` (or `eclipse.ini`, if we use Geppetto as plugin), we can set something as follows:

```
-XX:MaxPermSize=256m
-vmargs
-Xms384m
-Xmx512m
```

Vim

If we have to think of an evergreen tool that has accompanied many sys admins' keyboards for many years now, I think Vi(m) is one of the first names that comes to mind.

Its power and flexibility are well expressed in how it can be made effective to manage the Puppet code. There are two Vim bundles that are particularly useful for us:

- `vim-puppet` (`https://github.com/rodjek/vim-puppet`): This is a syntax highlighter and formatting tool written by Tim Sharpe, who is well known in the Puppet community for being the author of hugely popular tools such as `librarian-puppet`, `puppet-lint`, and `rspec-puppet` (all of which are going to be discussed in this chapter).
- `Syntastic`: This is a syntax-checking tool that works for many popular languages and has the ability to check the style and syntax of our manifests when we save them.

To install them easily, we first need to install **Pathogen** (a Vim extension that allows easy management of plugins) by copying the file `pathogen.vim` in `~/.vim/autoload/` from `https://raw.github.com/tpope/vim-pathogen/master/autoload/pathogen.vim`.

Then, be sure to have the following code in the `~/.vimrc` of our home directory:

```
call pathogen#infect()
syntax on
filetype indent plugin on
```

Once we have Pathogen loaded, we can easily add bundles in the `~/.vim/bundle` directory, as follows:

```
git clone git://github.com/rodjek/vim-puppet.git ~/.vim/bundle/puppet
git clone git://github.com/scrooloose/syntastic.git ~/.vim/bundle/
  syntastic
```

Now, we can use Vim with these powerful plugins that definitely make coding with Puppet DSL more comfortable.

 If, after these changes, we have problems when pasting multiple lines of text from the clipboard (each new line has one more indent level and # signs at the beginning), try to issue the Vim command `:set paste`.

Git workflows

If we want to work and prosper with Git, we have to grasp its principles. There are theories and some alternatives on how we can manage our Puppet code with Git in a safe and comfortable way.

In this section, we will review:

- Git's basic principles and commands
- Some useful Git hooks
- Two different workflows for Puppet code management with Git

Git's basic principles and commands

Git is generally available as a native package in every modern OS. Once we have installed it, we can configure our name and e-mail (that will appear in all our commits) with the following:

```
git config --global user.name "Alessandro Franceschi"
git config --global user.email al@lab42.it
```

These commands simply create the relevant entries in the ~/.gitconfig file. We can add more configurations by either editing this file directly or with the git config command.

To create a Git repository, we just have to move to the directory that we want to track and simply type git init. This command initializes a repository and creates a local .git directory where all Git data is stored.

Now, we can type git status to see the status of the files in our repository. If we have files in this directory, we will see them as untracked. This means that they are not managed under Git, and before being able to commit changes on our files, we have to stage them. This is done by the git add command, which adds all the files from the current working directory to Git's index (we can add only specific and selected files or changes). If we type git status again, we will notice that the files we added are ready to be committed. We can use git commit to create a commit with all the changes in the files we've previously staged. Our default editor is open, and we can type the title (first line) and the description of our commit.

For readability and better management later, it is important to make single and atomic commits that involve only the changes for a specific fix, feature, or ticket.

Now, we can type git log to see the history of our commits on this repository.

Git is a distributed SCM; we can work locally on a repository that is a clone of a remote one. To clone an existing repository, we can use the `git clone` command (we have seen some usage samples earlier with Vim bundles).

Once we have cloned a repository, we can use `git push` to update it with our local commits and `git pull` to retrieve all the changes (commits) made there since we cloned it (or made our latest pull).

We may want to work on separated branches where we can manage different versions of our code. To create a new branch, we use `git branch <branchname>`; to work inside a branch, we type `git checkout <branchname>`. When we are inside a branch, all the changes we make and commit are limited and confined in that branch; if we switch branches, we will see our changes to the local files magically disappearing. To incorporate the commits done in one branch to another branch, we can use the `git merge` or `git rebase` commands.

These are just the basics of Git; they just highlighted the kind of commands we may end up using when working with it. If we want to learn more, there are some great resources online, such as:

- `http://try.github.io`: This is a site with interactive tutorials to learn Git's basics
- `http://gitready.com`: This is a site full of hints and documentation

Git hooks

Git hooks are scripts that are executed when specific Git actions are performed. We can add a hook just by placing an executable file under our local `.git/hooks` directory. The name of the file reflects the phase when the hook is executed.

When we deal with Puppet, we generally have three different hooks that we can use. They are:

- `.git/hooks/pre-commit`: This is executed before finalizing the commit. Here, it makes sense to place syntax and lint checks that prevent us from committing code with errors.
- `.git/hooks/pre-receive`: This is executed before accepting a `git push` command; it may be placed on our central Git repository and can be quite similar to the pre-commit one. The difference here is that the checks are done on the central repository when changes already committed on remote working repositories are pushed.

- `.git/hooks/post-receive`: This is executed on the central repository server after a push. It can be used to distribute our committed code to a testing (or production) Puppet environment automatically.

Usage possibilities for hooks are endless; we can find some useful ones at `https://github.com/drwahl/puppet-Git-hooks`.

Environments and branches

When we want to manage our Puppet code with Git, we can follow different approaches. Our main objectives are:

- Be able to version our code
- Be able to distribute it
- Be able to test our code before pushing it into production

The first two points are implicit with Git usage; the third point can be achieved using Puppet's environments. Since we can set different paths on the Puppet Master for the `modulepath` directory and the `manifest` file, which are mapped to different Puppet environments, we can couple different Git branches or working repositories to them.

Here, we outline two possible approaches:

- The first is the officially recommended one, which is based on automatic environments and a well-established Git workflow, where a new branch is created for each new feature or bug fix. Here, we have to branch, merge, pull, and push from different branches.
- The second is a simplified approach, possibly easier to manage for Git beginners, where we always pull and push from the same branch.

Branch-based automatic environments

In the first approach, since we may have an unpredictable number of branches that are created and destroyed regularly, we use the possibility to create automatic environments with Puppet, which involves a configuration on `puppet.conf` as:

```
[main]
  server = puppet.example.com
  environment = production
  confdir = /etc/puppet
[master]
  environment = production
  manifest = $confdir/environments/$environment/manifests/site.pp
  modulepath = $confdir/environments/$environment/modules
```

This is coupled with the presence of a post-receive Git hook that automatically creates the relevant environment directories. Check `http://puppetlabs.com/blog/git-workflow-and-puppet-environments` for more detail.

Whoever writes Puppet code can work on any change in a separate Git branch, which can be tested on any client by specifying the namesake environment.

Passage to production is generally done by merging the separated branches in the master branch.

Simplified developer workdir environments

If our team has limited affinity with Git, we may find it easier to manage changes in a different, simpler way; people always work on the master branch and they have a local working copy of the Puppet code where they work, test, and commit. Code can be promoted to review for production with a simple `git push` command.

Also, in this case, it is possible to map the Puppet Master environments to the local working directories of the developers in `puppet.conf` so that they can test their code on real servers before pushing it to production.

We may evaluate variations on the described alternatives, which can adapt to our business requirements, team's skills, and preferred workflows. In any case, it is important to test the Puppet code before committing it, and a good way to do this is to use Puppet environments that map to the directories where this code is written.

Code review

When there's a team of people who work collaboratively on Puppet, it is important to have good communication among its members, a common vision on how the code is organized, where logic and data are placed, and what the principles behind some design decisions are.

Many mistakes made while working on Puppet are due to incomplete knowledge of the area of effect of code changes, and this is generally due to bad communication.

For this reason, any tool that can boost communication, peer review, and discussion about code can definitely help in having a saner development environment.

Gerrit

When we work with Git, the natural companion to manage peer review and workflow authorization schemes is **Gerrit**. This is a web interface made by Google for the development of Android. It integrates perfectly with Git and allows commenting on any commit, vote for them, and have users that may authorize their acceptance.

Different user roles with different permission schemes and authorization workflows can be defined. Once new repositories are added, they can be cloned via `git`, as shown:

```
git clone ssh://al@gerrit.example.com:29418/puppet-modules
```

When we work on repositories managed under Gerrit, we have to configure our Git to push to the special `for` ref, instead of the default `heads`. This is the key step that allows us to push our commits to a special intermediary place where they can be accepted or rejected.

```
git config remote.origin.push refs/heads/*:refs/for/*
```

We also need a pre-commit hook that automatically places the required `Change-Id` in our commits.

```
gitdir=$(git rev-parse --git-dir) ; scp -p -P 29418 \
  al@gerrit.example.com:hooks/commit-msg ${gitdir}/hooks/
```

Once we have made our setup, we can normally work on our local repo with Git. When we push our changes, they are submitted to Gerrit to the special `refs/for` for code peer review. When a commit is accepted, Gerrit moves it to `refs/heads` from where it can be pulled and distributed.

Gerrit can be introduced any time in our workflow to manage the acceptance of commits in a centrally managed way and, besides the client's configurations that we have seen, it doesn't require further changes in our architecture.

> A great tutorial on Gerrit can be seen at `http://www.vogella.com/tutorials/Gerrit/article.html`.

Online resources for peer review

There are various online services that can be used for peer review and be alternatives to an on-premise solution based on Gerrit. Some of them are:

- GitEnterprise (`https://gitent-scm.com`): This offers a Gerrit and code repository online service.
- Codifferous (`https://codifferous.com/`) presents an alternative approach based on single lines of code, instead of commits, for online collaborative code review.
- RBCommons (`https://rbcommons.com`): This is the SaaS version of the Review Board (`http://www.reviewboard.org/`) open source code review software.
- Repository management sites such as GitHub (`https://github.com`) and BitBucket (`https://bitbucket.com`): These offer an easy way to fork a repository via the web interface, make local changes, and push them back to the upstream repository with **pull requests** (**PR**) that can be discussed and approved by the upstream repository owner.

Testing the Puppet code

It has been clear for years that there is a strong need to be able to test how changes to our Puppet code can affect our infrastructure.

The topic is quite large and, to be honest, not completely solved, but there are tools and methods than can help us to work safely with Puppet in a production environment.

We can test our code with the following tools:

- The command `puppet parser validate` to check the syntax of our manifests
- The command `puppet-lint` to check the style of our code
- The tool rspec-puppet to test the catalog and the logic of our modules
- The tool rspec-system-puppet and Beaker to test what happens when our catalog is applied to a real system

We can also follow some procedures and techniques, such as:

- Use the `--noop` option to verify what the changes before applying them would be
- Use Puppet environments to try our code on test systems before pushing it into production

- Have canary nodes where Puppet is run and changes are verified
- Have a gradual and clustered deployment rollout procedure

Using rspec-puppet

The rspec-puppet tool (`http://rspec-puppet.com`) makes it possible to test Puppet manifests using rspec, a widely used Ruby behavior-driven development framework.

It can be installed as a gem:

```
gem install rspec-puppet
```

Once installed, we can move to the directory of a module and execute the following:

```
rspec-puppet-init
```

This command creates a basic rspec environment composed of the following:

- The `Rakefile` in our module's main directory, where the tasks we can run with the tool rake are defined and which can trigger the execution of our tests.
- The `spec/` directory that contains all the files needed to define our tests: `spec/spec_helper.rb` is a small Ruby script that helps in setting up Puppet's running environment during the tests' execution, and `spec/classes`, `spec/defines`, and `spec/functions` are subdirectories where the tests for classes, defines, and functions should be placed.
- The `spec/fixtures` directory is temporarily used to copy the Puppet code we need to fulfill our tests with during testing. It's eventually possible to define other dependency modules to fetch and use during the tests in a `.fixtures.yml` file.

Test files have names that reflect what they are testing. For example, if our module is called `apache`, the tests for the `apache` class are placed in `spec/classes/apache_spec.rb`, and the tests of a define called `apache::vhost` are in `spec/defines/apache_vhost_spec.rb`.

We have normal Ruby spec code in these files, where the test condition and the expected result are defined in terms of Puppet resources and their properties.

The following is a sample test file for an `apache` class (taken from Puppet Labs' apache module). The first line requires the `spec_helper.rb` file previously described, as shown:

```
require 'spec_helper'
```

Then, a 'Debian' context for which the relevant facts are provided is defined as follows:

```
describe 'apache', :type => :class do
  context "on a Debian OS" do
    let :facts do
      {
        :osfamily              => 'Debian',
        :operatingsystemrelease => '6',
        :concat_basedir        => '/dne',
      }
    end
```

Under this context (defined according to the specified facts or parameters) are listed the resources that we expect in a catalog; note that it is possible to use the `contain_*` matcher for any Puppet resource type, and each argument of that resource can be tested.

```
it { should contain_package("httpd").with(
  'notify' => 'Class[Apache::Service]',
  'ensure' => 'installed'
  )
}
it { should contain_user("www-data") }
}
```

We can also set specific parameters and test the behavior we expect when they are provided, as shown in the following code snippet:

```
describe "Don't create user resource" do
  context "when parameter manage_user is false" do
    let :params do
      { :manage_user => false }
    end

    it { should_not contain_user('www-data') }
    it { should
contain_file("/etc/apache2/apache2.conf").with_content %r{^User
www-data\n} }
  end
end
```

Note that the `with_content` matcher permits to verify the same contents of a file.

The intended usage of `rspec-puppet` is to verify if the logic of our module is correctly applied under different conditions, for example, testing its behavior when different parameters are provided or when different OSes are simulated. It is useful to prevent regressions during code refactoring and quickly validate PRs from contributors. It is not intended to validate the effect of our code when applied on a system.

A key point to understand is that `rspec-puppet` works on the catalog and checks whether Puppet resources are correctly provided; it does not test what happens when those resources are actually applied for real. In software testing terms, `rspec-puppet` is a unit-testing tool for modules.

rspec-system-puppet and Beaker

The rspec-system-puppet tools was written by Puppet Labs' Ken Barber to automate the testing of the effects of Puppet on a real system under Vagrant using rspec-style statements.

It was written to solve one of the limitations of catalog-based test tools such as `rspec-puppet`, automating the tests of the effects of a complete Puppet run on a system. We can consider it as an acceptance testing tool for modules.

Now, the project is deprecated in favor of Beaker (`https://github.com/puppetlabs/beaker`), which has been developed internally at Puppet Labs to manage acceptance tests for their products. So, we will refer to it, even if they share similar principles, which are:

- Tests are done on virtual machines that are created and destroyed on the fly
- Tests are described with rspec-style syntax
- In tests, the expected results are defined on a system where the tested code is applied

Beaker tests are executed on one or more **System Under Test (SUT)**, which may be run under VMWare, Vagrant, Solaris Zones, or Amazon EC2 instances.

Tests are configured in the `spec/acceptance` directory of a module, using one or more hosts that may have different roles and OSes. Their configuration is defined in YAML files generally placed in the `spec/acceptance/nodesets` directory.

Vagrant

Vagrant (`http://www.vagrantup.com`) is a very popular tool to quickly create **Virtual Machines (VM)**, mostly for testing and development purposes.

One of Vagrant's strong points is the ability to run provisioning scripts when a VM is created and, among others, the possibility to directly run Puppet with either the `apply` command pointing to a local manifest, or with `agent` pointing to Puppet Master.

This makes Vagrant a perfect tool to automate the testing of Puppet code and replicate development and test setups that can be aligned to the production setups in a local environment.

Once we have Vagrant and VirtualBox installed (its virtualization technology of reference, even if plugins are available to manage other VM backends), we just need to create a `Vagrantfile` where its configurations are defined.

This book's material is actually distributed as a repository that contains a `Vagrantfile` that allows easy usage of the sample Puppet code.

We can download it from Packt's site or from GitHub at `https://github.com/example42/puppet-architectures`. Be sure to have Vagrant, VirtualBox, and the `cachier` plugin installed (useful to cache frequently downloaded packages):

```
vagrant plugin install vagrant-cachier
```

If we have problems in provisioning a VM correctly, we may also need the `vbguest` plugin that automatically updates the VirtualBox additions on the VM with the VirtualBox version we are using (they are needed to support functionalities such as shared folders that are needed for Vagrant provisioning):

```
vagrant plugin install vagrant-vbguest
```

Vagrant works with base boxes, which are a sort of golden image of an OS downloaded from the Internet (once) and then used to create the virtual machines.

A good online reference for available public boxes is available at `http://www.vagrantbox.es`. It is maintained by Gareth Rushgrove, the author of the *DevOps Weekly* newsletter and well known in the Puppet community for having developed good modules.

Let's review a sample `Vagrantfile`, which is a bit more complex than a standard one, since it provides the following:

- A multi-VM environment
- The possibility to choose the OS for use from a selection of public base boxes
- The possibility to configure memory and CPU for any node
- Puppet provisioning with Hiera support

Our `Vagrantfile` begins with some variables that define how the boxes are created:

```
# Select the OS you want to use (see boxes list below)
default_os = 'Ubuntu1204_64'
# Define our domain
domain = 'example42.com'
# Default ram (can be overriden per node)
default_ram = '256'
# Default number of cpu  (can be overriden per node)
default_cpu = '1'
```

Then, there is the list of nodes that the multi-VM environment provides, as follows:

```
nodes = [
    { :hostname => 'puppet',    :ip => '10.42.42.10', cpu: '2'},
    { :hostname => 'lb01',      :ip => '10.42.42.91'},
    { :hostname => 'web01',     :ip => '10.42.42.101'},
    { :hostname => 'web02',     :ip => '10.42.42.102'},
    { :hostname => 'db01',      :ip => '10.42.42.141', ram: '512'},
    { :hostname => 'el01',      :ip => '10.42.42.151'},
    { :hostname => 'log',       :ip => '10.42.42.15'},
    { :hostname => 'mon',       :ip => '10.42.42.16'},
]
```

After this comes the list of public base boxes than can be used. Change the value of the `default_os` variable, which was previously assigned to the box name, to the one that we want to use for our VMs, using the following code snippet:

```
boxes = {
    :Centos64_64    => { :box => 'centos-64-x64-vbox4210',
:box_url => 'http://puppet-vagrant-boxes.puppetlabs.com/centos-64-x64-
vbox4210.box',              :breed => 'redhat' },
    [...]
}
```

Here comes Vagrant's actual configuration: it uses the `cachier` plugin to speed up the downloading of packages; parameters such as memory, networking, and hostnames are taken from the nodes' list:

```
Vagrant.configure("2") do |config|
  config.cache.auto_detect = true

  nodes.each do |node|
    config.vm.define node[:hostname] do |node_config|
```

```
node_config.vm.box = boxes[default_os.to_sym][:box]
node_config.vm.box_url = boxes[default_os.to_sym][:box_url]
node_config.vm.host_name = node[:hostname] + '.' + domain
node_config.vm.network :private_network, ip: node[:ip] if
  node[:ip]
if node[:forwards]
  node[:forwards].each do |from,to|
    node_config.vm.forward_port from, to
  end
end
memory = node[:ram] ? node[:ram] : default_ram ;
cpu = node[:cpu] ? node[:cpu] : default_cpu ;
node_config.vm.provider "virtualbox" do |v|
  v.customize [ 'modifyvm', :id, '--name', node[:hostname],
    '--memory', memory.to_s ]
  v.customize [ 'modifyvm', :id, '--cpus', cpu.to_s ]
  v.customize [ 'setextradata', :id,
    'VBoxInternal2/SharedFoldersEnableSymlinksCreate/v-
      root', '1']
  end
  end
end
```

Here, the provisioners are configured. First, a shell script is executed to install the latest version of Puppet on the VM, and then some other necessary plugins are used. The shell script is, according to the OS, in `bin/setup-debian` or `bin/setup-redhat`:

```
config.vm.provision "shell", path: 'bin/setup-' +
  boxes[default_os.to_sym][:breed] + '.sh'
```

Here comes the Puppet provisioner, where there are defined paths for modules, manifests, and Hiera data:

```
config.vm.provision :puppet do |puppet|
  puppet.hiera_config_path = 'hiera-vagrant.yaml'
  puppet.working_directory = '/vagrant'
  puppet.manifests_path = 'manifests'
  puppet.manifest_file = 'site.pp'
  puppet.module_path = [ 'modules' , 'site' ]
```

In the following code are defined the options used when Puppet is executed:

```
puppet.options = [
  '--verbose',
  '--report',
```

```
        '--show_diff',
        '--pluginsync',
#       '--debug',          # Uncomment to enable debugging
#       '--parser future',  # Uncomment to enable future parse
    ]
  end
end
```

We can run Vagrant without arguments to see the list of available actions. The most common ones are:

- `vagrant status`: This shows the current VM's status.
- `vagrant up [machine]`: This turns on all the existing VMs or the specified one. The VM is generated from a base box. If the box is not locally stored, then it's downloaded and saved in `~/.vagrant.d/boxes/`.
- `vagrant provision [machine]`: This runs the provisioning scripts on one or all VMs.
- `vagrant halt [machine]`: This stops one specific or all VMs.
- `vagrant destroy [machine]`: This destroys one specific or all VMs (their content will be erased; they can then be recreated with `vagrant up`).
- `vagrant ssh [machine]`: This makes an SSH connection to a running VM. Once logged in, we should be able to run `sudo -s` to gain root privileges without entering a password.

In our Vagrant environment, we can place Puppet modules in the `modules` and `site` directories. The first manifest file applied to nodes is `manifests/site.pp`; the Hiera configuration file is `hiera-vagrant.yaml`, and its data is in `hieradata`.

The repository also provides a simple `parc` script that allows the selection of alternative sample Puppet architectures.

The ability to quickly and easily create virtual machines where to run Puppet on makes Vagrant the perfect tool to test the effects of our changes on Puppet manifests on a real system in automated or manual ways.

Deploying the Puppet code

Deployment of the Puppet code is, most times, a matter of updating modules, manifests, and Hiera data on the relevant directories of the Puppet Master.

We deal with two logically different kinds of code that involve different management patterns, which are:

- Our modules, manifests, and data
- The public modules we are using

We can manage them in various ways. Some of them are:

- Eventually using **Git submodules** for each Puppet module in Git
- Using the `puppet module` command for the public modules published on the Forge
- Using tools such as `librarian-puppet` and `r10k`
- Using other tools or custom procedures that we may write specifically for our needs

Using librarian-puppet for deployments

The `librarian-puppet` tool (`http://librarian-puppet.com`) was developed to manage the installation of a set of modules from the Puppet Forge or any Git repository. It is based on `Puppetfile`, where the modules and the versions to install are defined:

```
forge "http://forge.puppetlabs.com"

# Install a module from the Forge
mod 'puppetlabs/concat'

# Install a specific version of a module from the Forge
mod 'puppetlabs/stdlib', '2.5.1'

# Install a module from a Git repository
mod 'mysql',
  :git => 'git://github.com/example42/puppet-mysql.git',

# Install a specific tag of a module from a Git repository
mod 'mysql',
  :git => 'git://github.com/example42/puppet-mysql.git',
  :ref => 'v2.0.2'

# Install a module from a Git repository at a defined branch
mod 'mysql',
```

```
    :git => 'git://github.com/example42/puppet-mysql.git',
    :ref => 'origin/develop'
```

We can install all the modules referenced in the local `Puppetfile` in our `modulepath` directory with the following:

```
librarian-puppet install
```

Deploying code with r10k

The `r10k` tool was written by Adrien Thebo, who works in Puppet Labs, to manage deployment of Puppet code from Git repositories or the Forge. It fully supports the format of `librarian-puppet` for `Puppetfile`, but it is also an alternative tool that empowers a workflow based on Puppet's dynamic environments.

It can be installed as `gem`:

```
gem install r10k
```

In the configuration file `/etc/r10k.yaml`, we define one or more source Git repositories to deploy in the defined `basedir` directory:

```
    :cachedir: '/var/cache/r10k'
    :sources:
      :site:
        remote: 'https://github.com/example/puppet-site'
        basedir: '/etc/puppet/environments'
```

The interesting thing is that we find a separate directory inside the defined `basedir` for each branch of our Git source, which can be dynamically mapped to Puppet environments.

To run a deploy from the repository where we have a `Puppetfile`, we can run the following:

```
r10k deploy environments -p
```

This creates a directory for each branch of our repository under `/etc/puppet/environments`. We find all the modules defined in `Puppetfile` under the `modules/` directory inside these directories.

Propagating Puppet changes

Deployment of the Puppet code on production is a matter of updating the files on the directories served by Puppet Master (or, in a Masterless setup, distributing these files on each node), but contrary to other typical application deployments, the process doesn't end here: we need to run Puppet on our nodes in order to apply the changes.

How this is done largely depends on the policy we follow to manage Puppet execution. We can manage Puppet runs in different ways, and this affects how our changes can be propagated:

- Running Puppet as a service: In this case, any change on the Puppet production environment (or what is configured as default) is propagated to the whole infrastructure in the `runinterval` timeframe.

- Running Puppet via a cron job has a similar behavior: Whatever is pushed to production is automatically propagated in the cron interval we defined. Also, in this case, if we want to make controlled executions of Puppet on selected servers, the only approach involves the usage of dedicated environments before the code is promoted to the production environment.

- Manage Puppet runs in a central way: MCollective (check `http://www.slideshare.net/PuppetLabs/presentation-16281121` for a good presentation on how to do it) is an option that can be used for managing Puppet centrally. Once our code has been pushed to production, we still have the possibility to manually run it on single machines before propagating it to the whole infrastructure. The complete rollout can then be controlled further by either using canary nodes, where changes are applied and monitored first, or by having different clusters of nodes in a large installation, where changes can be propagated in a controlled way.

Whatever pattern is used, it's very important and useful to keep an eye on the Puppet reports and spot quickly early signs of failures caused by Puppet's runs.

Puppet Continuous Integration tools

We reviewed the tools than can accompany our code from creation to production. Whatever happens after we commit and eventually approve our code can be automated.

It is basically a matter of executing commands on local or remote systems that use tools like the ones we have seen in this chapter for the various stages of a deployment workflow.

Once we have these single bricks that fulfill a specific function, we can automate the whole workflow with a **Continuous Integration** (CI) tool that can run each step in an unattended way, and proceed to the following if there are no errors.

There are various CI tools and services available; we will concentrate on a pair of them that are particularly popular in the Puppet community:

- **Travis**: This is an online Continuous Integration as a service project
- **Jenkins**: This is a well-known and widely used Hudson fork

Travis

Travis (`https://travis-ci.org`) is an online continuous integration service that perfectly integrates with Github.

It can be used to run tests of any kind; in the Puppet world, it is generally used to validate modules code with `rspec-puppet`. Refer to the online documentation (`http://docs.travis-ci.com/user/getting-started/`) on how to enable the Travis hooks on GitHub; on our repo, we configure it with a `.travis.yml` file like the following:

```
language: ruby
rvm:
  - 1.8.7
  - 1.9.3
script:
  - "rake spec SPEC_OPTS='--format documentation'"
env:
  - PUPPET_VERSION="~> 2.6.0"
  - PUPPET_VERSION="~> 2.7.0"
  - PUPPET_VERSION="~> 3.1.0"
matrix:
  exclude:
    - rvm: 1.9.3
      env: PUPPET_VERSION="~> 2.6.0"
      gemfile: .gemfile.travis

gemfile: .gemfile.travis
notifications:
  email:
    - al@lab42.it
```

As we can see from the previous lines, it is possible to test our code on different Ruby versions managed by **Ruby Version Manager (RVM)**, available at `https://rvm.io`, and different Puppet versions.

It's also possible to exclude some entries from the full matrix of the various combinations (for instance, the previous example executes the `rake spec` command to run the `puppet-rspec` tests in five different environments: 2 Ruby versions, 3 Puppet versions and - 1 matrix exclusion).

If we publish our shared Puppet modules on GitHub, Travis is particularly useful to automatically test the contributions we receive, as it is directly integrated on the GitHub pull requests workflow, which is commonly used to submit fixes or enhancements on the code to a repository author (check `https://help.github.com/categories/63/articles` for details).

Jenkins

Jenkins is by far the most popular open source CI tool. We are not going to describe how to install and use it; we will just point out useful plugins for our purposes.

A Puppet-related code workflow can follow common patterns; when a change is committed and accepted, Jenkins can trigger the execution of tests of different kinds and if they pass, can automatically (or after human confirmation) manage the deployment of the Puppet code on production (typically by updating the directories on Puppet Master, which are used by the production environment).

Among the multitude of Jenkins plugins (`https://wiki.jenkins-ci.org/display/JENKINS/Plugins`), the ones that are most useful for our purposes are:

- **ssh**: This allows execution of a command on a remote server. It can be used to manage deployments with `librarian-puppet` or `r10k`, or it can execute specific tests.

- **RVM/rbenv**: This integrates with RVM or rbenv to manage execution of tests in a controlled Ruby environment. It can be used for `rspec-puppet` and `puppet-lint` checks.

- **GitHub/Gerrit**: This integrates with GitHub and Gerrit to manage code workflow.

- **Vagrant**: This integrates with Vagrant for tests based on real running machines.

Testing can be done locally on the Jenkins server (using the RVM/rbenv plugins) or on any remote host (via the ssh plugin or similar tool); deployment of the code can be done in different ways, which will probably result in the execution of a remote command on Puppet Master.

Summary

In this chapter, we reviewed the tools that can help us to write our Puppet code, and manage, test, and deploy it.

We have seen how to enhance our writing experience on Geppetto, Puppet Labs official Puppet IDE, and Vim, a sysadmin's evergreen tool. We also learned how to version and manage code with Git, and how to introduce, eventually, a peer review and approval system such as Gerrit.

We have then seen the different tools and methodologies available to test our code: simple syntax checks that should be automated in Git hooks, style checks with `puppet-lint`, unit testing on modules with `puppet-rspec`, real-life (and ephemeral) acceptance tests on running virtual machines managed with Vagrant, and tools such as Beaker.

We have finally faced how the Puppet code can be delivered to production with tools such as `librarian-puppet` and `r10k`.

The execution of these individual tools can be automated with CI tools either to automatically trigger tests when a pull request is made on a GitHub repository such as Travis or to manage the whole workflow from code commit to production deployment with Jenkins.

The next chapter is about scaling, and focuses on how to make our Puppet setup grow with our infrastructure.

9
Scaling Puppet Infrastructures

There is one thing that I particularly like about Puppet: its usage patterns can grow with the user's involvement. We can start using it to explore and modify our system with puppet resource, we can use it with local manifests to configure our machine with puppet apply, and we can have a central server where a puppet master service provides configurations for all our nodes where we run the puppet agent command.

Then our nodes' number may grow and we may find ourselves with an overwhelmed Puppet Master that needs to scale accordingly.

In this chapter, we will review how to make our Master grow with our infrastructure and how to measure and optimize Puppet performances. We will learn the following:

- Optimizing the Puppet Master with **Passenger**
- Scaling the Puppet Masters horizontally
- Load balancing alternatives
- Masterless setups
- Store configs with PuppetDB
- Profiling Puppet performances
- Code optimization

Scaling Puppet

Generally, we don't have to care about the Puppet Master's performance when we have a few nodes to manage.

Few is definitely a relative word; I would say any number lower than one hundred of nodes, which varies according to various factors such as the following:

- **System resources**: The bare performances of the system, physical or virtual, where our Puppet Master is running are obviously a decisive point. Particularly needed is the CPU, which is devoured by the `puppet master` process when it compiles the catalogs for its clients and when it makes MD5 checksums of the files served via the fileserver. Memory can be a limit too while disk I/O should generally not be a bottleneck.

- **Average number of resources for node**: The more resources we manage in a node, the bigger becomes the catalog and the time required to compile it on the Puppet Master, deliver it via network, and finally receive and process the clients' reports.

- **Number of managed nodes**: The more nodes we have in our infrastructure, the more work is expected from the Puppet Master. More precisely, what really matters for the Master is how many catalogs it has to compile per unit of time. So the number of nodes is just a factor of a multiplication, which also involves the next point.

- **Frequency of Puppet runs for each node**: The default 30 minutes, when Puppet runs as a service, may be changed, and this has a big impact on the work submitted to the Master.

- **Exported resources**: If we use exported resources, we may have a huge impact on the performances, especially if we don't use PuppetDB as the backend for storeconfigs.

As simple as puppet apply

The simplest way we have to use Puppet is via the `apply` command. It is simple but powerful, because using it, we can apply exactly the same catalog that would be retrieved from the Puppet Master on the local node.

The manifest file we may apply locally can be similar to our `site.pp` file on the Puppet Master; we just have to specify the `modulepath` directory and eventually the `hiera_config` parameters to be able to reproduce the same result we would have with a client-server setup:

```
puppet apply --modulepath=/etc/puppet/modules:/etc/puppet/site \
             --hiera_config=/etc/puppet/hiera.yaml \
             /etc/puppet/manifests/site.pp
```

We can mimic an External Node Classifier by placing all the top scope variables and classes that would be provided by it on our manifest file. This usage pattern with Puppet is the most simple and direct and, curiously, is also a popular choice in some large installations. We will see later how a Masterless approach based on `puppet apply` can be an alternative for scaling.

Default Puppet Master

A basic Puppet Master installation is rather straightforward: we just have to install the server package and we have what is needed to start to work with Puppet. The following are the requirements:

- A `puppet master` service, which can start without any further configuration
- Automatic creation of the CA and the Master certificates
- Default configurations that involve the following settings:
    - First manifest file processed by the Master in `/etc/puppet/manifests/site.pp`
    - Modules searched in `/etc/puppet/modules` and `/usr/share/puppet/modules`

Now we just have to run Puppet on clients with `puppet agent -t --server <pupptmaster fqdn>` and sign their certificates on the master (`puppet cert sign <client certname>`) to have a working client-server environment.

We can work with such a setup if we have no more than a few dozens of nodes to manage.

We have already seen the elements that affect the Puppet Master's resources, but there is another key factor that should interest us: what are our acceptable catalog compilation and application times?

Compilation occurs on the Puppet Master, unless we operate in Masterless mode, and can last from a few seconds to minutes; it is heavily affected by the number of resources and relationships to manage, but also, obviously, by the load on the Puppet Master, which is directly related to how frequently it has to compile catalogs.

If the compilation time is too long for us, we will need to verify the following conditions:

- Compilation time is always long even with a single catalog processed at a time. In this case, we will have to work on two factors: code optimization and CPU power. Our manifests may have plenty of resources and we have to work on how to optimize our code (we will see later how). We can also provide more CPU power to our Puppet Master as that is needed during compilation. Of course, we should verify its overall sanity: it should not regularly swap memory pages to disk and should not have faulty hardware that might affect performance. If we use stored configs, we should definitely use PuppetDB as the backend, either on the same server or on a dedicated one.

- Compilation time becomes long because many concurrent catalogs are processed at the same time. Our default Puppet Master setup can't handle the quantity of nodes that interrogate it. Many options are available in this case. We will list them by their ease of implementation as follows:

    ◦ Reduce the frequency of each Puppet run (the default 30 minutes interval may be definitely longer, especially if we have a way to trigger Puppet runs in a centrally managed way, for example, via MCollective, so that we can easily force urgent runs).

    ◦ Use Apache Passenger instead of the default web server.

    ◦ Have a multi-Master setup with load-balanced servers. Of course, in this case also, we can work on code optimization and system's resources.

Puppet Master with Passenger

Passenger, also known as **mod_rails** or **mod_passenger**, is a fast application server that can work as a module with Apache or Nginx to serve Ruby, Python, Node.js, or Meteor web applications. Puppet is a Ruby application that uses HTTPS for client-server communication and it can gain great benefits by using Passenger, instead of the default and embedded **Webrick** as a web server.

The first element to consider when there is the need to scale the Puppet Master is definitely the introduction of Passenger. It brings a pair of major benefits that are listed as follows:

- General better performances in serving HTTP requests (either via Apache or Nginx, which are definitely more efficient than Webrick).

- Multi-CPU support. On a standalone Puppet Master, there is just one process that handles all the connections and that process uses only one CPU. With Passenger, you can have more concurrent processes that better use all the available CPUs.

On modern systems, where multiprocessors are the rule and not the exception, this leads to huge benefits.

Installing and configuring Passenger

Let's quickly see how to install and configure Passenger, using plain Puppet resources.

For the sake of brevity, here we simulate an installation on a RedHat 6 derivative. For other breeds, there are different methods to set up the source repo for packages and possibly different names and paths for resources.

The following Puppet code can be placed on a file such as setup.pp and run with puppet apply setup.pp.

First of all, we need to set up the following EPEL repo, which contains extra packages for RedHat Linux that we need:

```
yumrepo { 'epel':
  mirrorlist =>
    'http://mirrors.fedoraproject.org/mirrorlist?repo=epel-
      6&arch=$basearch',
  gpgcheck    => 1,
  enabled     => 1,
  gpgkey      => 'https://fedoraproject.org/static/0608B895.txt',
}
```

Then we set up the Passenger's upstream yum repo of Stealthy Monkeys as follows:

```
yumrepo { 'passenger':
  baseurl    =>
    'http://passenger.stealthymonkeys.com/rhel/$releasever/$basearch',
  mirrorlist =>
    'http://passenger.stealthymonkeys.com/rhel/mirrors',
  enabled    => 1,
  gpgkey     => 'http://passenger.stealthymonkeys.com/RPM-GPG-KEY-
    stealthymonkeys.asc',
}
```

We will then install all the required packages with the following code:

```
package { [ 'mod_passenger' , 'httpd' , 'mod_ssl' , 'rubygems']:
  ensure => present,
}
```

Since there is not a native RPM package, we install `rack`, a needed dependency, as a Ruby gem:

```
package { 'rack':
  ensure   => present,
  provider => gem,
}
```

We also need to configure an Apache virtual host file:

```
file { '/etc/httpd/conf.d/passenger.conf':
  ensure  => present,
  content => template('puppet/apache/passenger.conf.erb')
}
```

In our template (`$modulepath/puppet/templates/apache/passenger.conf.erb` would be its path for the previous sample), we need different parameters configured. The basic Passenger settings that can eventually be placed in a dedicated file are as follows:

```
PassengerHighPerformance on
PassengerMaxPoolSize 12 # Lower this if you have memory issues
PassengerPoolIdleTime 1500
PassengerStatThrottleRate 120
RackAutoDetect On
RailsAutoDetect Off
```

Then, we configure Apache to listen to the Puppet Master's port 8140 and create a virtual host on it:

```
Listen 8140
<VirtualHost *:8140>
```

On the virtual host, we terminate the SSL connection. Apache must behave as a Puppet Master when clients connect to it, so we have to configure the paths of the Puppet Master's SSL certificates as follows:

```
SSLEngine on
SSLProtocol -ALL +SSLv3 +TLSv1
SSLCipherSuite ALL:!ADH:RC4+RSA:+HIGH:+MEDIUM:-LOW:-SSLv2:-EXP
SSLCertificateFile /var/lib/puppet/ssl/certs/<%= @fqdn %>.pem
```

```
SSLCertificateKeyFile /var/lib/puppet/ssl/private_keys/<% @fqdn
    %>.pem
SSLCertificateChainFile /var/lib/puppet/ssl/certs/ca.pem
SSLCACertificateFile /var/lib/puppet/ssl/certs/ca.pem
SSLCARevocationFile /var/lib/puppet/ssl/certs/ca_crl.prm
SSLVerifyClient optional
SSLVerifyDepth 1
SSLOptions +StdEnvVars
```

We also need to add some extra HTTP headers to the connection that is made to the Puppet Master in order to let it identify the original client (details on this later) as follows:

```
RequestHeader set X-SSL-Subject %{SSL_CLIENT_S_DN}e
RequestHeader set X-Client-DN %{SSL_CLIENT_S_DN}e
RequestHeader set X-Client-Verify %{SSL_CLIENT_VERIFY}e
```

Then we enable Passenger and define a document root where we will create the Rack environment to run Puppet as follows:

```
PassengerEnabled On
DocumentRoot /etc/puppet/rack/public/
RackBaseURI /
<Directory /etc/puppet/rack/public/>
  Options None
  AllowOverride None
  Order allow,deny
  allow from all
</Directory>
```

Finally, we will add the normal logging directives as follows:

```
ErrorLog /var/log/httpd/passenger-error.log
CustomLog /var/log/httpd/passenger-access.log combined
</VirtualHost>
```

Then we need to create the Rack environment working directories and configuration as follows:

```
file { ['/etc/puppet/rack',
        '/etc/puppet/rack/public',
        '/etc/puppet/rack/tmp']:
  ensure => directory,
  owner  => 'puppet',
  group  => 'puppet',
}
```

```
file { '/etc/puppet/rack/config.ru':
  ensure => present,
  content => template('puppet/apache/config.ru.erb')
  owner  => 'puppet',
  group  => 'puppet',
}
```

In our `config.ru` file, we need to instruct Rack on how to run Puppet as follows:

```
# if puppet is not in your RUBYLIB:
# $LOAD_PATH.unshift('/opt/puppet/lib')
$0 = "master"
# ARGV << "--debug" # Uncomment to debug
ARGV << "--rack"
ARGV << "--confdir" << "/etc/puppet"
ARGV << "--vardir"  << "/var/lib/puppet"
require 'puppet/util/command_line'
run Puppet::Util::CommandLine.new.execute
```

Once these settings are configured, we can start our Apache. However, before doing this, we need to disable the standalone Puppet Master service as it listens to the same 8140 port and it would overlap with our Apache service:

```
service { 'puppetmaster':
  ensure => stopped,
  enable => false,
}
```

Then we can finally start our Apache with Passenger. Remember that whenever we make changes to Puppet's configuration, the service to restart to apply these changes is Apache. The Puppet Master standalone process should remain stopped.

```
service { 'httpd':
  ensure => running,
  enable => true,
  require => Service['puppetmaster'], # We start apache after
    having managed the puppetmaster service shutdown
}
```

All this code, with the ERB templates it uses, should be placed in a module that allows autoloading of classes and files.

Multi-Master scaling

A Puppet Master running under Passenger on a decently sized server (with at least four CPUs and 4 GB of memory) should be able to cope with hundreds of nodes.

When this number starts to enter in the range of thousands, a single server begins to have problems in handling all the traffic and we need to scale horizontally, adding more Puppet Masters to manage clients' requests in a balanced way.

There are some issues to manage in such a scenario; the most important ones are:

- How to manage the CA and the server certificates
- How to manage SSL termination
- How to manage Puppet code and data

Managing certificates

Puppet's certificates are issued by a Certificate Authority, which is automatically created on the Master when we start it the first time. We usually don't care much about it, we just sign certificate requests with `puppet cert` and have everything we need to work with clients.

On a multi-Master setup, an accurate management of the Puppet Certification Authority and Puppet Masters' certificates becomes essential.

The main element to consider is that the first time `puppet master` is executed, it automatically creates two different certificates, which are as follows:

- The CA certificate used to sign all the other certificates:
  - Public key is stored in `/var/lib/puppet/ssl/ca/ca_pub.pem`
  - Private key is in `/var/lib/puppet/ssl/ca/ca_key.pem`
  - Certificate file is in `/var/lib/puppet/ssl/ca/ca_crt.pem`

- The Puppet Master's own host certificate that is used to communicate with clients:
  - Public key is stored in `/var/lib/puppet/ssl/public_keys/<fqdn>`
  - Private key is stored in `/var/lib/puppet/ssl/private_keys/<fqdn>`; the same paths are used on clients for their own certificates

On the Puppet Master, all the clients' public keys that still need to be signed by the CA are placed in `/var/lib/puppet/ssl/ca/requests`. The ones that have been signed are in `/var/lib/puppet/ssl/ca/signed`.

The CA, which is managed via the `puppet ca` command, performs the following functions:

- Signs **Certificate Signing Requests (CSR)** from clients and transforms them in x509v3 certificates (when we issue `puppet cert sign <certname>`)

- Manages the **Certificate Revocation List (CRL)** of certificates we revoke with the `puppet cert revoke <certname>` command

- Authenticates Puppet clients and Masters making them establish a trustworthy relationship and communicate over SSL

There is a pair of important parameters that are related to certificates, which should be considered in `puppet.conf` before launching the Puppet Master for the first time:

- `dns_alt_names`: This allows us to define a comma-separated list of names with which a node can be referred to when using its certificate. This is useful for the Puppet Master when planning a multi-Master load-balanced setup, where we will have different masters with different hostnames. By default, Puppet creates a certificate that automatically adds to the host's `fqdn` the names `puppet` and `puppet.$domain`. We should be sure to have in this list of names both the local server hostname and the name the clients use to refer to the Puppet Master (probably associated with the IP of a load balancer).

- `ca_ttl`: This sets the duration, in seconds, of the certificates signed by the CA. The default value is 157,680,000, which means that after five years we have started for the first time our Puppet Master, its certificate expires and has to be reissued. This is an experience that many of us have already faced and involves the re-creation and signing of all their certificates.

Note that the whole `/var/lib/puppet/ssl` directory (which is the default value of the `ssldir` configuration parameter) and the certificates it contains are recreated from scratch if they don't exist when Puppet runs. Therefore, if we want to recreate our Puppet Master's certificates with corrected settings, we have to move that directory to a backup place (just as a precaution in case we change idea, we won't need it anymore otherwise), configure `puppet.conf` as needed, and restart the Puppet Master service.

This is an activity that we can do lightheartedly, on the Master, only when it has just been installed and there are no or few signed clients. This is because when we recreate the `ssldir` with new certificates on the Master, all the previously signed clients certificates are no longer valid and have to be recreated.

CA management in a multi-Master setup can be done in the following different ways:

- Configure one of the load-balanced Puppet Masters as a CA server, and have all the other ones using it for CA activities. In this case, all the servers act as Puppet Masters and one of them also does the CA.

- Configure an external, eventually in High Availability, Puppet Master that provides only the CA service and is not used to compile clients' catalogs.

In `puppet.conf`, the configuration is quite straightforward when the CA server is (or might be) different from the Puppet Master:

- On all the clients, explicitly set the `ca_server` hostname (by default, it is the same Puppet Master):

```
[agent]
  ca_server = puppetca.example42.com
```

- On the CA server, basically, no particular configuration is needed:

```
[master]
  certname = puppetca.example42.com
  ca = true
```

- On the other Puppet Masters, we just have to define that the local server is not a CA and to look, as done for all the clients, for another `ca_server`:

```
[agent]
  ca_server - puppetca.example42.com
[master]
  certname = puppet01.example42.com
  ca = false
```

Managing SSL termination

When we deal with Puppet's client server traffic, we can apply all the logics that are valid for HTTPS connections. We can, therefore, have different scenarios as follows:

- Clients' proxy (clients can use a proxy to reach remote or not directly accessible Puppet Masters)

- Master's reverse proxy (all clients communicate with frontend servers that proxy their requests to the backend workers)

- Load-balanced Masters at the network level (clients communicate directly with a load-balanced server)

- Load-balanced Master at the application level (clients communicate with an intermediate host that balances and reverse proxies the master)

While configuring the involved elements, we have to take care of the
following elements:

- The SSL certificates used where the SSL connection is terminated must
  always be the ones of the Puppet Master and of the CA. If they are on
  different servers, we need to copy them.

- We have to communicate the client's name to the Puppet Master. This is
  done by setting, where SSL is terminated, the HTTP headers **X-SSL-Subject**,
  X-Client-DN, and **X-Client-Verify**, the latter indicates to the Master if the
  certificate is authenticated.

In our `puppet.conf` file, there are always the following default settings, which
define the name of the HTTP header (with an `HTTP_` prefix and underscores instead
of dashes).

They contain the clients' SSL **Distinguished Name (DN)** and the name of the HTTP
header that contains the status message of the client verification (the expected value
for a trusted, not revoked, client certificate is `SUCCESS`):

```
ssl_client_header = HTTP_X_CLIENT_DN
ssl_client_verify_header = HTTP_X_CLIENT_VERIFY
```

On the web server(s) where SSL is terminated (it might be Passenger in a single
server setup or an Apache, which balances and reverse proxies backend Puppet
Masters), we need to set these HTTP headers extracting information from SSL
environment variables as follows:

```
RequestHeader set X-SSL-Subject %{SSL_CLIENT_S_DN}e
RequestHeader set X-Client-DN %{SSL_CLIENT_S_DN}e
RequestHeader set X-Client-Verify %{SSL_CLIENT_VERIFY}e
```

These servers are the ones that communicate directly with clients and terminate
the SSL connection; we can define them as **frontend** servers. They act as a proxy
and generate a new connection to the backend Puppet Masters that do the real
work and compile catalogs.

Since SSL has been terminated on the frontends, traffic from them to the backend
servers is in clear text (they are supposed to be in the same LAN) and on the backend
Apache we need to state where to get the client's certificates DN, using the previous
extra headers:

```
SetEnvIf X-Client-Verify "(.*)" SSL_CLIENT_VERIFY=$1
SetEnvIf X-SSL-Client-DN "(.*)" SSL_CLIENT_S_DN=$1
```

Also, on a backend server, we do not need to configure all the other SSL settings; we just need a VirtualHost with Rack configurations.

Given this information, we can compose our topology of web servers that handle Puppet traffic in a very flexible way, with one or more frontend servers that proxy requests to the backend Puppet Masters and terminate SSL, and with backend Puppet Masters that run Puppet via Passenger.

Managing code and data

Deployment of Puppet code and data is another factor to consider. We probably want the same code deployed on all our Puppet Masters. We can do this in various ways: all of them basically require the remote execution of some commands (if we want to avoid the need to log in to each server every time a change on Puppet is done) or a way to keep files synced across different servers.

How a deployment script or command may work is definitely tied to how we manage our code: we might execute r10k or librarian-puppet, or make a Git pull on our local directories to fetch changes from a central repo.

Alternatively, we might decide to have our Puppet code and data on a shared filesystem or keep them synced with tools such as rsync.

In any case, we have to copy/sync or share all the directories where our code and data are placed: the modules, manifest, and Hiera directories, if used.

Load balancing alternatives

When we have to balance a pool of Puppet Masters, we have different options which are as follows:

- **HTTP load balancing** with SSL termination done on the load balancer, which then proxies clients' requests to the Puppet Masters.

- **TCP load balancing** with SSL termination done on the Puppet Masters that directly communicate with clients. In this case, the load balancer listens to the virtual IP associated to the Master hostname configured on the clients. It then redirects all the TCP connections to the Puppet Masters (they need to have the name of the Puppet Master host configured on clients in their dns_alt_names configuration).

- DNS round robin can be considered the poor man alternative to TCP load balancing. Clients are configured to use a single hostname for the Puppet Master, which is resolved, via DNS, to the multiple masters' addresses. Also in this case, SSL connections are terminated directly on the masters and they must have in their `dns_alt_names` the name used by clients. This solution is quite easy to implement, as it does not require additional systems to manage load balancing, but has the (major) drawback of not being able to detect failures and remove nonresponding Puppet Masters from the pool of balanced servers.

- DNS SRV records can also be used to define the IP addresses of the Puppet Masters via DNS, allowing the possibility to set priorities and failovers. This feature is available only on Puppet 3 and later.

Masterless Puppet

An alternative approach to the Puppet Master scaling methods we have seen up to now is not to use it at all. Masterless setups involve the direct execution of `puppet apply` on each node, where all the needed Puppet code and data has to be stored.

In this case, we have to find a way to distribute our modules, manifests, and eventually Hiera data to all the clients. We still can use external components such as:

- **ENC**: The `external_nodes` script can work as it works on the Puppet Master: it can interrogate any external source of knowledge on how to classify nodes. A concern here is whether it makes sense to introduce a central point of authority when we want a distributed decentralized setup.

- **Report**: Also, the reporting function can work exactly as it works on the Puppet Master. Also here, as for the ENC, the basic difference is that whatever the tool used, it must allow access from any node in our infrastructure, and not just the Master.

- **Exported Resources**: These can be used too, with some caveats. If we use the active records backend, we need to access the database from all the nodes. If we use PuppetDB, we need to establish a trust between the certificates of the PuppetDB server and the ones of each client.

We also need a way to run Puppet on the clients in an automated or centrally managed way; it may be via a cron job or a remote command execution.

Distribution of Puppet code and data may be done in different ways as follows:

- Executing `git pull` to fetch updates from a central repository
- Updating native packages (`rpm`, `deb`, and so on) from a custom repo

- Running a command such as `rsync` or `rdiff`
- Mounting from NFS or another network or shared filesystem
- Using Bit Torrent with tools such as Murder (`https://github.com/lg/murder`)

Configurations and infrastructure optimizations

Whatever is the layout of our Puppet infrastructure, we may consider some other options to optimize its performance.

Traffic compression

A first quick attempt may be done by activating the compression of HTTPS traffic between the clients and the master. The following option has to be set on the `puppet.conf` on both ends:

```
http_compression = true
```

The case where it makes sense to enable it is mostly where we have clients that reach the server via a WAN link, generally via a VPN, where throughput is definitely not the one we have on LAN communications. If we have large catalogs and reports, their compression during transfer, since it involves mostly text files, can be quite effective.

Caching

Another area where we might operate is catalog caching. This is a delicate topic, as it is not easy to determine what has changed on the clients' side (some facts such as uptime always change by definition, others are supposed to be more stable) and on the server's side (changes on the Puppet code and data may or may not affect a specific node). The challenge, therefore, is to always provide the correct and updated catalog when a caching mechanism is in place.

Puppet provides some configuration options to manage caching. By default, Puppet doesn't recompile the catalog if it has a local version cached with an updated timestamp and facts that have not changed. When we want to be sure to obtain a new catalog, we have to enable the `ignorecache` option:

```
ignorecache = false # Default: false
```

Note that this is automatically done when we run the command `puppet agent -t`, which ensures that we always have a freshly compiled catalog.

We can also tell the client to always use a local cached copy of the catalog, instead of asking the Puppet Master:

```
use_cached_catalog = true # Default: false
```

This might be useful in cases where we want to temporarily "freeze" the configurations applied to a client without having to disable the Puppet service and without caring about eventual changes on the Puppet Master.

Distributing Puppet execution times

If we run Puppet via cron or other time-based mechanisms, we definitely need to avoid the problem of having all our clients hitting the Master and requesting their catalog at the same time. There are various options to distribute Puppet runs in order to avoid peaks of too many concurrent requests.

We can introduce a random sleep delay in the command we execute via cron, for example, with cron entries based on ERB templates such as:

```
0,30 * * * * root sleep <%= @sleep &> ; puppet agent --onetime
```

In the previous code, the `$sleep` variable with the number of seconds to wait may be randomly defined in Puppet manifests with the `fqdn_rand()` function, which returns a random value based on the node's full hostname (so it's random, not in a cryptographically usable way, but doesn't change at every catalog compilation):

```
$sleep = rqdn_rand('1800') # Returns a number from 0 to 1800
```

Alternatively, we can use the `splay` configuration option in `puppet.conf` that introduces a random (but consistent) delay at every Puppet run, which can be as long as defined by `splaylimit` (whose sane default is Puppet's run interval):

```
splay = true # Default: false
splaylimit = 1h # Default: $runinterval
```

Checking the interval for changes in files

On the Puppet Master, there is an option, `filetimeout`, which sets the minimum time to wait between checking for updates in configuration files (manifests, templates, and so on). This determines how quickly the Master checks whether a file has changed on the disk. The default value is 15 seconds, and can be changed in `puppet.conf`.

This setting has very limited effects on the performances (unless, I suppose, we lower it too much), but it's important to know that it exists, because this is the reason why, sometimes, nothing new happens on the client when we launch a Puppet run immediately after a change on some file of the Puppet Master.

This may lead to some confusion. We make a change on some manifests, we run Puppet, and nothing happens. Then we run Puppet again and the change is finally received and we wonder what is happening. Therefore, beware that there is such an option and, more importantly, this behavior on the Master, which "scans" the directories where our Puppet code and files are placed at regular intervals, might not immediately process the very latest changes made on these files.

Scaling stored configs

We have seen that the usage of exported resources allows resources declared on a node to be applied on another node. In order to achieve this, Puppet needs the storeconfigs option enabled and this involves the usage of an external database where all the information about the exported resources is stored.

The usage of store configs has been historically a big performance killer for Puppet. The amount of database transactions involved for each run makes it quite a resource-intensive activity.

There are various options in puppet.conf that permit us to tune our configurations. The default settings are as follows:

```
storeconfigs = false
storeconfigs_backend = active_record
dbadapter = sqlite3
thin_storeconfigs = false
```

If we enable them with storeconfigs = true, the default configuration involves the usage of the active_record backend and a SQLite database.

This is a solution that performs quite badly and, therefore, should be used only in test or small environments. It has the unique benefit that we don't need any other activity; we just have to install the SQLite Ruby bindings package on our system. With such a setup, we will quickly have access problems to the SQL backend with multiple concurrent Puppet runs.

The next step is to use a more performant backend for data persistence. Before the introduction of PuppetDB, MySQL was the only alternative. In order to enable it, we have to set the following options in `puppet.conf`:

```
dbadapter = mysql
dbname = puppet        # Default value
dbserver = localhost   # Default value
dbuser = puppet        # Default value
dbpassword = puppet    # Default value
```

Such a setup involves a local MySQL server where we have created a `puppet` database with the relevant grants. Thus, from our MySQL console, we should write something like the following code:

```
create database puppet;
GRANT ALL ON puppet.* to 'puppet'@'localhost' IDENTIFIED by 'puppet';
flush privileges;
```

This is enough to have a Puppet Master storing its data on a local MySQL backend. If the load on our systems grows, we can move the MySQL service to another dedicated server and can tune our MySQL server.

Brice Figureau, who heavily contributed to the original store configs code, made an interesting presentation at the first Puppet Camp on the topic, which is available at `http://www.slideshare.net/masterzen/all-about-storeconfigs-2123814`, where useful hints to configure MySQL are provided to scale for the inserts:

```
innodb_buffer_pool_size = 70% of physical RAM
innodb_log_file_size = up to 5% of physical RAM
innodb_flush_method = O_DIRECT
innodb_flush_log_at_trx_commit = 2
```

Also, to optimize the most common queries on Puppet's Wiki, it is suggested to create this index from the MySQL console as follows:

```
use database puppet;
create index exported_restype_title on resources (exported,
  restype, title(50));
```

We can limit the amount of information stored by setting `thin_storeconfigs = true`. This makes Puppet store just facts and exported resources on the database and not the whole catalog and its related data. This option is useful with the `active_record` backend (with PuppetDB this is not necessary).

Finally, there is the possibility to set an option that processes stored configs in an asynchronous way; in this way, the Puppet Master can compile the catalog without being locked to database operations:

```
async_storeconfigs = true
queue_source = stomp://localhost:61613
queue_type = stomp
```

This requires the usage of the puppet queue command and the setup of a queue service. It is a rarely used option, which is now obsolete.

What we have written up to now about store configs using the active records backend made a lot of sense some years ago, and we referenced it here to have a view on how to scale with store configs. The truth is that the best and recommended way to use store configs is via the PuppetDB backend; this is done by placing the following settings in `puppet.conf`:

```
storeconfigs = true
storeconfigs_backend = puppetdb
```

We have dedicated the whole of *Chapter 3*, *PuppetDB*, to PuppetDB because it is definitely a major player in the Puppet ecosystem. The performance improvements it brings are huge so there is really no reason not to use it.

The components of PuppetDB can be distributed to scale better as follows:

- PuppetDB can be horizontally scaled. It's a stateless service entirely based on a REST-like interface. Different PuppetDB servers can be load balanced either at TCP or HTTP level.

- PostgreSQL server may be moved to a dedicated host and then scaled or configured in high-availability mode following PostgreSQL's best practices.

Measuring performance

When we start to have a remarkable number of resources on a node (in the order of several hundreds or thousands), the compilation and application time of a node catalog grows to uncomfortable levels.

If the number of the nodes to manage is big, even small tunings and optimizations of our code can bring interesting results.

For this reason, it is useful to have at disposal tools and techniques that permit us to measure Puppet's performance metrics.

Puppet metrics

Puppet itself provides some options that help us in understanding where time is spent during its execution.

At the end of each Puppet run, it is possible to see a detailed report on the time spent on each kind of activity. In `puppet.conf`, we can enable reports with the following option:

```
report = true # Enable client's reporting
```

We can have a summary of the run times with the following option:

```
summarize = true # Print a summary of the Puppet transaction
```

At the end of a Puppet run, we can have metrics that let us understand how much time the Master spent in compiling and delivering the catalog (**Config retrieval time**) and how much has been spent to manage each of the most common types of resources: package installation, files management, commands executions, and so on.

Of these metrics, the one related to configuration retrieval time is probably the most interesting as it is directly related to the work that the Puppet Master has to do.

This key metric can be retrieved directly on the Puppet Master with a quick glance at the logs, where for each generated catalog the compilation time is reported. On RedHat-based systems, we can get this with the following command:

```
grep 'Compiled catalog' /var/log/messages
```

On other distros or OSes, just look for the log file where syslog stores messages with the daemon facility (or what's configured by the option, `syslogfacility`).

If we want to see how much time Puppet takes to evaluate each resource of the catalog, we can enable the option as follows:

```
evaltrace = true
```

This, actually more than for performance reasons (evaluation times should always be in the order of 0.0x seconds), might be useful when we want to see Puppet's exact order in evaluating and applying resources.

Since Puppet 3.4.0, we also have a very useful option for profiling at our disposal, which is as follows:

```
profile = true
```

This gives a lot of useful information for troubleshooting performance issues.

If we want to load test our Puppet code and setup, we have two useful tools at our disposal, which are as follows:

- The `puppet-load.rb` script is distributed with Puppet code in the `ext` directory and can be used to simulate multiple Puppet runs via the command line.

- There is also a Jenkins plugin that can be used to load test Puppet with the stress tool Gatling (`http://gatling-tool.org/`). For more information, visit `http://puppetlabs.com/blog/puppet-gatling-and-jenkins-together`.

Optimizing code

Every Puppet user complains about catalog compilation times. That's a fact. Sooner or later, seldom or always, depending on our patience and time, we have our moment of frustration for how much time it takes to churn out the catalogs of our nodes. There is something we can do for this.

The first basic rule is that the more resources we manage, the longer is the Puppet run: for each resource, there's something to parse and compile on the Master, write in the catalog, send to clients, apply locally, report back to the master, and handle to the report backend.

This is hardly an issue for few resources, but when we have nodes with several hundred, or sometimes thousands of them, things definitely change.

The overall number of resources managed in our nodes can grow with the following factors:

- The extension of Puppet coverage on more services and managed resources. This is quite obvious: more the number of components of a system we have to manage with Puppet, more will be the relevant resources we will have to declare in our manifests.

- A single defined type used many, too many, times. For example, we manage local system users via Puppet and we have many of them or we have a server with hundreds or thousands of Apache Virtual Hosts managed by a specific define.

- Excessive usage of a setting-based approach for configuration files (for example, with Augeas or other in-file line-management defines). In these cases, the number of resources of our nodes can explode easily (one resource for each line of each configuration file of each node: the result of these multiplying factors can easily get out of control).

- An excessive use of classes and subclasses that fragment our code. For example, in my very personal opinion, the pattern that suggests the division of a module in three major subclasses (for example, `openssh::package`, `openssh::service`, and `openssh::config`) makes little sense when we have only one resource for each subclass. A small module that manages a typical package-service-config application can have its overall number of resources raise from four (the main class and the package, service, and file resources) to seven (all the previous plus the three containing subclasses).

When we have the same resource type used many times on the same catalog, we may study alternatives that deliver great benefits for our performances:

- When they are used to manage setting-based configuration files (Augeas or `file_line`—from stdlib module—or others), we may question if it makes sense to manage those files in this way or use a simple ERB template, eventually using their parameters such as `config_file_hash` that allow us to manage any custom configuration entry in a file via a hash.

- When a single define is used to create fragments of configuration files, such as hypothetical `apache::vhost`, we might evaluate the usage of a function that returns the whole content of a single huge file based on a datasource with the information about all the virtual hosts. The result would be a single resource instead of many.

Besides optimizations on the number of resources, we can consider a few other general recommendations as follows:

- Do not use the `file` type to deliver too large files or binaries. For each file, Puppet has to make a checksum to verify if it has changed.

- Whenever the `source =>` argument is used to provide a file, a new connection is made to the PuppetMaster during catalog application time, with `content =>` instead, the whole content of the file is placed in the catalog.

- Avoid too many elements in a source array for file retrieval as follows:

```
source => [ "site/openssh/sshd.conf---$::hostname" ,
            "site/openssh/sshd.conf--$::env-$::role",
            "site/openssh/sshd.conf-$::role" ,
            "site/openssh/sshd.conf" ],
```

This checks three files (and eventually gets three 404 errors from the server) before getting the default one.

When we have many files provided by the Puppet Master's fileserver (whenever we use the `source` argument in a file type), we might evaluate the opportunity of moving the fileserver functionality to a separate dedicated node. Here we can set up a normal Puppet Master, which just serves static files and is not used to compile catalogs. We can then refer to it in our code as follows:

```
file { '/tmp/sample':
  source => "puppet://$fileserver_name/path/to/file",
}
```

Testing different Puppet versions

In the `ext/` directory of the Puppet code repository, there is `envpuppet`, a smart bash script written by Jeff McCune that makes it easy to test different Puppet versions.

The usage is easy. We create a directory and clone the official Puppet repos from GitHub using the following commands:

```
cd /usr/src
git clone git://github.com/puppetlabs/puppet.git
git clone git://github.com/puppetlabs/facter.git
git clone git://github.com/puppetlabs/hiera.git
```

Then we can switch to the version we want to test using the following command:

```
cd /usr/src/puppet && git checkout tags/3.0.2
cd /usr/src/facter && git checkout tags/1.6.17
```

We then set an environment variable that defines the `basedir` directory for `envpuppet` using the following command:

```
export ENVPUPPET_BASEDIR=/usr/src
```

Now we can test Puppet prepending the `envpuppet` to any Puppet, Facter, or Hiera command as follows:

```
envpuppet puppet --version
envpuppet facter --version
```

Alternatively, it can be possible to use the `code` configuration parameter to use `envpuppet` as a default executable for Puppet.

Summary

In this chapter, we have seen how Puppet can scale while our infrastructure grows. We have to consider all the components involved.

For test or small environments, we may have an all-in-one server, but it makes sense to separate these components from the beginning on dedicated nodes:

- A Puppet Master under Passenger
- PuppetDB and its backend database (we might decide to move the PostgreSQL service to a dedicated server too)
- Eventually an ENC such as Foreman and its backend database (which might be moved to a dedicated node too)

When we need to scale further, or want high availability on these components, we can start to scale out horizontally and load balance the Puppet Master, Foreman, and PuppetDB systems (they all provide stateless HTTP(s) services) and cluster our database services (following the available solutions for PostgreSQL and MySQL).

When the bottleneck of a centralized Puppet Master service becomes an issue or simply not a preferred solution, we might decide to go Masterless. This might be more complex to set up and may add some security concerns (Puppet data about all nodes are stored on all the other nodes). However, it has the benefit of having all our clients compiling and running their own manifests independently, without the bottleneck of a central server. Besides changes at the infrastructure level, we can scale better if our code performs well.

We have seen how to measure Puppet times and where code and configuration tuning may improve performances. In particular, we have reviewed the first, most obvious, and most basic element that affects Puppet times: the number of managed resources for a node. We also reviewed how we can deal with edge cases where some of them are used multiple times.

In the next chapter, we are going to dive more deeply into Puppet's internal details and discover how we can extend its functionalities.

10
Writing Puppet Plugins

Puppet is impressively extendable. Almost every key component of the software can be extended and replaced by the code provided by users.

Most of the time, we can use modules to distribute our code to clients. However, Puppet goes a step further; surprising things are possible, for example, with the indirector and its termini (somehow strange words that are going to be clearer in the following pages).

This chapter is about understanding and extending Puppet code. We are going to review the following topics:

- Anatomy of a Puppet run; what happens under the hood
- What are Puppet extension alternatives
- How to develop custom functions
- How to develop custom facts
- How to develop custom types and providers
- How to develop custom report handlers
- How to develop custom faces

The subject is large; we are going to have an overview and show examples that let us dive in some details. For more information about how Puppet works and its inner beauties, check these great sources in crescent detail:

- The Puppet Extension Points and Puppet Internals series of blog posts by Brice Figureau are by far the most intriguing, fascinating, and better-explained sources of documentation about Puppet's inner workings; they can be found at http://www.masterzen.fr.

- Puppet on the edge, the blog of Puppet Labs' Henrik Lindberg (`http://puppet-on-the-edge.blogspot.it/`), focuses on the new features of Puppet, which we will see in *Chapter 12, Future Puppet*.

- The puppet-dev discussion group, where ideas are discussed and questions are answered, can be found at `https://groups.google.com/forum/#!forum/puppet-dev`.

- The official developer reference at `https://docs.puppetlabs.com/references/latest/developer/`.

- The official ticketing system (`https://tickets.puppetlabs.com`), where we can see how the actual discussion and work on the code is delivered.

Anatomy of a Puppet run, under the hood

We have seen the output of a Puppet run in *Chapter 1, Puppet Essentials*. Now, let's explore what happens behind these messages.

We can identify the following stages that turn our Puppet code into a catalog that is applied on clients:

- **Parsing and compiling**: In this phase, the Puppet manifests are fed to the `Puppet::Parser` class, which does basic syntax checks and produces an **Abstract Syntax Tree (AST)** object. This represents the same objects we have defined in our manifests in a machine-friendly format. Both the facts received from the client and the AST are passed to the compiler. The facts and manifests are interpreted, and the result is converted into a tree of transportable objects, that is, the resource catalog (commonly called catalog). This phase happens on the server, unless we use the `puppet apply` command.

- **Transport**: In this phase, the Master serializes the catalog in the PSON format (a Puppet version of JSON) and sends it over HTTPS to the client. Here, it is deserialized and stored locally. The transport phase doesn't occur in a Masterless setup.

- **Instantiation**: Here, the objects present in the resource catalog (instances of `Puppet::Resource`) are converted to instances of the `Puppet::Type` class, and a RAL catalog is generated. Note that the resource catalog and RAL catalog are two different things.

- **Configuration**: This is where the real action happens inside a Puppet transaction. The RAL catalog is passed to a new `Puppet::Transaction` instance; relationships and resources are evaluated and applied to the system.

- **Report**: A report of the transaction is generated on the client and eventually sent back to the Master.

The involved nodes (client/master), components, actions, and classes are summarized in the following table (these steps generally refer to Puppet 3; they may change according to different versions):

Node	Component	Action	Class#method
Client	Configurer	Plugins are downloaded and loaded	`Puppet::Configurer::PluginHandler#download_plugins`
Client	Configurer	Local facts are collected and sent to the Master	`Puppet::Configurer#prepare_and_retrieve_catalog`
Master	Compiler	Compilation is started by the indirection of the REST call	`Puppet::Resource::Catalog::Compiler`
Master	Parser	Manifests are parsed and an AST is generated	`Puppet::Parser::Parser#parse`
Master	Compiler	A graph of Puppet resources is elaborated from this AST	`Puppet::Parser::Compiler#compile`
Master	Compiler	The output of this operation is the resource catalog	`Puppet::Resource::Catalog`
Master	Network	The catalog is serialized as a PSON object and sent over the network	`Puppet::Network::HTTP::API::V1#do_find`
Client	Configurer	The catalog is received, deserialized, and cached locally	`Puppet::Configurer#prepare_and_retrieve_catalog`
Client	Configurer	The catalog is transformed to a RAL catalog	`Puppet::Type`
Client	Transaction	Each instance of `Puppet::Type` in the catalog is applied	`Puppet::Transaction#evaluate`
Agent	Configurer	The transaction report is saved to the configured report termini	`Puppet::Configure#send_report`

Anatomy of a Puppet run

Extendibility has always been a widely pursued concept in Puppet; we can practically provide custom code to extend any activity or component of the software.

We can customize and extend Puppet's functionalities in many different ways operating at different levels as follows:

- Key activities such as nodes' classification via an ENC or variable definition and management via Hiera can be customized to adapt to most of the users' needs.

- Our code can be distributed via modules using the pluginsync functionality. This is typically used to provide our facts, types, providers, and functions, but it may basically apply to any piece of Puppet code.

- We can configure indirections for the main Puppet subsystems and use different backends (called termini) to manage the locations from where we can retrieve their data.

ENC and Hiera extendibility

We have already seen in the earlier chapters of this book how it is possible to manage some key aspects of our Puppet infrastructure in many different ways:

- We can manage the location where our nodes and the classes are defined and which variables and environment they use. This can be done via an ENC that may be any kind of system that feeds us this data in YAML format via the execution of a custom script, which may interrogate whatever backend we may have.

- We can manage the location where our Hiera data is stored, having the possibility to choose from many different backends for data persistence.

We are not going to talk again about these extension possibilities; we just have to remember how powerful they are and how much freedom they give us in managing two key aspects of our Puppet infrastructure.

Modules' pluginsync

When we set `pluginsync=true` (this is default from Puppet 3; it had to be explicitly set on the earlier versions) in our `puppet.conf`, we activate the automatic synchronization of plugins. When Puppet is invoked and before doing any other operation, the clients retrieve the content of the `lib` directories from all the modules in the Master's `modulepath` and copy them in their own `libdir` (`/var/lib/puppet/lib` by default), keeping the same directory tree.

In this way, all the extra plugins provided by modules can be used on the client exactly as the core code. The structure of the `lib` directory of a module is as follows:

```
{modulepath}
└── {module}
    └── lib
        ├── augeas
        │   └── lenses
        ├── hiera
        │   └── backend
        ├── puppetdb
        ├── facter
        └── puppet
            ├── parser
            │   └── functions
            ├── provider
            │   └── $type
            ├── type
            ├── face
            └── application
```

The previous layout suggests that we can use modules to distribute custom facts, Augeas lenses, faces, types, and providers to clients. We can also distribute custom functions and Hiera backends, but this is not useful for the clients, as they are used during the catalog compilation phase, which usually occurs on the Master (a notable exception is in Masterless setups when `pluginsync` is not necessary).

A small intriguing note is that the plugin synchronization done at the beginning of a Puppet run is actually performed using a normal file type, which looks like the following code:

```
file { $libdir:
  ensure  => directory,
  recurse => true,
  source  => 'puppet:///plugins',
  force   => true,
  purge   => true,
  backup  => false,
  noop    => false,
  owner   => puppet, # (The Puppet process uid)
  group   => puppet, # (The Puppet process gid)
}
```

Similarly, all the files and directories configured in `puppet.conf` are managed using normal Puppet resources, which are included in a small settings catalog that is applied on the client as the very first step.

Some notes about the file resource mentioned earlier are as follows:

- The `purge` and `recurse` arguments ensure that the plugins that are removed from the Master are also removed from the client, and new ones are added recursively.

- The `noop => false` parameter ensures that a regular pluginsync is done even when we want to test a Puppet run with the `--noop` argument passed at the command line.

- The `source => puppet:///plugins` source is based on an automatic fileserver mount point that maps to the lib directory of every module. This can be modified via the `pluginsource` configuration entry.

- `$libdir` can be configured via the homonymous configuration entry.

In this chapter, we are going to review how to write the most common custom plugins, which can be distributed via user modules, that is, functions, facts, types, providers, report handlers, and faces.

Puppet indirector and its termini

Puppet has different subsystems to manage objects such as catalogs, nodes, facts, and certificates. Each subsystem is able to retrieve and manipulate the managed object data with REST verbs such as `find`, `search`, `head`, and `destroy`.

Each subsystem has an indirector that allows the usage of different backends, called termini, which define the location from where data is retrieved.

Each time we deal with objects such as nodes, certificates, and so on, we can see (in the following table) that we work on an instance of a model class for the object that is indirected to a specific terminus.

A terminus is a backend that allows the retrieval and manipulation of simple key values related to the indirected class.

This allows the Puppet programmer to deal with model instances without caring about the details of where the data is coming from.

Here is a complete list of the available indirections, the class they indirect, and the relevant termini. For more details, refer to `http://docs.puppetlabs.com/references/latest/indirection.html`.

Indirection	Indirected class	Available termini
catalog	Puppet::Resource::Catalog	active_record, compiler, json, queue, rest, static_ compiler, store_ configs, yaml
certificate	Puppet::SSL::Certificate	ca, disabled_ca, file, rest
certificate_ request	Puppet::SSL:: CertificateRequest	ca, disabled_ca, file, memory, rest.
certificate_ revocation_list	Puppet::SSL:: CertificateRevocationList	ca, disabled_ca, file, rest
certificate_ status	Puppet::SSL::Host	file, rest
data_binding	Puppet::DataBinding	hiera, none
facts	Puppet::Node::Facts	active_record, couch, facter, inventory_ active_record, inventory_service, memory, network_ device, rest, store_ configs, yaml
file_bucket_file	Puppet::FileBucket:: File	file, rest, selector
file_content	Puppet::FileServing:: Content	file, file_server, rest, selector
file_metadata	Puppet::FileServing:: Metadata	file, file_server, rest, selector
instrumentation_ data	Puppet::Util:: Instrumentation::Data	local, rest
instrumentation_ listener	Puppet::Util:: Instrumentation::Listener	local, rest
instrumentation_ probe	Puppet::Util:: Instrumentation:: IndirectionProbe	local, rest
key	Puppet::SSL::Key	ca, disabled_ca, file, memory
node	Puppet::Node	active_record, exec, ldap, memory, plain, rest, store_configs, yaml, write_only_yaml

Indirection	Indirected class	Available termini
report	Puppet::Transaction::Report	processor, rest, yaml
resource	Puppet::Resource	active_record, ral, rest, store_configs
resource_type	Puppet::Resource::Type	parser, rest
status	Puppet::Status	local, rest

Puppet uses the indirectors mentioned earlier and some of their termini every time we run it. For example, in a scenario with a Puppet Master, an ENC, and a PuppetDB, the following are the indirectors, REST verbs, and termini involved:

1. On the agent, Puppet collects local facts via Facter:
   `facts find from terminus facter`

2. On the agent, a catalog is requested from the Master:
   `catalog find from terminus rest`

3. On the Master, the client's facts are stored in PuppetDB:
   `facts save to terminus puppetdb`

4. On the Master, node classification is requested from an ENC:
   `node find from terminus exec`

5. On the Master, a catalog is compiled:
   `catalog find from terminus compiler`

6. On the master, the catalog is stored in PuppetDB:
   `catalog save to terminus puppetdb`

7. On the agent, the received catalog is applied and a report is sent:
   `report save to terminus rest`

8. On the master, the report is managed with the configured handler:
   `report save to terminus processor`

We can configure the termini to use for each indirector either with specific entries in `puppet.conf` or via the `/etc/puppet/routes.yaml` file that overrides any configuration setting.

On `puppet.conf`, we have the following settings by default:

```
catalog_cache_terminus =
catalog_terminus = compiler
data_binding_terminus = hiera
default_file_terminus = rest
facts_terminus = facter
inventory_terminus = facter
node_cache_terminus =
node_terminus = plain
```

Just by having a look at these values, we can deduce the following interesting things:

- The ENC functionality is enabled specifying `node_terminus = exec`, which is an alternative terminus to fetch the resources and parameters to assign to a node.

- The catalog is retrieved using the Puppet `compiler` by default, but we might use other termini, such as `json`, `yaml`, or `rest` to retrieve catalogs from local files or remote REST services. This is exactly what happens, with the `rest` terminus, when an agent requests a catalog to the Master server.

- Hiera lookups for every class parameter (the data binding functionality introduced on Puppet 3) can be replaced with a custom terminus with other lookup alternatives.

- The `*_cache_terminus` settings are used, for some cases, to define secondary termini in case of failures of the default primary ones. The data retrieved from the default terminus is always written to the correspondent cache terminus in order to keep it updated.

We have seen in *Chapter 3, PuppetDB*, how a modification to the `routes.yaml` file is necessary to set up PuppetDB as a backend for the facts terminus; let's use it as an example:

```
---
master:
  facts:
    terminus: puppetdb
    cache: yaml
```

Note that we refer to the puppet mode (`master`), the indirection (`facts`), and the `terminus` to use and its eventual `cache`. Other termini that do not have a dedicated configuration entry in `puppet.conf` may be set here as needed.

We can deal with indirectors and their termini when we use the Puppet command; many of its subcommands refer directly to the indirectors reported in the previous table and let us specify, with the `--terminus` option, which terminus to use.

We will come back to this later in the chapter when we will talk about Puppet faces.

Custom functions

Functions are an important area where we can extend Puppet. They are used when Puppet parses our manifests and can greatly enhance our ability to fetch data from custom sources and filter, elaborate, and manipulate it.

We can distribute a function just by placing a file in `lib/puppet/parser/<function_name>.rb` in a module of ours.

Even if they are automatically distributed to all our clients via the modules' pluginsync mechanism, it's important to remember that they are needed only on the Puppet Master, since they are used only during catalog compilation.

 Note that as they are loaded in memory when Puppet starts, if we change a function on the Master, we have to restart its service in order to load the latest version.

There are two kinds of functions; they are as follows:

- The `:rvalue` functions return a value; they are typically assigned to a variable or resource argument. Sample core `rvalue` functions are `template`, `hiera`, `regsubst`, `versioncmp`, and `inline_template`.

- The `:statement` functions perform an action without returning any value. Samples from the Puppet core are `include`, `fail`, `hiera_include`, and `realize`.

Let's see a real case, starting from a function called `options_lookup` that returns the value of a key from a hash.

Such a function is quite useful in ERB templates where we want to use arbitrary data provided by users using a class parameter whose expected content is a hash.

We can place it inside any of our modules in a file called `lib/puppet/parser/options_lookup.rb`.

The first line invokes the `newfunction` method of the `Puppet::Parser::Functions` class. Here, we define the name of the function and its type (if it's an `rvalue`, we have to specify it; by default, a function's type is `statement`):

```
module Puppet::Parser::Functions newfunction(:options_lookup, :type =>
:rvalue, :doc => <<-EOF
```

A description of what the function does and how it can be used is passed with the `doc` argument; here, the whole description is inside a Heredoc block ended by the EOF marker:

```
This function takes two arguments (option, and default value) and
looks for the given
option key in the calling modules options hash, and returns the value.
[...]
EOF
  ) do |args|
```

After the parameters are passed to the `newfunction` method, we have the function body; here, we catch all the arguments passed to our function in the `args` variable.

We can raise an error if their number is not what we expected (2 or 3):

```
    raise ArgumentError, ("options_lookup(): wrong number of arguments
(#{args.length}; must be 2 or 3)") if (args.length != 2 and args.
length != 3)
```

Then, we assign local variables to each argument. Note that as `args` is managed as an array, the first argument passed to our function is referred by `args[0]`. We also assign the value of Puppet's `parent_module_name` internal variable to our `mod_name` variable:

```
    value = ''
    option_name = args[0]
    default_val = args[1]
    hash_name = args[2]
    mod_name = parent_module_name
```

We set the default name (`options`) of the class parameter that contains the hash to be used. Note that we have had to cope with different Puppet versions where a missing variable is referenced in different ways (with the `:undefined` symbol, an empty string, or `nil`):

```
    hash_name = "options" if (hash_name == :undefined || hash_name ==
'' || hash_name == nil)
```

Then, we set the `value` to return using the `lookupvar` Puppet function, the fully qualified name of the hash variable, and its key:

```
    value = lookupvar("#{mod_name}::#{hash_name}")["#{option_name}"]
if (lookupvar("#{mod_name}::#{hash_name}").size > 0)
```

If no value is returned, then the default value expected from the second argument passed to the function is used:

```
    value = "#{default_val}" if (value == :undefined || value == '' ||
value == nil)
```

The output of the function is, finally, the calculated `value`:

```
    return value
  end
end
```

We can use this function in ERB templates in a similar way:

```
Listen <%= scope.function_options_lookup(['Listen','127.0.0.1'])%>
```

Let's see also a statement function like Puppet's core `fail` function.

The structure is very similar; we don't have to specify the type of function and each argument that is provided is collected on a variable called `vals`:

```
Puppet::Parser::Functions::newfunction(:fail, :arity => -1, :doc =>
"Fail with a parse error.") do |vals|
```

If the argument is an array, its members are converted to a space-separated string:

```
vals = vals.collect { |s| s.to_s }.join(" ") if vals.is_a? Array
```

Then, an exception with a message containing a string with the arguments provided to the function (this is a function that enforces a failure, after all) is simply raised:

```
    raise Puppet::ParseError, vals.to_s
end
```

We can use functions for a wide variety of needs:

- Many functions in Puppet Labs' `stdlib` module such as `chomp`, `chop`, `downcase`, `flatten`, `join`, `strip`, and so on, reproduce common Ruby functions that manipulate data and make them directly available in the Puppet language
- Others are used to validate data types (`validate_array`, `validate_hash`, `validate_re`)
- We can also use functions to get data from any source (the output of a command, a YAML file, a database, or a REST interface) and make it directly available in our manifests

The possibilities are endless; whatever is possible in Ruby can be made available within our manifests with a custom function.

Custom facts

Facts are the most comfortable kind of variables to work with:

- They are at top scope; therefore, they are easily accessible in every part of our code
- They provide direct and trusted information, being executed on the client

- They are computed; their values are set automatically, and we don't have to manage them manually

Out of the box, depending on the Facter version and the underlying OS, they give us:

- Hardware information (`architecture bios_* board* memory* processor virtual`)
- Operating system details (`kernel* osfamily operatingsystem* lsb* sp_* selinux ssh* timezone uptime*`)
- Network configuration (`hostname domain fqdn interfaces ipaddress_* macaddress_* network*`)
- Disks and filesystems (`blockdevice_* filesystems swap* `)
- Puppet-related software versions (`facterversion puppetversion ruby*`)

We already use some of these facts to manage the right resources to apply for our operating systems in modules, and we already classify nodes according to their hostnames.

There is a lot more that we can do with them; we can create custom facts useful to:

- Classify our nodes according to their functions and locations (using custom facts that might be named `dc`, `env`, `region`, `role`, or `node_number`)
- Determine the version and status of a program (`php_version`, `mysql_cluster`, `glassfish_registered`)
- Return local metrics of any kind (`apache_error_rate`, `network_connections`)

Just think about any possible command we can run on our servers and how its output might be useful in our manifests to model the resources we provide to our servers.

We can write custom facts in the following two ways:

- As Ruby code in our modules distributed to clients via `pluginsync`
- Using the `/etc/facter/facts.d` directory where we can place plain text, JSON, YAML files, or executable scripts

Ruby facts distributed via pluginsync

We can create a custom fact by placing files called `lib/facter/<fact_name>.rb` in one of our modules. For example, a fact named `role` should be placed in a file called `lib/facter/role.rb` and may have the following content:

```
require 'facter'
```

We require the `facter` class, and then, we use the `add` method for our custom fact called `role`:

```
Facter.add("role") do
```

We can restrict the execution of this fact only to specific hosts according to any other fact value. This is done using the `confine` statement, which is based on the `kernel` fact here:

```
confine :kernel => [ 'Linux' , 'SunOS' , 'FreeBSD' , 'Darwin' ]
```

We can also set the maximum number of seconds to wait for its execution:

```
timeout = 10
```

We can even have different facts with the same name and give a weight to each of them; facts with a higher weight value are executed first, and facts with a lower weight value are executed only if no value is already returned:

```
has_weight = 40
```

We use the `setcode` method of the `Facter` class to define what our fact does. What is returned from the block of code contained here (between `do` and `end`) is the value of our fact:

```
setcode do
```

We can have access to other fact values with `Facter.value`. In our case, the `role` value is a simple extrapolation of the `hostname` (basically, the hostname without numbers). If we have different naming schemes for our nodes and we can deduce their roles from their names, we can easily use other Ruby string functions to extrapolate the value we need:

```
host = Facter.value(:hostname)
host.gsub(/\d|\W/,"")
end
end
```

Often, the output of a fact is simply the execution of a command. In this case, there is a specific wrapper method called `Facter::Util::Resolution.exec` that expects the command to execute as a parameter.

The following fact, called `last_run`, simply contains the output of the `date` command:

```
require 'facter'
Facter.add("last_run") do
  confine :kernel => [ 'Linux' , 'SunOS' , 'FreeBSD' , 'Darwin' ]
  setcode do
```

```
      Facter::Util::Resolution.exec('date')
    end
  end
```

We can have different facts with different names on the same Ruby file, and we can also provide dynamic facts. For example, the following code creates several different facts, returning the installed version for each package. Here, the confinement according to osfamily is done outside the fact's definition:

```
if Facter.osfamily == 'RedHat'
  IO.popen('yum list installed').readlines.collect do |line|
      array = line.split
      Facter.add("#{array[0]}_version") do
          setcode do
              "#{array[1]}"
          end
      end
  end
end
if Facter.osfamily == 'Debian'
  IO.popen('dpkg -l').readlines.collect do |line|
      array = line.split
      Facter.add("#{array[1]}_version") do
          setcode do
              "#{array[2]}"
          end
      end
  end
end
```

Remember that to have access from the shell to the facts that we distribute via pluginsync, we need to use the --puppet (-p) argument:

facter -p

Alternatively, we need to set the FACTERLIB environment variable pointing to the lib directory of the module that provides it, for example:

export FACTERLIB=/etc/puppet/modules/site/lib

External facts in the facts.d directory

Puppet Labs's stdlib module provides a very powerful addendum to custom facts: a feature called external facts, which has proven to be so useful that it has been included directly into the core Facter since Version 1.7.

We can define new facts without having to write Ruby code; we can just place files in the `/etc/facter/facts.d` directory (`/etc/puppetlabs/facter/facts.d` with Puppet Enterprise and `C:\ProgramData\PuppetLabs\facter\facts.d\` on Windows).

These files can be simple `.txt` files such as `/etc/facter/facts.d/node.txt` with facts declared with the following syntax:

```
role=webserver
env=prod
```

YAML files such as `/etc/facter/facts.d/node.yaml` with the same sample facts would appear as:

```
---
  role: webserver
  env: prod
```

Also, JSON files such as `/etc/facter/facts.d/node.json` would look as:

```
{
  'role': 'webserver',
  'env': 'prod'
}
```

We can also place plain commands in any language. On Unix, any executable file present in `/etc/facter/facts.d/` is run and expected to return facts' values with an output like:

```
role=webserver
env=prod
```

On Windows, we can place files with the `.com`, `.exe`, `.bat`, `.cmd`, or `.ps1` extension.

Since Puppet 3.4.0, external facts can be automatically propagated to clients with pluginsync. In this case, the directory synced is `<modulename>/facts.d` (note that this is at the same level as the lib directory).

Alternatively, we can use other methods to place our external facts, for example, in the postinstallation scripts during the initial provisioning of a server, using Puppet's file resources directly, or having them generated by custom scripts or cron jobs.

Custom types and providers

If we had to name a single feature that defines Puppet, it would probably be its approach to the management of the system's resources.

The abstraction layer that types and providers provide saves us from caring about implementations of the resources we want on different operating systems.

This is a strong and powerful competitive edge of Puppet, and the thing that makes it even more interesting is the possibility to easily create custom types and provides and seamlessly distribute them to clients.

Types and providers are the components of Puppet's resource abstraction layer; even if they are strongly coupled, they do different things:

- Types abstract a physical resource and specify the interface to its management, exposing parameters and properties that allow users to model the resource as desired.

- Providers implement the types' specifications on the system, adapting to different operating systems. They need to be able to query the current status of a resource and configure it to reflect the expected state.

For each type, there must be at least one provider, and each provider may be tied to one and only one type.

Custom types can be placed inside a module; in files such as `lib/puppet/type/<type_name>.rb`, providers are placed in `lib/puppet/provider/<type_name>/<provider_name>.rb`.

Before analyzing a sample piece of code, we will recapitulate what types are all about:

- They abstract the resources of a system.
- They expose parameters to shape resources in the desired state.
- They have a title that must be unique across the catalog.
- One of their parameters is the `namevar`. If not set explicitly, its value is taken from the title.

Let's see a sample custom native type; what follows manages the execution of `psql` commands and is from Puppet Labs' Postgresql module (`https://github.com/puppetlabs/puppetlabs-postgresql`). We can find it in `lib/puppet/type/postgresql_psql.rb`:

```
Puppet::Type.newtype(:postgresql_psql) do
```

A type is created by calling the `newtype` method of the `Puppet::Type` class. We pass the type name as a symbol and a block of code with the type's content.

Here, we just have to define the parameters and properties of the type, exactly the ones our users will deal with.

Parameters are set with the `newparam` method; here, the `name` parameter is defined with a brief description and is marked as `namevar` with the `isnamevar` method:

```
newparam(:name) do
    desc "An arbitrary tag for your own reference; the name of the
message."
    isnamevar
end
```

> An alternative and currently preferred method to set a `namevar` parameter is:
>
> `newparam(:name, :namevar => true) do`

Types may have parameters, which are instances of the `Puppet::Parameter` class and properties, which are instances of `Puppet::Property` that inherit `Puppet::Parameter` and all its methods.

The main difference between a property and parameter is that a property models a part of the state of the managed resource (it defines a characteristic), whereas a parameter gives information that the provider will use to manage the properties of the resource.

We should be able to discover the status of a resource's property and modify it.

In the type, we define them. In the providers, we query their status and change them.

For example, the built-in `service` type has different arguments: `ensure` and `enable` are properties; all the others are parameters.

The `file` type has the `content`, `ctime`, `group`, `mode`, `mtime`, `owner`, `seluser`, `selrole`, `seltype`, `selrange`, `target`, and `type` properties; they represent the characteristics of the file resource on the system.

On the other side, its parameters are `path`, `backup`, `recurse`, `recurselimit`, `replace`, `force`, `ignore`, `links`, `purge`, `sourceselect`, `show_diff`, `source`, `source_permissions`, `checksum`, and `selinux_ignore_defaults`. They allow us to manage the file in various ways but are not a direct expression of the characteristics of the file on the system.

A property is set with the `newproperty` method. Here is how the `postgresql_psql` type sets the `command` property, which is the SQL query we have to execute:

```
newproperty(:command) do
    desc 'The SQL command to execute via psql.'
```

A default value can be defined here. In this case, it is the resource name:

```
defaultto { @resource[:name] }
```

In this specific case, the `sync` method of `Puppet::Property` is redefined to manage this particular case:

```
def sync(refreshing = false)
  if (!@resource.refreshonly? || refreshing)
    super()
  else
    nil
  end
end
end
```

Other parameters have the same structure:

```
newparam(:db) do
    desc "The name of the database to execute the SQL command
against."
  end

  newparam(:search_path) do
    desc "The schema search path to use when executing the SQL
command"
  end

  newparam(:psql_user) do
    desc "The system user account under which the psql command should
be executed."
    defaultto("postgres")
  end
[...]
end
```

The `postgresql_psql` type continues with the definition of other parameters, their description, and wherever possible, the default values.

If a parameter or property is required, we set this with the `isrequired` method; we can also `validate` the input values if we need to force specific data types or values and normalize them with the `munge` method.

A type can also be made ensurable, that is, have an `ensure` property that can be set to `present` or `absent`. The property is automatically added just by calling the `ensurable` method.

We can also set automatic dependencies for a type; for example, the `exec` native type has an automatic dependency for a user resource that creates the user who is supposed to run the command as if this is set by its name and not its `uid`; here is how this is done in `lib/puppet/type/exec.rb`:

```
autorequire(:user) do
  # Autorequire users if they are specified by name
  if user = self[:user] and user !~ /^\d+$/
    user
  end
end
```

We can use such a type in our manifests; here is, for example, how it's used in the `postgresql::server::grant` define of Puppet Labs' `postgresql` module:

```
$grant_cmd = "GRANT ${_privilege} ON ${_object_type} \"${objectname}\"
TO \"${role}\""
  postgresql_psql { $grant_cmd:
    db           => $on_db,
    port         => $port,
    psql_user    => $psql_user,
    psql_group   => $group,
    psql_path    => $psql_path,
    unless       => "SELECT 1 WHERE ${unless_function}('${role}',
'${object_name}', '${unless_privilege}')",
    require       => Class['postgresql::server']
  }
```

For each type, there must be at least one provider. When the implementation of the resource defined by the type is different according to factors such as the operating system, we may have different providers for a given type.

A provider must be able to query the current state of a resource and eventually configure it according to the desired state, as defined by the parameters we've provided to the type.

We define a provider by calling the `provide` method of `Puppet::Type.type()`; the block passed to it is the content of our provider.

We can restrict a provider to a specific platform with the `confine` method and, in case of alternatives, use the `defaultfor` method to make it the default one.

For example, the `portage` provider of the `package` type has something like:

```
Puppet::Type.type(:package).provide :portage, :parent =>
Puppet::Provider::Package do
  desc "Provides packaging support for Gentoo's portage system."
  has_feature :versionable
  confine :operatingsystem => :gentoo
  defaultfor :operatingsystem => :gentoo
[...]
```

In the preceding example, `confine` has matched a fact value, but it can also be used to check for a file's existence, a system's feature, or any piece of code:

```
confine :exists => '/usr/sbin/portage'
confine :feature => :selinux
confine :true => begin
  [Any block of code that enables the provider if returns true]
end
```

Also note the `desc` method used to set a description of the provider and the `has_feature` method used to define the supported features of the relevant `type`.

The provider has to execute commands on the system. These are defined via the `command` or `optional_command` methods; the latter defines a command that might not exist on the system and is not required by the provider.

For example, the `useradd` provider of the `user` type has the following commands defined:

```
Puppet::Type.type(:user).provide :useradd, :parent => Puppet::Provider
::NameService::ObjectAdd do
  commands :add => "useradd", :delete => "userdel", :modify =>
"usermod", :password => "chage"
  optional_commands :localadd => "luseradd"
```

When we define a command, a new method is created; we can use it wherever it is needed, passing eventual arguments via an array. The defined command is searched in the path, unless specified with an absolute path.

All the types' property and parameter values are accessible via the `[]` method of the `resource` object: `resource[:uid]`, `resource[:groups]`.

When a type is `ensurable`, its providers must support the `create`, `exists?`, and `destroy` methods, which are used, respectively, to create the resource type, check if it exists, and remove it.

The `exists?` method in particular is at the basis of Puppet's idempotence, as it verifies whether the resource is in the desired state or needs to be synced.

For example, the `zfs` provider of the `zfs` zone implements the methods that run the (defined earlier) `zfs` command:

```
def create
  zfs *([:create] + add_properties + [@resource[:name]])
end

def destroy
  zfs(:destroy, @resource[:name])
end

def exists?
  if zfs(:list).split("\n").detect { |line| line.split("\s")[0]
    == @resource[:name] }
    true
  else
    false
  end
end
```

For every property of a type, the provider must have methods to read (getter) and modify (setter) its status. These methods have exactly the same name as the property, with the setter method having an ending equal symbol (=).

For example, the `ruby` provider of the `postgresql_psql` type we have seen earlier has these methods to manage the command to execute (here, we have removed the implementation code):

```
Puppet::Type.type(:postgresql_psql).provide(:ruby) do

  def command()
    [ Code to check if sql command has to be executed ]
  end

  def command=(val)
    [ Code that executes the sql command ]
  end
```

If a property is out of sync, the setter method is invoked to configure the system as desired.

Custom report handlers

Puppet can generate data about what happens during a run, and we can gather this data in reports. They contain the output of what is executed on the client, details on every action taken during the execution, and performance metrics.

Needless to say that we can also extend Puppet reports and deliver them to a variety of destinations: logging systems, database backends, e-mail, chat roots, notification and alerting systems, trouble ticketing software, and web dashboards.

Reports may contain the whole output of a Puppet run, a part of it (for example, just the list of resources that failed), or just the metrics (as it happens with the rrd report that graphs key metrics such as Puppet compilation and run times).

We can distribute our custom report handlers via the pluginsync functionality too. We just need to place them in the lib/puppet/reports/<report_name>.rb path so that the file name matches the handler name.

> James Turnbull, the author of the most popular Puppet books, has written many custom reports for Puppet; check his blog for detailed posts about report handlers at http://kartar.net/category/ puppet/.

Here, we analyze the structure of one of James Turnbull's report handlers that sends notifications of failed reports to the PagerDuty online service (https://github. com/jamtur01/puppet-pagerduty); it should be placed in a module with the lib/ puppet/reports/pagerduty.rb path.

First, we need to include some required classes. The Puppet class is always required; the other ones may be required depending on the kind of report.

```
require 'puppet'
require 'json'
require 'yaml'

begin
  require 'redphone/pagerduty'
rescue LoadError => e
  Puppet.info "You need the `redphone` gem to use the PagerDuty
    report"
end
```

Then, we call the `register_report` method of the `Puppet::Reports` class, passing the handler name to it as a symbol and its code in a block.

```
Puppet::Reports.register_report(:pagerduty) do
```

Here, the report handler uses an external configuration file, `/etc/puppet/pagerduty.yaml` (note how we can access Puppet configuration entries with `Puppet.settings[]`), where users can place specific settings (in this case, the PagerDuty API key):

```
config_file = File.join(File.dirname(Puppet.settings[:config]),
  "pagerduty.yaml")
raise(Puppet::ParseError, "PagerDuty report config file
  #{config_file} not readable") unless File.exist?(config_file)
config = YAML.load_file(config_file)
PAGERDUTY_API = config[:pagerduty_api]
```

We can use the familiar `desc` method to place a description of the report:

```
desc <<-DESC
Send notification of failed reports to a PagerDuty service. You
  will need to create a receiving service
in PagerDuty that uses the Generic API and add the API key to
  configuration file.
DESC
```

All the reporting logic is defined in the `process` method. Here, we can have access to a variety of information about the report, available as variables of the `self` object; for example, `self.status` contains the status of the Puppet run, `self.logs` contains all the output text, and `self.host` contains the host where Puppet has been executed. In this case, the `trigger_incident` method of the `Redphone::Pagerduty` class is called and information about a Puppet run is sent if the report `status` is `failed`:

```
def process
  if self.status == "failed"
    Puppet.debug "Sending status for #{self.host} to PagerDuty."
    details = Array.new
    self.logs.each do |log|
      details << log
    end
    response = Redphone::Pagerduty.trigger_incident(
      :service_key => PAGERDUTY_API,
      :incident_key => "puppet/#{self.host}",
      :description => "Puppet run for #{self.host}
        #{self.status} at #{Time.now.asctime}",
```

```
      :details => details
    )
    case response['status']
    when "success"
      Puppet.debug "Created PagerDuty incident:
        puppet/#{self.host}"
    else
      Puppet.debug "Failed to create PagerDuty incident:
        puppet/#{self.host}"
    end
  end
  end
end
```

Custom faces

With the release of Puppet 2.6, a brand new concept was introduced: Puppet Faces.

Faces is an API that allows the easy creation of new Puppet (sub) commands. Whenever we execute Puppet, we specify at least one command that provides access to the functionalities of its subsystems.

The most common commands are `agent`, `apply`, `master`, and `cert`, and have existed for a long time. However, there are a lot more (we can see their full list with `puppet help`), and most of them are defined via the Faces API.

As you can guess, we can easily add new faces and, therefore, new subcommands to the puppet executable just by placing some files in a module of ours.

The typical synopsis of the Puppet command is as follows:

```
puppet [FACE] [ACTION] [ARGUMENTS] [OPTIONS]
```

Here, [FACE] is the Puppet subcommand to be executed, [ACTION] is the face's action we want to invoke, [ARGUMENTS] are its arguments, and [OPTIONS] are general Puppet options.

To create a face, we have to work on two files: `lib/puppet/application/<face_name>.rb` and `lib/puppet/face/<face_name>.rb`. The code in the `application` directory simply adds the subcommand to Puppet, extending the `Puppet::Application::FaceBase` class; the code in the `face` directory manages all its logic and what to do for each action.

An interesting point to consider when writing and using faces is that we have access to the whole Puppet environment, and its indirectors and termini, and we can interact with its subsystems via the other faces.

The `secret_agent` face is a good example of how to use other faces inside a face. It reproduces, using the faces API, the activity of the `agent` command, which is currently not implemented via the faces API. A quick look at the code in `lib/puppet/face/secret_agent.rb`, amended of documentation and marginal code, reveals the basic structure of a face and how other faces can be used:

```ruby
require 'puppet/face'
Puppet::Face.define(:secret_agent, '0.0.1') do
  action(:synchronize) do
    default
    summary "Run secret_agent once."
[...]
    when_invoked do |options|
      Puppet::Face[:plugin, '0.0.1'].download
      Puppet::Face[:facts, '0.0.1'].upload
      Puppet::Face[:catalog, '0.0.1'].download
      report = Puppet::Face[:catalog, '0.0.1'].apply
      Puppet::Face[:report, '0.0.1'].submit(report)
      return report
    end
  end
end
```

The `Puppet::Face` class exposes various methods. Some of them are used to provide documentation both for the command line and the help pages: `summary`, `arguments`, `license`, `copyright`, `author`, `notes`, and `examples`.

For example, the `module` face uses these methods to describe what it does in Puppet core's `lib/puppet/face/module.rb` file:

```ruby
require 'puppet/face'
require 'puppet/module_tool'
require 'puppet/util/colors'

Puppet::Face.define(:module, '1.0.0') do
  extend Puppet::Util::Colors

  copyright "Puppet Labs", 2012
  license   "Apache 2 license; see COPYING"

  summary "Creates, installs and searches for modules on the
    Puppet Forge."
  description <<-EOT
```

```
    This subcommand can find, install, and manage modules from the
        Puppet Forge,
    a repository of user-contributed Puppet code. It can also
        generate empty
    modules, and prepare locally developed modules for release on
        the Forge.
  EOT

    display_global_options "environment", "modulepath"
  end
```

The `action` method is invoked for each action of a face. Here, we pass the action name as a symbol and a block of code that implements our action using various other methods:

- Methods used for documentation and inline help: `description`, `summary`, and `returns`

- Methods used to manage the parameters used in the command line: `option` and `arguments`

- Methods used to implement specific actions: `when_invoked` (its return value is the output of the command) and `when_rendering`

Let's see the implementation of the `install` action of the `module` face. The following code is in the `lib/puppet/face/module/install.rb` file. It's possible to add the code for each action in separate files, like in this case, or on the main face file.

We are dealing with a Ruby class that may require other classes:

```
require 'puppet/forge'
require 'puppet/module_tool/install_directory'
require 'pathname'
```

This is followed by the face definition and the code applied for the `install` action:

```
Puppet::Face.define(:module, '1.0.0') do
  action(:install) do
```

Then, some description methods are called:

```
    summary "Install a module from the Puppet Forge or a release
        archive."

    description <<-EOT
      [...]
    EOT
```

```
returns "Pathname object representing the path to the
  installed module."

examples <<-'EOT'
  [...]
EOT
```

Then, the expected arguments and the available options (here, only the block relative to the `--target-dir` option is copied; various others are present in the original file and are defined in a similar way) are defined:

```
arguments "<name>"

option "--target-dir DIR", "-i DIR" do
  summary "The directory into which modules are installed."
  description <<-EOT
    [...]
  EOT
end
```

Then, when the `install` action is called, the `when_invoked` block is executed. Here is where the real work is done; in this case, methods from the `Puppet::ModuleTool` class and related classes are called:

```
when_invoked do |name, options|
  Puppet::ModuleTool.set_option_defaults options
  Puppet.notice "Preparing to install into
    #{options[:target_dir]} ..."

  forge = Puppet::Forge.new("PMT", self.version)
  install_dir = Puppet::ModuleTool::InstallDirectory.
    new(Pathname.new(options[:target_dir]))
  installer = Puppet::ModuleTool::Applications::Installer.
new(name, forge, install_dir, options)

  installer.run
end
```

This action also invokes the `when_rendering` block to format the console output:

```
when_rendering :console do |return_value, name, options|
  if return_value[:result] == :failure
    Puppet.err(return_value[:error][:multiline])
    exit 1
```

```
      else          tree = Puppet::ModuleTool.build_tree(return_
value[:installed_modules], return_value[:install_dir])
        return_value[:install_dir] + "\n" +
        Puppet::ModuleTool.format_tree(tree)
      end
    end
  end
end
```

As it happens for many faces, most of the code is in the `face` directory; the other component of the face placed in `lib/puppet/application/module.rb` is just an extension of the `Puppet::Application::FaceBase` class:

```
require 'puppet/application/face_base'

class Puppet::Application::Module < Puppet::Application::FaceBase
end
```

Summary

This chapter has been entirely dedicated to how we can extend Puppet functionalities using Ruby code. We have reviewed the different areas where Puppet can be customized, from the indirector and its termini to the plugins we can deliver via modules.

We have reviewed the most common plugins, facts, functions, types and providers, reports, and faces, trying to outline the needed code components without indulging much in specific implementation details.

The best place to look for samples is the Puppet code itself; under the `lib/puppet` directory, we can find the actual implementation of the core components.

How often we find ourselves working on custom plugins written in Ruby will depend on our needs and skills; we might never need to write any of them, but it is useful to know what they are and the principles behind them.

The scope of this chapter was to provide an overall view in order to be able to find where plugins are placed in a module, know how they integrate into Puppet, and have a high-level view of how they can be implemented.

The next chapter enters brand new territories. We are going to explore how we can extend Puppet usage to devices different from the usual operating systems: network equipment, storage devices, and cloud instances.

Believe it or not, we can manage them with Puppet as well.

11
Beyond the System

Puppet was designed as a configuration management tool for Unix-like systems. It runs on Linux, Solaris, FreeBSD, OpenBSD, AIX, Mac OS, and since Version 2.7.6, also on Windows.

Over the years, however, it became clear that automation in a data center must also involve other families of devices such as network equipments, storage devices, and virtualization solutions.

The same interest of companies such as Cisco and VMware, who are investors and technological partners of Puppet Labs, could only facilitate Puppet's steps into these territories. We are already seeing the results of these partnerships, and the vision of a software-defined data center is also taking shape under a Puppet-driven perspective.

In this chapter, we will review the current status of the projects that allow us to use Puppet in the following categories of devices and technologies:

- Network equipments such as switches, routers, and load balancers from Cisco, Juniper, and F5
- Cloud and virtualization with VMware, Amazon, Google, Eucalyptus, and OpenStack
- Storage equipment from NetApp

Puppet on a network equipment

The automation of network equipments' configuration is a common need. When we provision a new system, besides its own settings, we often need to manage switching ports to assign it to the correct VLAN, firewalls to open the relevant ports, and load balancers to add the server to a balanced pool.

It is obvious that the possibility of automating the configuration of the whole infrastructure, network included, is a powerful and welcomed point.

There are two main challenges in front of Puppet when it has to deal with network devices. They are as follows:

- **Technical**: This is simply due to the impossibility of having the `puppet` executable running on the device to be managed

- **Cultural**: This is because at many places, network administrators don't know or use Puppet

For the technical challenge, there is good news. Alternative approaches have been taken to manage Puppet network equipments of various natures and from different vendors:

- **Proxy mode**: In our manifests, we declare network-related resource types and apply them to normal nodes, running Linux or another Puppet-supported OS. On these servers, the relevant providers execute local commands that interact with remote network devices and configure them as needed. Generally, how this can be done depends on the following available configuration methods:

    ° **Telnet** or **SSH**: Connections (Telnet or SSH) are made to the device, and from there, local commands are executed to check the status of a resource (interface, VLAN, pool member, and so on) and eventually, to modify it using the local CLI syntax.

    ° **Web API**: Some devices expose a web interface to their configuration and allow remote management. On the Puppet proxy node, providers make remote connections to these web APIs to check and sync the status of resources.

    ° **SNMP**: Most of the network devices have an SNMP interface, and this can be used for their remote management. Even if I am not aware of any module using this approach, this is theoretically possible.

- **Native mode**: Some network devices can run Puppet natively. They may be based on Linux or FreeBSD and, therefore, can potentially host the needed Puppet stack. Puppet Labs' partnerships with other vendors are providing good results: Cisco Nexus 9000 switches with Cisco NX-OS can run Puppet natively in a dedicated Linux container, and Juniper provides a native Puppet package for its Junos OS.

Besides the technical challenges for which there are some solutions (but there is still much to do), there are also cultural and operational issues to deal with.

At many places, network and system administrators are of different breeds; they operate in different groups and are responsible for their infrastructures, using their own instrumentation.

Puppet's programmatic approach to configuration is likely to be pushed by sysadmins. This approach might not be well accepted by network people, who are probably less obsessed by automation and more used to dealing with static configurations.

Here is where the DevOps culture can make a difference. There are great tools that can automate our processes. There are also common sense practices such as collaboration, sharing of responsibilities, and good communication across teams. If we put together these elements, we can achieve great results.

Puppet users need just the basic management of network devices, not their whole configurations. Most of the time, it is a matter of setting parameters and VLANs on switch interfaces.

Many products provide authorization profiles that can limit the users' permissions, so a sane compromise can be to allow automatic management only for simple port settings and prevent changes to the more global and risky core configurations.

A Proxy mode with the puppet device application

Many Puppet features originate from community contribution. One of the most versatile and long-standing contributors is definitely Brice Figureau (the fact that he is a personal friend and technical reviewer of this book is really irrelevant here). When there was still nothing around on the topic, he proposed an approach to the management of network devices. This approach has been the foundation for the proxy mode we mentioned earlier.

In his blog post at http://puppetlabs.com/blog/puppet-network-device-management, he introduced the puppet device application in Puppet 2.7 to manage external devices where Puppet cannot run natively.

This command uses, by default, /etc/puppet/device.conf as a configuration file, and the hostnames of the equipment to be managed, their types, and the method to connect to them can be placed here. A sample entry may look like the following code:

```
[switch01.example42.lan]
  type cisco
  url ssh://puppet:my_password@switch01.example42.lan/
```

```
[router01.example42.lan]
  type cisco
  url telnet://puppet:my_pass@router01.example42.lan/
?enable=enablepassword
```

With such a file in place, we can use the `puppet device` command on the host we want to act as proxy for the configuration of remote devices.

The first time this command is executed, it creates certificates for all the devices we have defined in `device.conf`. These certificates have to be signed by the Puppet Master as a normal node's certificates.

The implementation provides two core native types, `interface` and `vlan`, with a provider to manage Cisco IOS-based devices. We can execute `puppet describe interface` and `puppet describe vlan` for details on their attributes.

To manage switch interfaces (speed and duplex, VLAN, port mode (access/trunk), description, and so on), we can write resources as follows:

```
interface { 'FastEthernet 0/1':
  description => "Server ${server_name}",
  mode        => access,
  native_vlan => 1000,
  duplex      => auto,
  speed       => auto,
}
```

To manage routers interfaces, we can use the following code:

```
interface { 'Vlan12':
  ipaddress => [ "192.168.14.14/24", "2001:2674:8C23::1/64" ]
}
```

To manage VLANS (their ID, which is `105` in the following example is the title of the `vlan` resource), the following code is enough:

```
vlan { '105':
  description => 'DMZ',
}
```

These resources can be declared in nodes' definitions that match the device names specified in `device.conf`. When `puppet device` is executed, it behaves like `puppet apply`, but it operates on a remote device. This means that it retrieves facts from the network device, retrieves a catalog from the Puppet Master for the locally configured devices, and runs it by providing a normal transaction report. A notable difference between `puppet device` and a normal Puppet run is that the providers that implement the types mentioned earlier perform configurations on remote network devices.

On the Puppet core source, there is currently just the provider for Cisco devices, and the supported transport methods are just `telnet` and `ssh`. However, we can find modules that use the same approach and implement it on different devices.

For example, Puppet Labs' F5 module, which is available at `https://github.com/puppetlabs/puppetlabs-f5`, introduces several F5-specific resource types but is based on the network device application and has similar usage patterns. A sample entry in `device.conf` might be like the following code:

```
[f5.example42.lan]
  type f5
  url https://username:password@f5.example42.lan/
```

Note that in this case, the network device type is `f5` and the access is created via `https`.

A further demonstration of Puppet's expandability is a module such as the one available at `https://github.com/uniak/puppet-networkdevice`, which is written by two community members, Markus Burger and David Schmitt. It provides wider support for Cisco devices and implements, in addition to the Puppet device application, a new device type (`cisco_ios`). A sample entry in `device.conf` looks like the following:

```
[switch01.example42.lan]
  type cisco_ios
  url sshios://user:password@switch01.example42.lan:22/?$flags
```

The module features a more complete set of resource types to manage different elements of a Cisco IOS configuration (access lists, SNMP configuration, interfaces, VLANS, users, and so on).

A thing to consider is that the Puppet agent that normally runs as a service on a node does not implement any device activity. To manage the configured devices on a regular basis, we need to place a cron job that executes `puppet device` on the proxy host.

Native Puppet on the network equipment

A proxy-based approach based on `puppet device` has the benefit of letting us manage virtually any device that in some way allows programmatic remote configuration. However, it has some cons related to scale, authentication management, and the fact that it behaves differently as compared to any other Puppet command.

A step further can be taken when Puppet runs natively on the device to be managed and can apply configurations directly. This is an emerging field where we are already seeing some implementations, and this field will probably grow with the same concept of the software-defined data center.

Cisco onePK

In 2013, Cisco released **onePK**, a software development toolkit that consists of a set of API libraries that allow monitoring and management of different families of Cisco devices and operating systems (IOS/XE, NXOS, and IOS XR), exposing an abstracted interface that may be used by libraries in different languages.

The Nexus 9000 enterprise switches execute a native Puppet agent in a Linux VM container running inside the NXOS. This agent allows the usage of dedicated resource types such as `cisco_device`, `cisco_interface` and `cisco_vlan` in a normal Agent/Master setup. We can place the following code in a device node:

```
node 'switch01.example42.lan' {
  # Definition of the Device, needed for each device
  cisco_device { 'switch01.example42.lan':
    ensure => present,
  }

  # Configuration of a VLAN on an access interface
  cisco_interface { 'Ethernet1/5':
    switchport  => access,
    access_vlan => 1000,
  }

  # Configuration of a VLAN
  cisco_vlan { '1000':
    ensure    => present,
    vlan_name => 'DMZ',
    state     => active,
  }
}
```

Directly from the device's CLI, we can issue commands such as `onep application puppet v0.8 puppet_agent` to run Puppet from the local device, which has its normal certificate and communicates with the Puppet Master as any other node.

The previous resources, when applied on the Linux container where Puppet runs, actually don't operate directly on the switch's configuration; they rather use the onePK presentation API to interface with onePK API infrastructure running on the device.

 For more information about Cisco onePK and Puppet, refer to the presentation at `http://puppetlabs.com/presentations/managing-cisco-devices-using-puppet`.

Juniper and netdev_stdlib

Juniper Network offers a deeper approach to Puppet integration. It provides native `jpuppet` packages for its Junos OS supported on all releases after 12.3R2. On Juniper devices, these packages install Ruby, the required gems, and Puppet, which runs locally and behaves absolutely like any other client, with its certificates and node definition.

Juniper has also developed two modules:

- The `netdev_stdlib` module is a general, open source, and abstracted interface to network configurations (now, it is under Puppet Lab's control and can be found at `https://github.com/puppetlabs/puppet-netdev-stdlib`), which contains the `netdev_*` types

- A vendor-specific one (`https://github.com/Juniper/puppet-netdev-stdlib-junos`) where just the relevant provider for Junos devices is present

The Puppet code for a switch node looks like the following code:

```
node 'switch02.example42.lan' {

  # A single netdev_device resource must be present
  netdev_device { $hostname: }

  # Sample configuration of an interface
  netdev_interface { 'ge-0/0/0':
    admin => down,
    mtu   => 2000,
  }
```

```
# Sample configuration of a VLAN
netdev_vlan { 'vlan102':
  vlan_id     => '102',
  description => 'Public network',
}


# Configuration of an access port without VLAN tag
netdev_l2_interface { 'ge-0/0/0':
   untagged_vlan => Red
}


# Configuration of a trunk port with multiple VLAN tags
# And untagged packets go to 'native VLAN'
netdev_l2_interface { 'xe-0/0/2':
   tagged_vlans  => [ Red, Green, Blue ],
   untagged_vlan => Yellow
}


# Configuration of Link Aggregation ports (bonding)
netdev_lag { 'ae0':
   links => [ 'ge-0/0/0', 'ge-1/0/0', 'ge-0/0/2', 'ge-1/0/2' ],
   lacp  => active,
   minimum_links => 2
}
}
```

The idea of the authors is that `netdev_stdlib` might become a standard interface for network devices configurations with different modules providing support for different vendors.

This approach looks definitively more vendor-neutral than Cisco's approach, which is based on onePK and has already implementations from Arista Networks (`https://github.com/aristanetworks/puppet-eos`) and Mellanox (`https://github.com/Mellanox/mellanox-netdev-stdlib-mlnxos`).

This means that the same code mentioned earlier with the `netdev_*` resource types can be used on network devices from different vendors. This is a good example of the power of Puppet's resource abstraction model and the great work of a wonderful community.

Puppet for cloud and virtualization

Puppet is a child of our times; the boom of virtualization and cloud computing have boosted the need and diffusion of software-management tools that can accelerate the deployment and scaling of new systems.

Puppet can be used to manage the following aspects related to cloud computing and virtualization:

- Configure virtualization and cloud solutions such as VMware, OpenStack, and Eucalyptus. This is done with different modules for different operating systems.
- Provide commands to provision instances on different clouds such as Amazon AWS, Google Compute Engine, and VMware. This is done with the cloud provisioner module.

Let's review the most relevant projects in these fields.

VMware

VMware is a major investor in Puppet Labs, and technological collaborations have been done at various levels. Let's see the most interesting projects.

VM provisioning on vCenter and vSphere

Puppet Enterprise provides support to manage virtual machine instances using vSphere and vCenter. This is done via a new face that provides the `node_vmware` Puppet subcommand. Once the local environment is configured (for details you read the documentation on `http://docs.puppetlabs.com/pe/latest/cloudprovisioner_vmware.html`), we can create a new VM based on an existing template with the following command:

```
puppet node_vmware create --name=myserver --
  template="/Datacenters/Solutions/vm/master_template"
```

We can start and stop an existing VM with these commands:

```
puppet node_vmware start /Datacenters/Solutions/vm/myserver
puppet node_vmware stop /Datacenters/Solutions/vm/myserver
```

The integration of vCloud Automation Center

Integration with Puppet is possible directly from within the VMware vCloud Automation Center, which incorporates the features of a product that was previously named vFabric Application Director.

It is a component of the vCloud suite that allows deployment of full application stacks on a dynamically composable number of nodes. The Automation Center uses blueprints to manage application stacks; the end user can provide parameters to manage their configurations.

Deep integration is possible via a specific module given at `http://forge.puppetlabs.com/puppetlabs/appdirector`, which provides commands and scripts that allow any kind of Puppet module to be used and parameterized in blueprints.

In this scenario, users operate on the Automation Center console, and the operations they perform with the blueprints are basically based on bash scripts that install Puppet and run `puppet apply` on properly parameterized manifests.

The configuration of vCenter

Puppet Labs and VMware products interoperate also on the setup and configuration of vCenter, the VMware application that allows the management of the virtual infrastructure. The module available at `https://github.com/puppetlabs/puppetlabs-vcenter` can be used to install (on Windows) and configure vCenter.

It provides native resource types to manage objects such as folders (`vc_folder`), data centers (`vc_datacenter`), clusters (`vc_cluster`), and hosts (`vc_host`).

The Puppet code to manage the installation of vCenter on Windows and the configuration of some basic elements may look as follows:

```
class vcenter {
  media            => 'e:\\',
  jvm_memory_option => 'M',
}

vc_folder { '/prod':
  ensure => present,
}

vc_datacenter { [ '/prod/uk', '/prod/it' ]:
  ensure => present,
}
```

```
vc_cluster { [ '/prod/uk/fe', '/prod/it/fe' ]:
  ensure => present,
}

vc_host { '10.42.20.11':
  ensure   => 'present',
  username => 'root',
  password => 'password',
  tag      => 'fe',
}

vc_host { '10.42.20.12':
  ensure   => 'present',
  username => 'root',
  password => 'password',
  tag      => 'fe',
}
```

Amazon Web Services

Puppet-based solutions to manage **Amazon Web Services (AWS)** have been around
for some time. There are contributions both from Puppet Labs and the community,
and they relate to different Amazon services.

Cloud provisioning on AWS

Puppet Labs has released a Cloud Provisioner module that provides faces to manage
instances on AWS and Google Compute Engine. We can install it with:

```
puppet module install puppetlabs-cloud_provisioner
```

A new node_aws face is provided, and it allows operations on AWS instances. They
are performed via Fog, a Ruby cloud services library, and need some prerequisites.
We can install them with:

```
gem install fog
```

```
gem install guid
```

 On Puppet Enterprise, all the cloud provisioner tools and their
dependencies can be easily installed on the Puppet Master or any
other node directly during Puppet installation.

In order to be able to interface to AWS services, we have to generate access credentials from the AWS Management Console. If we use the now-recommended **AWS Identity and Access Management (IAM)** interface, remember to set at least a power user policy to the user for which access keys are created. For more details, visit https://aws.amazon.com/iam/. We can place the access key ID and secret access key in ~/.fog, which is the configuration file of Fog:

```
:default:
  aws_access_key_id: AKIAILAJ3HL2DQC37HZA
  aws_secret_access_key: /vweKQmA5jTzCem1NeQnLaZMdGlOnk10jsZ2
```

Once done, we can interact with AWS. To see the SSH key pair names we have on AWS, we run:

```
puppet node_aws list_keynames
```

To create a new instance, we can execute:

```
puppet node_aws create --type t1.micro --image ami-2f726546 --keyname
  my_key
```

We have specified the instance type, the **Amazon Machine Image (AMI)** to use, and the SSH key we want to use to connect to it.

The output of the command reports the hostname of the newly created instance so that we can log in to it with a command such as the following one (if you have issues with connecting via SSH, review your instance's security group on the AWS console and verify that inbound SSH traffic is permitted):

```
ssh -i .ssh/aws_id_rsa root@ec2-54-81-87-78.compute-1.amazonaws.com
```

To list all our instances (both stopped and running), we use:

```
puppet node_aws list
```

To destroy a running instance (it is going to be wiped off forever), we use:

```
puppet node_aws terminate ec2-54-81-87-78.compute-1.amazonaws.com
```

We can specify the AWS region where instances are created with the `--region` option (the default value is us-east-1).

AWS provisioning and configuration with resource types

Puppet Labs' Cloud Provisioner is not the only solution we have to create AWS instances with Puppet. There are at least a couple of community modules that tackle the same challenge from another point of view: instead of adding a Puppet subcommand, they provide extra resource types that allow us to declare the instances we want to create or various AWS configuration objects in our Puppet manifests.

Dave McCormick's module, which is given at `https://github.com/practicalclouds/pclouds-aws`, provides the `ec2instance` native type, which can be used to manage AWS instances.

Setup of the module `pclouds-aws` is quite easy. We need the Fog gem installed and the module from GitHub or the Forge:

```
puppet module install pclouds-aws
```

We configure the AWS credentials with:

```
awsaccess { 'default':,
  ensure                => 'present',
  aws_access_key_id     => 'AKIAILAJ3HL2DQC37HZA',
  aws_secret_access_key => '/vweKQmA5jTzCem1NeQnLaZMdGlOnk10jsZ2',
  regions               => [ 'eu-west-1', 'us-east-1' ]
}
```

We can manage instances with something as easy as:

```
ec2instance { 'test1':
  ensure   => 'present',
  region   => 'eu-west-1',
  image_id => 'ami-90dbd0e4',
}
```

A very neat thing is that as `ec2instance` is a normal type, we can see many details (and configurable arguments) of all our instances on the regions for which we configured `awsaccess` with the following command:

```
puppet resource ec2instance
```

This approach, in my very personal opinion, really gives a meaning to Puppet integration, and it allows us do to the same things we can do with Cloud Provisioner (the management of instances via the command line), plus much more (such as the management of instances on Puppet manifests).

For example, to terminate the previously created instance, we can execute the following command:

```
puppet resource ec2instance test1 ensure=absent
```

The same author has written other AWS-related modules such as `pclouds-ebsvol` to manage EBS volumes.

Another interesting module is `https://github.com/bobtfish/puppet-aws_api` by Tomas Doran; it does not strictly manage AWS instances, but it allows us to configure many AWS resources in manifests, in particular the configurations related to VPC (the AWS service that allows the creation of instances on a virtual private cloud). It provides native types such as `aws_vpc`, `aws_subnet`, `aws_cgw`, `aws_dopts`, `aws_igw`, `aws_routetable`, `aws_vgw`, `aws_vpn`, `aws_iam_user`, and `aws_iam_group`.

The ability to express such configuration settings in Puppet language makes the setup of a AWS-based infrastructure much more reliable and reproducible and becomes particularly valuable, for example, when we need to reproduce our configurations on different regions or availability zones.

Managing CloudFormation

We have seen how Puppet functionalities can be extended with modules, either by providing resource types that enrich the language or additional faces that add actions to the application.

One of these extra faces is provided by Puppet Labs' CloudFormation module (`https://github.com/puppetlabs/puppetlabs-cloudformation`). It adds the `puppet cloudformation` subcommand, which can be used to deploy a whole Puppet Enterprise stack via Amazon's CloudFormation service.

The module, besides installing a Master based on Puppet Enterprise, configures various AWS resources (security groups, IAM users, and ec2 instances) and Puppet-specific components (modules, dashboard groups, and agents).

Cloud provisioning on Google Compute Engine

The Puppet Labs' cloud provisioner module, which we mentioned earlier, can be used to create AWS instances and can work with **Google Compute Engine (GCE)** as well.

A new face, `node_gce`, is provided. This enables various actions to manage GCE instances; for the official documentation check `http://docs.puppetlabs.com/pe/latest/cloudprovisioner_gce.html`.

Its usage patterns are similar to the ones of the `node_aws` face; a new subcommand is added to Puppet to interactively manage instances on GCE, but no new dedicated resource types are provided.

Puppet on storage devices

Puppet management on storage devices is still in the early stages; there are not many implementations around, but something is moving, for example, Gavin Williams' module to manage NetApp filers available at `https://forge.puppetlabs.com/fatmcgav/netapp`.

In addition, this module is based on `puppet device`; the configuration is something like the following lines of code:

```
[netapp.example42.lan]
  type netapp
  url https://root:password@netapp.example42.lan
```

The module provides native types to manage volumes (`netapp_volume`), NFS shares (`netapp_export`), users (`netapp_user`), snap mirrors (`netapp_snapmirror`), and other configuration items. It also provides a defined resource (`netapp::vqe`) for the easy creation and exportation of a volume.

Summary

In this chapter, we have explored new territories for Puppet. We have gone beyond server operating systems and have seen how it is possible to also manage network and storage equipments and how Puppet can help us work with the cloud.

We have seen that there are two general approaches to the management of devices: the proxy one, which is mostly implemented by the `puppet device` application and has a specific operational approach, and the native one, where Puppet runs directly on the managed devices and behaves like it does in a normal node.

We have also reviewed the modules available to manage virtualization and cloud-related setups. Some of them configure normal resources on a system; others expand Puppet applications to allow the creation of and interaction with cloud instances.

Puppet is well placed for the future challenges that a software-defined data center involves, but its evolution is an ongoing process in many fields.

In the next chapter, we are going to explore how Puppet is evolving and what we can expect from Puppet Version 4.

12
Future Puppet

Time is relative.

My future is your present.

When you read this, Puppet 4 has probably been released, largely based on the experimental features presented in Puppet 3.x releases, which we are going to review in this chapter.

Puppet 4 is a real (r)evolution.

New versatile and powerful features are going to stimulate smart implementations and very new approaches to the management of Puppet logic and data.

The grounds are being placed for future evolutions based on what we are seeing here.

Still, the familiar Puppet elements are all there; all the ones we have seen in the previous chapters: variables, resource types, nodes, modules, code and data to manage, plugins, integration with different devices, and so on. They are going to stay and evolve.

Most of the changes introduced as an experiment in the 3.x tree and enabled by default in Puppet 4 can be activated with the configuration option `parser = future`, so that they can be tested on Puppet 3 before trying a version switch.

Experimental features are not officially supported and don't follow semantic versioning rules as they may change any time. So, it's not advisable to enable them on production systems, without proper testing of each new version.

Puppet developers refined many parts and completely redesigned some key areas of the code. Among the many great authors, we have to name a single person responsible for the most profound changes: Henrik Lindberg.

Check out his blog (http://puppet-on-the-edge.blogspot.it/) for up-to-date and thoughtful insights on the development of many new features in Puppet 4.

In this chapter, we are going to explore the following topics:

- **The Future Parser**: The code that interprets our manifests has been rewritten from scratch and now allows a much richer and more powerful DSL

- **The Type System**: This allows the definition of different data types in Puppet, and also involves easier and powerful validation of the data we manage

- **The EPP templates**: This is where we can directly use Puppet DSL instead of Ruby as we do in ERB templates

- Various other features like heredoc support, msgpack serialization, an improved error system, the contain function, and directory environments

- **Data in modules**: This is a long-standing and desired feature, which allows smarter management of a module's internal data and defaults

- **Facter 2**: With support for structured facts and other features

- **The Trapperkeeper framework**: This is possibly the base of the future Puppet's ecosystem

Introducing the future parser

The parser is the part of the Puppet code that interprets our manifests.

It has been rewritten from scratch and its new incarnation, nicknamed future parser, introduces many new features, which greatly enhance the power of the Puppet DSL.

The most relevant additions are:

- Lambdas which are blocks of code that have parameters and can be passed directly to the new iteration functions

- Powerful filtering and concatenation functions for data collection like hashes and arrays, also thanks to the new type system

The overall impression is that the whole set of innovations expected with Puppet 4 will allow better and more versatile management of data, which should ease the adoption of paradigms such as infrastructure as data, and maybe, radically change the way we write and compose our Puppet code.

For example, in future modules, we might face a wider and more dynamic usage of functions like create_resources or resource declarations based on iterations over data and see less repetitions of normal resource type declarations.

Lambdas and Iterations

Lambdas are parameterized blocks of code. Think of them as anonymous functions which can be defined, used, and thrown away without naming them. They are typically used as arguments to other functions, and this brings great power and flexibility.

Lambdas' code is enclosed in braces ({ }). Inside them, we can place any Puppet code except node statements, and class and defines definitions. Lambdas can have parameters declared within pipes (|). The basic syntax of a lambda is therefore:

```
| <parameters> | { <expressions> }
```

An example may definitively help in understanding possible usage cases. In the following code, an array of sites is passed to a lambda to create their apache virtual hosts and FTP users:

```
$sites = ['example42.com','lab42.it','google.com']
each($sites) |$my_site| {
  apache::virtualhost { $my_site: }
  ftp::user { $my_site: }
}
```

In the preceding example, we used the new `each` function. Each element of the `$sites` array is used as a parameter, here called `$my_site`, for a lambda that declares an `apache::virtualhost` and a `ftp::user` define (there can be any other piece of Puppet code here).

The parameters inside the pipe can be separated by commas and may have default values:

```
| $user , $group = 'admins' |
```

Various new functions have been introduced to work with lambdas; they allow iteration and manipulation of collections (arrays or hashes), as shown in the following list:

- `each`: This iterates over collections. It takes two arguments; the first is an array or a hash, the second is the lambda.
- `map`: This transforms an array or a hash (the first argument) into a new array (the result of the lambda invocation).
- `filter`: This filters an array or a hash (first argument) and produces an array based on the evaluation done in the lambda (second argument).

- `reduce`: This returns a single value from an array or a hash (first argument) as computed by a lambda (second argument).
- `slice`: This slices an array or hash (first argument) according to defined elements (second argument), which are optionally iterated over a lambda (third argument).

These functions can be invoked using different syntaxes; all the following examples are valid and do the same thing:

```
each($x)   |$value| { ... }
$x.each    |$value| { ... }
$x.each()  |$value| { ... }
```

The `slice` function, which takes an additional argument, can be used in these ways:

```
slice($x, 2) |$value| { ... }
$x.slice(2)  |$value| { ... }
```

When used with these preceding functions, lambdas can have one or two parameters whose value depends on the type of data they are dealing with.

When the lambda is used with an array, if it has one parameter, that parameter is the array value. If it has two parameters, the first one is the array index and the second one the value:

```
$my_array = [ 'al' , 'joe' ]
$my_array.each |$x| { notice "${x} is the array value" }
$my_array.each |$index, $value| {
  notice "${index} is the array index (Starts from 0)"
  notice "${value} is the array value"
}
```

When we use a hash with a lambda, we can express it with a single parameter that represents a complete key-value pair, or, if there are two parameters, the first is the key and the second is the value:

```
$my_hash = { name => 'al' , group => 'admins' }
$my_hash.each |$x| {
  notice "${x[0]} is the hash key"
  notice "${x[1]} is the hash value"
}
$my_hash.each |$key, $value| {
  notice "${key} is the hash key"
  notice "${value} is the hash value"
}
```

The lambda parameters can be used as variables only inside its body (they belong to a local scope, which is not accessible outside the lambda code block).

Inside the code block, we can, however, use any variable available in the containing scopes (top, node, and class).

For example, the following code works, but we cannot use the variable `$user` outside the lambda body:

```
$names = ['fred','al']
$names.each |$user| { notice "User ${user} available on ${::fqdn}"}
```

Manipulating and validating hashes and arrays

The future parser, thanks to the new type system we will see later, allows easier manipulation of arrays and hashes, and permits operations directly in the Puppet DSL that were possible only via custom functions before.

Arrays and hashes can be concatenated with the + sign:

```
[1,2,3] + [4,5,6]   # produces [1,2,3,4,5,6]
{a => 1} + {b => 2} # produces {a=>1, b=>2}
```

The `stdlib` equivalents are:

```
concat ( [1,2,3] , [4,5,6] )
merge ( {a => 1} , {b => 2} )
```

We can append values to arrays with <<:

```
[1,2,3] << 2,    # produces [1,2,3,2,]
[1,2,3] << [2,4]    # produces [1,2,3,[2,4]]
```

The type of a variable can be verified and evaluated with the =~ operator.

To test, for example, whether a variable is an array:

```
    if $users =~ Array { .. }
```

This applies to any recognized data type. The following output shows the stdlib equivalent functions of the =~ operator:

```
# StdLib                    # Puppet 4 Type System
is_array($x)                $x =~ Array
is_bool($x)                 $x =~ Boolean
is_float($x)                $x =~ Float
is_hash($x)                 $x =~ Hash
```

```
is_integer($x)              $x =~ Integer
is_numeric($x)              $x =~ Numeric
is_string($x)               $x =~ String
not available               $x =~ Regexp
```

Similarly, the new `assert_type` function allows validation of data types. It's equivalent to the various `validate_*` stdlib functions:

```
# StdLib                    # Puppet 4 Type System
validate_array($x)          assert_type(Array, $x)
validate_bool($x)           assert_type(Boolean, $x)
validate_hash($x)           assert_type(Hash, $x)
validate_re($x)             assert_type(Regexp, $x)
validate_string($x)         assert_type(String, $x)
```

The `assert_type` function can check only one argument, so if we want to validate multiple values, we have to place them in an array and then check the parameterized array properly:

```
# StdLib                    # Puppet 4 Type System
validate_array($x, $y)      assert_type(Array[Array], [$x, y])
validate_bool($x, $y)       assert_type(Array[Boolean], [$x, $y])
validate_hash($x, $y)       assert_type(Array[Hash], [$x, $y])
validate_re($x, $y)         assert_type(Array[Regexp], [$x, $y])
validate_string($x, $y)     assert_type(Array[String], [$x, $y])
```

A very interesting feature is the possibility to validate the length of types when we refer to them. This is done by specifying minimum and maximum values inside square brackets:

```
$x =~ String[min, max]
[$x, $y] =~ Array[String[min, max]]
assert_type(String[min,max], $x)
assert_type(Array[String[min,max]], [$x, $y])
```

To execute some code only if a string is not empty, we can write:

```
if $package_name=~String[1] { ... }
```

This might not impress us, as it was possible to check for a string existence before as well, but these checks can be more elaborated, for example, to declare some resources only if the string length is between two and four characters:

```
if $package_name=~String[2,4] { ... }
```

Similar checks can also be done for the single values of an array. To execute code for an array whose values can have only two characters, we can write:

```
if $country =~ (Array[String[2,2]) { ... }
```

We can also emulate the functionality of the `values_at` stdlib function with the `[]` operator. This allows us to select only the specified values from a given array (we indicate the range, starting from 0):

```
notice [one,two,three,four,five][1,3]
=> two three four
```

Other features

Various other smaller features and language constructs are now possible, as shown in the following points:

- We can interpolate the value of a function (into a double-quoted string) without the need to previously assign it to a variable:

  ```
  "Random value is ${fqdn_rand()}"
  ```

- Hashes and arrays can be used directly in function arguments:

  ```
  notice [ 'one','two' ]
  ```

- We can use a semicolon to separate expressions on the same line:

  ```
  $package_name = 'httpd' ; $service_name = 'httpd'
  ```

- We can also chain variable assignments:

  ```
  $package_name = $service_name = 'httpd'
  ```

- The `unless` statement now has an `else` clause:

  ```
  unless [condition] { code } else { code }
  ```

Restrictions and backward incompatibilities

The introduction of a more structured type of system and the rewriting of the Parser has been an occasion to clean up some idiosyncrasies in the language and deprecate some constructs that were previously possible.

These are the cases where the earlier code won't be compatible with Puppet 4; they are not so common, but are worth mentioning:

- Variable and parameters names can't be only numbers or contain capital letters. In order to avoid bad surprises, use only names with lowercase letters, numbers (but not alone), and underscores. These are all illegal statements:

```
$42 = 'the answer'
$Answer = '42'
```

- When assigning numerical values to variables, they are validated according to their type if they are not quoted. The following code will throw an error:

```
$a = 0x0EZ # Not a valid HEX number
$b = 0778  # Not a valid octal number
```

Directory environments

The usual approach to environments management using settings such as manifest, modulepath, or config_version inside an [environment] stanza of the Master's puppet.conf is going to be deprecated and we see notices about this from Puppet 3.6. Starting with Puppet 4, environments are managed by default with a directory-based approach.

The configuration setting environmentpath defines the directory that contains our environments. Its default value is /etc/puppet/environments, where we can have a different environment in each subdirectory. They are immediately available to the clients, we can call them, as often done, production, testing, and devel, but also use very volatile names which may map to temporary Git branch names, such as 0ed1434e or pupp_376, where we can test specific fixes or features.

In each environment directory, we can place a modules directory specific to that environment, a manifests directory, and an environment.conf file, where we can place environment-specific settings that override the general default ones.

We can define, with the basemodulepath parameter, a global directory where we can place modules shared by all the environments. The actual modulepath used to load our modules is $environmentpath/$environment/modules:$basemodulepath so that the modules directory inside an environment has higher priority than the general base one.

Heredoc support

Heredoc support is introduced in Puppet 3.5 and is done in a cool way.

We can now write text anywhere in the code where a string is expected without caring about managing quotes and escaping it with backslashes.

The basic syntax is @(WORD) to open the heredoc block and WORD to end it, where WORD is any sequence of characters of your choice (of course, we should not have it in our heredoc content). For example, we can assign content with newlines, quotes, and any character to a string:

```
$my_content = @(HERE)
This is a sample heredoc test.
With "double quotes" and 'single quotes' happily coexisting.
New lines are present:
  - and indentations
HERE
```

We can use the $my_content variable wherever we want (for example, in the content argument of a file resource).

There is more. We can use variables in our text (referenced with $ or ${}) by quoting our starting word with ". The normal dollar sign ($) is escaped with \$:

```
$my_content = @("HERE")
# File Managed by Puppet. Great \$\$\$ value for money.
search ${::domain}
nameserver $dns_server
HERE
```

We can manage the indentation of the text, aligning it to the | char in the ending tag (this is very useful to help our code look good without keeping the indentation used for code alignment in our resulting heredoc text):

```
if $::osfamily == 'RedHat' {
  $my_content = @(DOC)
  # This is present on RedHat systems
  | DOC
}
```

The new type system

The new type system is another major pillar of Puppet 4. We have already seen the beneficial side effects of its existence when exploring the future parser.

All the data we manage with Puppet is now expressed by a rich type system.

Everything inside our DSL has its type: the resources we declare, the parameters of our defines, our Hiera data, facts, and all the variables used in our code.

The type system is hierarchical, and besides common Scalars (`Numeric`, `String`, `Boolean`, `Regexp`) and Collections (`Array`, `Hash`), it can represent catalog entries (`Resource`, `Node`, `Class`, `Stage`) or more esoteric data types, such as Ruby class names and undefined values.

Following is the full, hierarchical list of the available data types. It's quite useful to understand how they are organized and the different data types we can deal with:

```
Object
 |- Scalar
 |   |- Numeric
 |   |   |- Integer[from, to]
 |   |   |   |- (Integer with range inside another Integer)
 |   |   |
 |   |   |- Float[from, to]
 |   |   |   |- (Float with range inside another Float)
 |   |
 |   |- String
 |   |   |- Enum[*strings]
 |   |   |- Pattern[*patterns]
 |   |   |- Regexp[regexp]
 |   |
 |   |- Boolean
 |   |- Regexp
 |
 |- Collection[size_from, size_to]
 |   |- Array[element_type, size_from, size_to]
 |   [   |- (type compatible array with size within range)
 |   |
 |   |- Hash[key_type, value_type, size_from, size_to]
 |       |- (type compatible hash with size within range)
 |
```

```
|- Data
|  |- Scalar
|  |- Array[Data]
|  |- Hash[Scalar, Data]
|
|- CatalogEntry
|  |- Resource[resource_type_name, title]
|  |- Class[class_name]
|  |- Node[node_name]
|  |- Stage[stage_name]
|
|- Variant[*types]
|- Optional[type]
|- Undef
|
|- Type[T]
|
|- Ruby[class_name]
```

Other new features

Besides the functionalities strictly related to the new parser and type system, many other new features have been introduced.

EPP Templates

We are used to managing the contents of configuration files using ERB templates, where it is possible to embed the Ruby code and variables interpolation inside the text to be used in the files deployed to our nodes.

Puppet 3.5 introduces Embedded Puppet (EPP) Templates, where we can directly use Puppet code inside our templates. They are supposed to be placed in the same template's directory of our nodes; they are expected to have a `.epp` extension and are invoked via the `epp` and `inline_epp` functions, which are equivalent to the `template` and `inline_template` ones.

The tags to be used to insert Puppet code inside files' text are the same ones used for ERB templates:

- `<%`: Switches to the code mode. From here, normal Puppet DSL can be used.

- `<%=`: Switches to the expression mode. Variables can be directly referenced (using `$` instead of `@`).

- `<%-`: Switches to the code mode, and any whitespaces preceding the tag are not included in the output.

- `<%#`: Comment, not included in the output (up to the next `%>`).

- `%>`: Ends the puppet mode.

- `-%>`: Ends the puppet mode and trims any generated trailing whitespaces.

Inside the code block, the normal Puppet DSL can be used. At the beginning of the template, we can declare the parameters the template uses and, eventually, their default values:

```
<%- ( $dns_servers , $options, $timeout => 2 )-%>
```

In EPP templates, variables scoping works differently compared to what we used with ERB templates:

- Top scope and node scope variables (also defined as global scope variables) are always available

- If parameters are declared at the beginning of the template with the syntax we have just seen, only those variables are available

- If no parameters are explicitly declared in the template, then local scope variables (the ones coming from the class or the define that uses the template) are available

The contain function

We have seen in *Chapter 5, Using and Writing Reusable Modules*, that we need to use the anchor pattern when we manage relationships with classes that contain other classes.

Puppet 3.4 introduced a new function, called `contain`, which is used as the `include` function but adds a strict containment to the included classes. All the classes that are declared inside the class we contain are applied together, avoiding the risk to have some of these classes applied in other uncontrolled parts of the catalog.

Usage of `contain` does not involve parameterized-class-style declaration and accepts more than one class name (either comma separated or in an array). An example for this is as follows:

```
contain apache
contain apache, php, myql
contain [ 'apache' , 'php' , 'mysql' ]
```

So, for example, when we have a `wordpress` class that just installs the WordPress application and we want to apply it after the other classes are applied, we can safely use a syntax shown as follows:

```
contain wordpress
Class['apache'] -> Class['mysql'] -> Class['wordpress']
```

Serialization with MessagePack

Puppet Master and clients exchange a remarkable amount of data: facts, catalogs, and reports. All this data has to be serialized, that is, converted into a format that can be stored to a file, managed in a memory buffer, and sent on a network connection.

There are different serialization formats. Puppet, during its years of existence, has used XML-RPC, YAML, and PSON (a custom variation of JSON, which allows inclusion of binary objects), the latter being the currently preferred choice.

A new and very promising protocol called `MessagePack` has entered the programming scene and is gaining consensus. It's a binary format more compact and efficient (some tests suggest that it can be 50 percent more compact than JSON). So, it reduces the quantity of data to transmit over the wire and the computational resources needed to manage it.

A simple test shows what an array such as `['one', 'two', 'three']` can look like in different formats. Expressed in the YAML format, this becomes (24 bytes, newlines included):

```
---
- one
- two
- three
```

In the JSON format, this becomes (21 bytes):

```
["one","two","three"]
```

In `MessagePack`, this becomes (15 bytes (a string like \x93 represents a single byte in hexadecimal notation)):

```
\x93\xA3one\xA3two\xA5three
```

If we consider that Puppet is constantly making serialization and deserialization of data, it's clear that the introduction of such a format may deliver great performance benefits.

To enable the `MessagePack` serialization, we need to install the `msgpack` gem on both the client and Master (it might become an automatic dependency in future Puppet packages):

```
gem install msgpack
```

Set in the `[main]` section of their `puppet.conf`:

```
preferred_serialization_format = msgpack
```

Clients where `msgpack` is not supported can keep the default PSON format and continue to operate normally.

Improved error system

Various enhancements have also been made to how Puppet reports errors.

Now, in most of the error messages, besides the filename and the line where the error is caught, the position inside the line is also indicated (the format is `filename:line:position`).

The same error messages have been improved to ease readability and troubleshooting.

It's also possible to configure the parameters `max_errors`, `max_warnings`, and `max_deprecations` (by default, 10 for each of them) in `puppet.conf` to set the maximum lines to print for each of these error categories. If the limit is reached, the last line with the total count of the found errors is printed.

Data in modules

We have already mentioned the data in the modules feature and its long and difficult path inside Puppet in *Chapter 5, Using and Writing Reusable Modules*.

At the moment of writing, the feature is still not released on the core Puppet; however, it's expected for Puppet 4.

The implementation details are still not defined, but for modules' authors, the usage patterns should be similar to the ones suggested by R.I.Pienaar in his experimental module-based proposal, which can be found at `https://github.com/ripienaar/puppet-module-data`.

The basic idea is that all the internal variables of a module and, where needed, the default values of parameters should be based on a Hiera YAML backend directly placed inside the module, with a module-specific hierarchy that does not interfere with users' local hierarchies.

Basically, we can define the hierarchy to manage the module data in our module's `data/hiera.yaml` file:

```
---
    :hierarchy:
      - "osfamily/%{::osfamily}"
      - common
```

Such a (simple) configuration would look for Hiera data in YAML files such as `data/osfamily/RedHat.yaml`, `data/osfamily/Debian.yaml`, and `data/common.yaml`.

Here, we can place the correct values for the module's internal variables and parameters. A `RedHat.yaml` file in a `postgresql` module could look like:

```
---
postgresql::version: '8.4'
postgresql::package_name: 'postgresql-server'
postgresql::service_name: 'postgresql'
postgresql::config_path: '/var/lib/pgsql/data/postgresql.conf'
postgresql::config_dir_path: '/var/lib/pgsql/data'
postgresql::hba_file_path:  '/var/lib/pgsql/data/pg_hba.conf'
```

This will allow us to completely remove the Puppet code, usually placed in the `manifests/params.pp` file, that computes internal variables according to the underlying operating systems.

One of the reasons why I personally find this feature particularly useful, besides the obvious benefits of having all the data nicely managed in a hierarchical way, is the possibility to insert the same parameters of the module's classes in the hierarchy.

For example, if we want to provide the option to install PostgreSQL in custom ways (for example, using upstream repositories, or downloading and eventually compiling the software) in our `postgresql` module, we can add a specific parameter that defines the name of the installation class. Consider a possible hierarchy such as:

```
---
    :hierarchy:
      - "install_class/%{install_class}"
      - "osfamily/%{::osfamily}"
      - common
```

If we have a class named `postgresql::install::postgresql_org_redhat`, we can place the specific module data for the packages provided by this installation method in a file named `data/install_class/postgresql::install::postgresql_org_redhat.yaml`, shown as follows:

```
---
postgresql::version: '9.3'
postgresql::package_name: "postgresql-%{::postgresql::version}"
postgresql::service_name: "postgresql-%{::postgresql::version}"
postgresql::configpath:
  "/etc/postgresql/%{::postgresql::version}/main/postgresql.conf"
postgresql::config_dir_path:
  "/etc/postgresql/%{::postgresql::version}/main"
postgresql::hba_file_path:
  "/etc/postgresql/%{::postgresql::version}/main/pg_hba.conf"
```

I can assure you that to manage such a scenario in a normal module requires a lot of boilerplate code, and can't be done via a `params` class since some of the values that are expected to be defined there depend not only on facts, but also on parameters passed by users.

Be warned. This implementation is based on R.I.Pienaar's proposal, and at the time of writing, it is not sure if its usage patterns will be exactly like the ones of these examples.

Also, it's probable that the final implementation will allow different methods to provide the module's data in a similar fashion of the data binding feature for each class parameter, which currently has only Hiera as an available backend, but which might be open to other implementations.

Facter 2

Strictly speaking, Facter is an autonomous software project and does not follow Puppet's versioning and release schedule. It is not a surprise, therefore, that Facter 2 was released more or less when Puppet 3.5 was already out.

> The first official version of Facter 2 is 2.0.1.
>
> Version 2.0.0 was skipped because previously some 2.0.0.rcX release candidate versions, based on older and deprecated code, were released, and the guys at Puppet Labs preferred to avoid confusion, since the code in 2.0.1 is totally new and unrelated to the one in 2.0.0.rcX.

The main features of Facter 2 (`http://docs.puppetlabs.com/facter/2.0/`) are:

- **New return types**: In Facter 1, all facts were simple strings. Now, facts values can be expressed in different data types, such as `Integer`, `Float`, `TrueClass`, `FalseClass`, `NilClass`, `String`, `Array`, and `Hash`.

- **Structured facts**: Facts can have complex structures and represent data with arrays or hashes. This greatly enhances their power and expressiveness.

- **Aggregate resolutions**: The content of a fact can be built merging different chunks of code allowing more elaborate results.

- **Pluginsync for external facts**: From Puppet 3.4 and Facter 2.0.1, it is possible to provide external facts directly via modules, using the `pluginsync` functionality and copying the content of the `MODULE/facts.d` directory to clients' `/etc/facter/facts.d` automatically.

Let's analyze a sample fact, `yumplugins`, written by Dean Wilson, a proficient community member and author of the website `http://www.puppetcookbook.com`.

This example gives us a great idea of the usefulness and power of structured facts.

Fact declaration and structure is completely the same as Facter 1:

```
Facter.add("yumplugins") do
  confine :osfamily => "RedHat"
  setcode do
    plugin_directory = '/etc/yum/pluginconf.d'
```

Here, we begin with the interesting things; a hash called `plugins`, which will be the result of the fact, is defined with three different keys that expect an array of values:

```
plugins = {}
plugins['plugin']   = []
plugins['enabled']  = []
plugins['disabled'] = []
```

The fact analyzes all the `.conf` files in the `plugins` directory, and for each of them, the plugin name is added to the `plugins['plugin']` key:

```
Dir[plugin_directory + '/*.conf'].each do | file |
  plugin_name = File.basename( file, '.conf')
  plugins['plugin'] << plugin_name
```

If the plugin is enabled (the enabled string is searched), an entry is added to the `plugins['enabled']` array, otherwise it is added to the `plugins['disabled']` one:

```
    enabled = File.open(file).read.grep(/^(\s*enabled\s*=\s*[01])/).
to_s.split('=')[1]
      if enabled.to_i.zero?
        plugins['disabled'] << plugin_name
      else
        plugins['enabled'] << plugin_name
      end
    end
```

At the end, the `plugins` hash is returned after a sort of its keys to preserve consistency on different executions:

```
    plugins.keys.each do |key|
      plugins[key].sort!
    end
    plugins
  end
end
```

The resulting fact, expressed in the YAML format, might be something like:

```
  ---
  yumplugins:
    plugin:
    - blacklist
    - presto
    - refresh-packagekit
    enabled:
    - presto
    - refresh-packagekit
    disabled:
    - blacklist
```

Another important addition is the possibility to compute the content of a fact aggregating different parts of the code.

Let's see the official example of a fact (`networking`) with an aggregate resolution. It's declared as any other fact but specifies that its type is aggregate:

```
  Facter.add(:networking, :type => :aggregate) do
    confine :kernel => "Linux"
```

The internal code, instead of being defined with the `setcode` statement, is separated into different chunks of code. The next one gathers the MAC addresses of the interfaces:

```
chunk(:macaddrs) do
  interfaces = {}
  Sysfs.net_devs.each do |dev|
    interfaces[dev.name] = {
      'macaddr' => dev.macaddr,
      'macbrd'  => dev.macbrd,
    }
  end
  interfaces
end
```

A second one defines the IPv4 addresses:

```
chunk(:ipv4) do
  interfaces = {}
  Facter::Util::IP.get_interfaces.each do |interface|
    interfaces[interface] = {
      'ipaddress' => Facter::Util::IP.get_ipaddress_
value(interface),
      'netmask'   => Facter::Util::IP.get_netmask_value(interface),
    }
  end
  interfaces
  end
end
```

The values of the two chunks are merged and returned in a single hash. Optionally, we can find an `aggregate` block in facts with aggregate resolutions, which can summarize and merge the values from the existing `chunks` with a particular logic.

Trapperkeeper

A few days before these lines were written, Puppet Labs released a new open source project called TrapperKeeper, which can be found at https://github.com/puppetlabs/trapperkeeper:

"TrapperKeeper is a clojure framework for hosting long-running applications and services."

It has been presented in a blog post by Chris Price at `http://puppetlabs.com/blog/new-era-application-services-puppet-labs`, and currently there is really not much to say on how this product will affect the Puppet's ecosystem.

From what can be read and heard around, the impression is that TrapperKeeper will earn a lot of attention from Puppet Labs in the future. They talk about a new era after all.

My easy guess is that all the current and future projects written in Clojure by Puppet Labs will be based on this framework, starting from the same PuppetDB.

Given the terrific work they have done with PuppetDB, we can have great expectations on many different services that gravitate around Puppet.

I wouldn't be surprised to see external Puppet data backends, alternative or complementary to Hiera, or Node Classifiers, or even orchestration and data correlation services in the future.

I wouldn't be surprised, also, to see more and more components of Puppet being developed in Clojure instead of Ruby, probably with remarkable performance benefits.

Here, we are really into pure speculation, so take these as personal fantasies.

Maybe we will have to start playing with Clojure, which can't be a bad thing in itself, or just use beautifully engineered applications by Puppet Labs, but I have a strong feeling that we will have to deal frequently with TrapperKeeper.

Summary

In this chapter, we have given a peek to what is the future of Puppet. We have explored the new Parser and most of its language enhancements, such as the Lambdas and the iteration functions.

We have seen how the new type system allows a much more structured approach to data validation and management and how this can enrich our possibilities to use and manipulate data.

We have mentioned some other features, such as support for heredoc, the `contain` function, the EPP templates, data in modules, and directory environments.

We have also reviewed Facter 2, with support for structured facts and aggregations, and finally took a quick look at TrapperKeeper, which will be the basis of the future Puppet Labs applications written in Clojure.

The number of changes introduced in Puppet 4 is quite relevant, and they will definitely make complex operations on data easier.

Maybe we will partly lose the unique feeling of the Puppet declarative DSL, where a system administrator can easily understand what's configured on a system by taking a look at the declared resource types in his manifests.

We will probably move more and more towards an infrastructure as data approach, where the Puppet code will probably look more complex but will deal, in powerful ways, with our data, whether it is placed in Hiera or other parts.

The jump from Puppet 3 to Puppet 4 is probably going to have more impact than in any major version change, and the new possibilities of the language will probably be used and abused by the community in the most unexpected and imaginative ways.

Some of them will probably become best practices, others will be considered bad patterns, but none of them, strictly speaking, will be required. We can continue writing the Puppet code similar to how we used to write in Puppet 0.24.

Best practices are relative; they depend on time, conditions, and also personal taste. Our best practice is what works best for us, and this is the only thing that really matters.

So close this book and open your laptop. It's time to play the Puppet Master!

Index

B

backend-specific settings, Hiera
  :datadir 46
  :datasource 46
Beaker 190
BitBucket
  URL 187
blog post, Craig Dunn
  URL 103
built-in variables
  variables, set by client 27
  variables, set by parser 27
  variables, set by server 27

C

CA certificate
  about 209
  managing, via puppet ca command 210
Certificate Revocation List (CRL) 210
Certificate Signing Requests (CSR) 210
Cisco onePK 260
class
  declaring 20
  defining 19
  parameterized class 20
classes key 65
class inheritance
  about 22
  using 22
class scope 28
class variables 28
cloud computing and virtualization
  aspects 263
  projects 263
CloudFormation
  managing 268
Cloud Provisioner module 265
Cloud provisioning
  on AWS 265
  on Google Compute Engine 268
code review
  about 185
  Gerrit 186
  peer review 187

code workflow management
  about 179
  Geppetto 180
  Puppet code, writing 179, 180
  Vim 181
Codifferous
  URL 187
command line
  working with, on Hiera YAML
    backend 48-53
command method 245
**Command/Query Responsibility Separation
    (CQRS) pattern 79**
comparison operators
  about 33
  equal == 33
  expressions combinations 34
  greater than > 33
  greater than or equal to >= 33
  in operator 34
  less than < 33
  less than or equal to <= 33
  not equal != 33
  regex match =~ 33
conditionals
  case statements 32
  else statements 32
  elsif statements 32
  if statements 32
  managing 32
config_file_options_hash parameter 131
configuration directory 132
configuration files
  defining, custom fileserver mounts
    used 101
  defining, Hiera used 100
  defining, public modules used 100
  defining, site modules used 100
configuration hash patterns, modules
  managing 130-132
configuration management
  benefits 9, 10
configuration management tools
  Ansible 9
  CFEngine 9
  Chef 9

error system enhancement
  about 284
  max_deprecations parameter 284
  max_errors parameter 284
  max_warnings parameter 284
exists? method 246
exported resources
  about 34, 214
  virtual resources 36
External Node Classifier. *See* ENC
external_nodes parameter 95
extlookup function 44, 121
extra files 132
extra resources, modules
  managing 137, 138

F

Faces 249
Facter 9, 24
Facter 2
  about 286
  aggregate resolutions 287
  declaration and structure 287, 288
  features 287
  pluginsync for external facts 287
  return types 287
  structured facts 287
facter class 238
facts 24
filebucket
  files, restoring from 40
files, managing in modules
  configuration hash patterns,
      managing 130-132
  extra resources, managing 137, 138
  installation options, managing 135, 136
  multiple configuration files,
      managing 132, 133
  users and dependencies, managing 134, 135
file type
  about 242
  parameters 242
  properties 242
filter function 273

foreman-cli command 102
foreman() function 102
frontend servers 212
future parser
  about 272
  arrays and hashes, manipulating 275, 276
  directory environments 278
  each function 273
  features 277
  filter function 273
  incompatibilities 277
  iterations 273
  lambdas 273, 274
  language constructs 277
  map function 273
  reduce function 274
  slice function 274

G

general-purpose define 132
Geppetto
  about 9, 180
  features 180
  URL 180
Gerrit 186
Git 179
Git commands
  git add 182
  git branch 183
  git checkout 183
  git clone 183
  git commit 182
  git config 182
  git init 182
  git log 182
  git merge 183
  git pull 183
  git push 183
  git rebase 183
  git status 182
GitEnterprise
  URL 187
Git hooks 183

Thank you for buying
Extending Puppet

About Packt Publishing

Packt, pronounced 'packed', published its first book "*Mastering phpMyAdmin for Effective MySQL Management*" in April 2004 and subsequently continued to specialize in publishing highly focused books on specific technologies and solutions.

Our books and publications share the experiences of your fellow IT professionals in adapting and customizing today's systems, applications, and frameworks. Our solution based books give you the knowledge and power to customize the software and technologies you're using to get the job done. Packt books are more specific and less general than the IT books you have seen in the past. Our unique business model allows us to bring you more focused information, giving you more of what you need to know, and less of what you don't.

Packt is a modern, yet unique publishing company, which focuses on producing quality, cutting-edge books for communities of developers, administrators, and newbies alike. For more information, please visit our website: www.packtpub.com.

About Packt Open Source

In 2010, Packt launched two new brands, Packt Open Source and Packt Enterprise, in order to continue its focus on specialization. This book is part of the Packt Open Source brand, home to books published on software built around Open Source licenses, and offering information to anybody from advanced developers to budding web designers. The Open Source brand also runs Packt's Open Source Royalty Scheme, by which Packt gives a royalty to each Open Source project about whose software a book is sold.

Writing for Packt

We welcome all inquiries from people who are interested in authoring. Book proposals should be sent to author@packtpub.com. If your book idea is still at an early stage and you would like to discuss it first before writing a formal book proposal, contact us; one of our commissioning editors will get in touch with you.

We're not just looking for published authors; if you have strong technical skills but no writing experience, our experienced editors can help you develop a writing career, or simply get some additional reward for your expertise.

Puppet 3 Cookbook

ISBN: 978-1-78216-976-5   Paperback: 274 pages

Build reliable, scalable, secure, and high-performance systems to fully utilize the power of cloud computing

1. Use Puppet 3 to take control of your servers and desktops, with detailed step-by-step instructions.

2. Covers all the popular tools and frameworks used with Puppet: Dashboard, Foreman, and more.

3. Teaches you how to extend Puppet with custom functions, types, and providers.

Instant Puppet 3 Starter

ISBN: 978-1-78216-174-5   Paperback: 50 pages

Gain complete consistency from your systems with minimal effort using Instant Puppet 3 Starter

1. Learn something new in an Instant! A short, fast, focused guide delivering immediate results.

2. Learn how deterministic results can vastly reduce your workload.

3. Deploy Puppet Server as a Ruby-on-Rails application to handle thousands of clients.

4. Design your own module for complex configurations.

Please check **www.PacktPub.com** for information on our titles

16306049R00185

Made in the USA
Middletown, DE
10 December 2014